FROM *GLASNOST* TO THE INTERNET

Also by Frank Ellis

VASILY GROSSMAN: The Genesis and Evolution of a Russian Heretic

From *Glasnost* to the Internet

Russia's New Infosphere

Frank Ellis
Reuter Foundation Lecturer in Russian and
East European Media
University of Leeds

First published in Great Britain 1999 by
MACMILLAN PRESS LTD
Houndmills, Basingstoke, Hampshire RG21 6XS and London
Companies and representatives throughout the world

A catalogue record for this book is available from the British Library.

ISBN 0–333–67095–7

First published in the United States of America 1999 by
ST. MARTIN'S PRESS, INC.,
Scholarly and Reference Division,
175 Fifth Avenue, New York, N.Y. 10010

ISBN 0–312–21765–X

Library of Congress Cataloging-in-Publication Data
Ellis, Frank, 1953–
From glasnost to the internet : Russia's new infosphere / Frank
Ellis.
 p. cm.
Includes full text of the 1992 Russian mass media law in English.
Includes bibliographical references and index.
ISBN 0–312–21765–X (cloth)
1. Mass media—Russia (Federation) 2. Internet (Computer
network)—Russia (Federation) I. Title.
P92.R9E45 1998
302.2'0947—dc21   98–20783
                                                                CIP

This book is printed on paper suitable for recycling and made from fully managed and sustained forest sources.

10 9 8 7 6 5 4 3 2
08 07 06 05 04 03 02 01 00

Printed and bound in Great Britain by
Antony Rowe Ltd, Chippenham, Wiltshire

To the memory of
Viktor Kravchenko (1905–66)
Soviet defector, freedom-fighter and
truth-teller

Contents

Preface

When embarking on this book, it was my intention to use media, the standard term, in the title. The more, however, I pondered the changes which had taken place since the mid-eighties, and which had then accelerated after 1991, the greater the inadequacy of the term media seemed to be. It is, I think, a question of perceptions. For better or for worse, the term media is overwhelmingly associated with the print and broadcast media, with their physical, tangible existence. This association does not, I argue, do justice to some of the profound changes and shifts taking place not just in the Russian Federation, but worldwide. The traditional term media was being overshadowed by something more powerful and more comprehensive. That phenomenon I call the infosphere. The change from media to infosphere has been forced on us by the astonishing advances brought about by computers and information technology (IT) generally. As configurations in products and services available to consumers multiply, so the legislative background becomes ever more complicated. Such configurations also imply huge changes in the physical infrastructure.

While 1991 can possibly be regarded as the starting point of this study, it must, for obvious reasons, take note of the historical legacy whose malignancies will be felt for many years to come. More than any other state, Russia's new infosphere is a combination of the old and the new.

1991 has a double significance for the Russian people. First and foremost, it is the year of the Great August Liberation, the end of the Leninist experiment in mass enslavement which was launched with a *coup d'état* in 1917. 1991 also marks the fiftieth anniversary of the German invasion, and in a strange way these two events – liberation from Leninist enslavement and the attempt by the Nazis to impose another – are related. For Hitler's failure to take the Soviet Union – and it was there for the taking – stemmed from the overweening belief in violence accompanied by the will to power. Hitler's empire was acquired by violence but it could not be sustained by violence. It lacked any idea that could hold it together outside of war. The Soviet empire, on the other hand, had what its ideologues believed was the great idea – socialism – but this, too, could only be sustained by violence of much greater severity and duration than that of the Nazis.

Nor, when it came to the crunch, could violence sustain the Soviet empire indefinitely. The costs were too high. The Soviet collapse of 1991 was both the recognition that these costs could no longer be sustained, and the failure of will. Above all, it demonstrated the total exhaustion of Leninist agitation and propaganda. It was no longer possible to live on slogans.

The failure of Soviet *agitprop* highlights the consequences of Soviet censorship, the latter being a unique institution in human thought, or rather, anti-thought. Part I of this survey begins with an examination of the way in which censorship attacked the system it was designed to protect. Part II examines some of the problems now confronting journalists, beginning with media legislation, the impact of crime and the recent Chechen war. Part III considers the fate of the writer in a society that has found its own voice and ends with an examination of some of the issues raised by Russia's moving into the Global Information Infrastructure (GII).

This book grew out of a number of lectures on media themes delivered to full-time and retired members of the Reuter News Agency under the auspices of the Reuter Foundation between 1994 and 1997. I found the response from these media professionals both stimulating and demanding. On more occasions than I care to remember I was hard put to provide answers to some penetrating questions. Those of us who study the media in academe have much to learn from the hands-on media professionals. I would especially like to thank the following members of the Reuter Foundation: Mr Stephen Somerville for all his help and his cornucopian hospitality; Mr John Entwisle, the Reuter archivist; and Jo Weir, Irina Taylor and Jane Collins, the energetic, efficient and dedicated foot-soldiers that made things happen on time and in good order.

I would also like to thank the following: Mr Jeff Gardner of the Open Media Research Institute (OMRI) for allowing me unrestricted access to the archive in Prague, and the help extended to me while in Prague by the Russian specialists Silja Haas and Elena Corti; Mr Michael Nelson, formerly of Reuters, for allowing me unrestricted access to his personal library, for allowing me to copy much of his archive and finally for giving me a manuscript-copy of his forthcoming book, *War of the Black Heavens: The Battles of Western Broadcasting in the Cold War*; Professor Peter Krug for giving me copies of various articles; Professor Monroe Price of the Benjamin Cardozo Law School, for giving me a copy of his book, *Television, The Public Sphere, and National Identity* (1995); Mr Nicholas Pilugin of the

United States Information Agency for all the information provided via e-mail; Mr Aleksey Simonov for sending me copies of books and information which were unavailable in England; Ināra Rudaka, Department of Communications, Latvia; G. Berzins, former Director of the Department of Telecommunications, Latvia; Richard Cummings, formerly of Radio Free Europe/Radio Liberty for his material on the Markov murder. Copies of the manuscript were sent to Mr Melvin Kean, Head of School for English and Communication Studies, Southgate College of Further Education, London and Mr Ctibor Peciva, former Political and Military Affairs Specialist, Czechoslovak Broadcasting Service, Radio Free Europe/Radio Liberty, Munich for comments; I gratefully acknowledge their help and kindness.

Unless otherwise stated all translations from the Russian are mine. Transliteration conforms to British Standard (Modified) with the exception of established usage such as Dostoevsky.

When writing this book I have been mindful throughout of the admirable advice given by the late Sir Karl Popper in *The Poverty of Historicism* (1957), namely, to state one's point of view as plainly as possible and to be aware that it is one of a number 'and that even if it should amount to a theory, it may not be testable' (p. 152). All views and interpretations expressed in this book are mine alone.

FRANK ELLIS
University of Leeds

Glossary of Soviet and Russian Media Terms

agitatsiya/agitation. One of the functions of mass propaganda. A crucial element in Marxist-Leninist indoctrination.

antikommunizm:
> a constituent part of the ideology and politics of imperialism, the pivot of its class strategy, the aggregate of its aggressive political and ideological actions, including the comprehensive, universal use of propaganda channels with the aim of falsifying the ideology of communism and of discrediting the practice of real socialism and undermining the revolutionary movement of the working class worldwide (Beglov, 1984, p. 356).

antisovietizm:
> the basic manifestation of anti-communism aimed at discrediting and undermining the internal and external policies of the Soviet Union as the first country of victorious socialism and at undermining the foundations of international solidarity of contemporary progressive forces (Beglov, 1984, p. 356).

de-ideologizatsiya/de-ideologization/the renouncing of ideology:
> the anti-scientific bourgeois concept about the 'end of ideology' on the strength of an allegedly growing preponderance of scientific-technical 'administrative-control' factors in the development of society over factors determined by the class nature of society and the ideology of the ruling class (Beglov, 1984, p. 358).

eklektizm/eclecticism:
> used by Lenin to criticize opponents who did not strive for ideological and theoretical purity.

Federal'noe agentstvo pravitel'stvennoy svyazi i informatsii pri Prezidente Rossiyskoy Federatsii/Federal Agency of Communications and Information Attached to the Presidential Office of the Russian Federation:
> official body for determining questions of access to computer and other networks in matters of international information exchange.

Federal'naya komissiya po teleradioveshchaniyu/Federal Commission for Television and Radio Broadcasting.

Federal'nyy informatsionnyy tsentr Rossii (FITsR)/Russian Federal Information Centre.

Federal'naya sluzhba Rossii po televideniyu i radioveshchaniyu/The Federal Service of Russia for Television and Radio Broadcasting.

Fond zashchity Glasnosti/ The Glasnost Defence Foundation.

fotoreportazh/Picture story.

glasnost'/openness. Synonymous with the Gorbachev reforms.

Glavnoe upravlenie po okhrane gosudarstvennykh tayn v pechati/ GLAVLIT/Chief Directorate for the Protection of State Secrets in the Press:

the body responsible for censorship throughout most of the Soviet period.

Gosudarstvennaya inspektsiya po zashchite svobody pechati i massovoy informatsii pri Ministerstve pechati i informatsii Rossiyskoy Federatsii/ State Inspectorate for the Protection of the Freedom of the Press and Mass Information attached to the Ministry of the Press and Information of the Russian Federation.

Gosudarstvennaya tekhnicheskaya komissiya pri Prezidente Rossiyskoy Federatsii/ The State Technical Commission of the Presidential Office of the Russian Federation:

Official body for determining questions of access to computer and other networks in matters of international information exchange.

ideynost'/ideological correctness.

Informatsionnoe telegrafnoe agentsvo Rossii (ITAR)/Information Telegraph Agency of Russia:

successor agency to the Soviet agency TASS (see below) though TASS is retained in the title (ITAR/TASS).

informatsiya dokumentirovannaya/documentary information (Russian Federation).

——, *konfidentsial'naya*/confidential information access restricted in accordance with the legislation of the Russian Federation.

——, *massovaya*/mass information designed for an unlimited circle of persons (Russian Federation).

kinofikatsiya/Cinemafication:

programme of building cinemas, or using mobile ones, so as to disseminate party propaganda.

Komissiya po svobode dostupa k informatsii (KSDI)/Freedom of Information Commission.

Komissiya po raspredeleniyu gosdotatsiy redaktsiyam, gazetam i zhurnalam/Commission for the Allocation of State Subsidies to Editorial Staffs, Newspapers and Journals.

Komitet pri Prezidente Rossiyskoy Federatsii po politike informatizatsii (*Roskominform*)/The Presidential Committee of the Russian Federation on the Policy of Informatization.

Komitet po zashchite prav zhurnalistov pri Rossiyskom Soyuze zhurnalistov/Committee for the Protection of Journalists' Rights of the Russian Union of Journalists.

Komitet Rossiyskoy Federatsii po pechati (*Roskompechat'*)/successor body to the Federal Information Centre of Russia and the Ministry of Press and Information of the Russian Federation.

Komitet Rossiyskoy Federatsii po standartizatsii, metrologii i sertifikatsii/ Russian Federation Committee on Standardization, Metrology and Certification.

kommunikativnaya deyatel'nost'/the translation of ideas and images arising in the journalist's mind into a language accessible and comprehensible to a wider public.

kritika/criticism:
  criterion of socialist realism and Marxist-Leninist press theory.

massovost'/mass appeal or relevance:
  criterion of socialist-realism and Marxist-Leninist press theory.

Mezhvedomstvennaya Komissiya po zashchite gosudarstvennoy tayny/ The Inter-Departmental Commission for the Protection of State Secrets.

Ministerstvo pechati i informatsii Rossiyskoy Federatsii/ The Ministry of Press and Information of the Russian Federation.

napravlennost'/the focusing of a number of points as they affect a question, and addressed to a specific audience.

narodnost'/national character or traits:
  criterion of socialist realism and Marxist-Leninist press theory.

nastupatel'nost'/Soviet propaganda's 'uncompromising exposure of the flaws and contradictions of the capitalist structure' (Beglov, 1984, p. 360).

nauchnost/the scientific basis of Marxist-Leninist ideology.

nekontroliruemyy podtekst/uncontrollable subtext:
  the use of hints, allusions and ambiguity, which, as the Russian suggests, poses problems for the censor.

Neposredstvennoe televizionnoe veshchanie/Live Television Broadcasting. Also referred to as satellite broadcasting.

Nezavisimoe televidenie (NTV)/Independent Television.

oblichitel'naya literatura/literature of exposure:
  a term coined by Lenin. Part of Bolshevik attacks on capitalism before 1917.

Obmeny informatsionnye/Information Exchanges:
    a form of international intercourse provided for by the mass media
    and foreign-policy propaganda, by cultural channels, economic and
    scientific links, as well as by the activities of international organiza-
    tions. In contrast to the imperialist doctrine and practice of the
    'free flow of information', the principles of original internal
    exchanges in the sphere of information are based on the aggregate
    of the widely recognized norms of international law, on the right of
    every country to participate in such an exchange in conditions of
    full equality, respect for the structure of the life and traditional
    forms of the dissemination of information of other countries and
    the reinforcement of peace and mutual understanding among
    nations (Beglov, 1984, p. 361).

obobshchenie/generalizing:
    Lenin's term for drawing conclusions on the nature of the class
    struggle as reflected, according to Lenin, in discrete incidents.

Obshchestvennoe rossiyskoe televidenie (ORT)/Public Russian Television.

otechestvennost'/ of, or relating to, the Fatherland:
    criterion of socialist realism and Marxist-Leninist press theory.

partiynost'/ party-mindedness, party spirit or political correctness. The
most important criterion of socialist realism and Marxist-Leninist
press theory. Note the following definition:

    Partyinost' in communist propaganda is fidelity to the higher, class
    interests of the working class and its mission of the revolutionary
    transformation of the nature of social relations. The principle
    of *partyinost'* rejects the pretensions of bourgeois ideology and
    propaganda to 'non-*partiynost*'', 'objectivity' and 'pluralism' as
    masking the bourgeois mechanism of social control (Beglov,
    1984, p. 362).

*Perechen' svedeniy, ne podlezhashchikh opublikovaniyu v otkrytoy
pechati*/List of Information Not Suitable for Publication in the Open
Press:
    the Soviet censor's manual. Referred to as the 'List' and sometimes
    'The Talmud'.

poznavatel'naya deyatel'nost'/the methods and means by which the
journalist acquires and conceptualizes information.

pravdivost'/ truthfulness (to Marxism-Leninism):
    Criterion of socialist realism and Marxist-Leninist press theory.

proektivnaya deyatel'nost'/the mastery of procedures which make it
possible for the journalist to process effective images for the benefit
of himself and others.

propaganda kommunisticheskaya:
   Communist propaganda is a scientifically-based system of spiritual activity in the dissemination of Marxist-Leninist ideology and policy with the aim of enlightening, educating and organizing the masses. It is one of the means by which the party leads the processes of the revolutionary struggle, the building of communism and socialism. Its basic principles are: *nauchnost'*, *partiynost'*, a close link with life and the unity of propagandistic and organizational work. Bourgeois propaganda has as its aim the forcing onto the masses of false ideas, theories and unobjective information in the interests of the ruling classes (Beglov, 1984, p. 363).

radiofikatsiya/Radiofication:
   programme analogous to cinemafication carried out through the medium of radio.

Rossiyskoe agentstvo po pravovoy okhrane programm dlya EVM, baz dannykh i topologiy integral'nykh mikroskhem/The Russian Agency for the Legal Storage of Computer Programs, Databases and Topologies of Integrated Microsystems.

Rossiyskoe informatsionnoe agentstvo 'Novosti' (RIA)/Russian Information Agency 'Novosti.'

samokritika/self-criticism:
   criterion of socialist realism and Marxist-Leninist press theory.

Russian Institute for Public Networks (RIPN).

soznatel'nost'/consciousness or political awareness.

Sredstva massovoy informatsii (SMI)/ The means of mass information, the mass media:
   in the Soviet period this would have been referred to as *sredstva massovoy informatsii i propagandy*, the mass media and propaganda.

stikhiynost'/elementalism. Lenin's term for the political immaturity of the masses.

Sudebnaya Palata po Informatsionnym Sporam pri Prezidente Rossiskoy Federatsii/The Judicial Chamber for Information Disputes attached to the President of the Russian Federation. 'Successor' body to the Information Arbitration Tribunal).

Telegrafnoe Agentstvo Sovetskogo Soyuza (TASS)

telefonizatsiya/development and investment needed to create a universal telephone network.

tipichnost'/typicalness:
   criterion of socialist realism and Marxist-Leninist press theory.

Treteyskiy informatsionnyy sud/Information Arbitration Tribunal. Set up to monitor access to the media during the 1993 elections.

Upravlenie repertuarnogo kontrolya/Repertory Control Administration.
Vremenny informatsionnyy tsentr pri Komitete RF po pechati (VITs)/The Provisional Information Centre Attached to the Russian Federation Press Committee.
Vserossiyskaya gosudarstvennaya televizionnaya i radioveshchatel'naya kompaniya (VGTRK)/All-Russian State Television and Radio Broadcasting Company.
Vsesoyuznyy tsentr izucheniya obshchestvennogo mneniya (Vtsiom)/ All-Union Centre for the Study of Public Opinion.
zametka/ short piece of reporting.

Chronology

1943. COLOSSUS, a British computer used for code-breaking at Bletchley Park

1945. Arthur C. Clarke's concept of the geosynchronous communications satellite published.

1946–53. *Zhdanovshchina*. Named after Stalin's Commissar for Culture. Period of cultural purges and savage attacks on writers, artists and scientists.

24 June 1948. Soviet authorities start blockade of West Berlin.

1948. Soviet Union's first televised outside broadcast.

1948. William Shockley invents the transistor.

1948. Claude Shannon publishes his theory of information.

1948. Publication of Norbert Wiener's *Cybernetics: Or, Control and Communication in the Animal and the Machine*.

1949. Publication of George Orwell's *1984*.

13 January 1953. An announcement in *Pravda* that Jewish doctors were conspiring to kill senior members of the Soviet establishment. Vicious anti-Jewish campaign ensues in the Soviet media.

17 June 1953. Workers' Uprising in East Berlin, part of the Soviet occupation zone.

1953. Publication of Czesław Miłosz's *The Captive Mind*.

24 February 1956. Khrushchev attacks Stalin and Stalinism in a closed session of the 20th Congress of the CPSU.

4 November 1956. Soviet troops invade Hungary.

26 October 1958. Article in *Pravda* attacks Boris Pasternak and his book *Dr Zhivago*, 'Reactionary Propaganda over a Literary Weed'.

1959. Xerox markets the photocopier.

14 February 1961. KGB seizes the manuscript of Grossman's *Life and Fate*.

13 August 1961. Work starts on the Berlin Wall.

10–14 February 1966. Daniel and Sinyavsky trial in Moscow.

1966. International Covenant of Civil and Political Rights (ICCPR) (adopted).

1968. Underground journal *Chronicle of Current Events* starts to be circulated in the Soviet Union.

1968. Andrei Sakharov's *Progress, Coexistence, and Intellectual Freedom* completed.

21 August 1968. Soviet troops invade Czechoslovakia.

1969. The Advanced Research Project Agency (ARPANET) initiated. Military and defence-related computer networks linked to share research findings. Beginnings of the Internet.

1971. Tef Hoff (Intel employee) invents microprocessor.

1972 c. Gary Kildall, a computer science teacher at the Naval Post-Graduate school, Monterey California, invents the first microcomputer operating system.

1972–74. Watergate. President Nixon resigns.

1974. Ray Tomlinson invents electronic mail, sends first e-mail message.

1975. Soviet Union launches its first geo-stationary satellite (*Raduga*) followed by *Ekran* in 1976 and *Gorizont* in 1978.

1977. Polish Censor, number C-36, Tomasz Stryżewski, defects to Sweden. Brings with him documents revealing the full extent of the Polish censorship apparatus. Documents translated and published under the title *The Black Book of Polish Censorship*.

7 October 1977. Fourth Soviet Constitution (adopted).

7 September 1978. Bulgarian Dissident writer, Georgi Markov, murdered in London on orders of Todor Zhivkov.

1980. Josip Broz Tito dies. Throughout the 1980s the republics comprising Yugoslavia assert themselves. Media in all republics crucial.

10 December 1981. Martial Law declared in Poland. Crackdown on *Solidarity*.

26 April 1986. Chernobyl reactor explodes. Pace of *glasnost'* accelerates.

15 May 1986. Full transcript of Gorbachev's televised address on the Chernobyl disaster published in *Pravda*.

1986–90. Publication of major Russian authors hitherto banned and censored. Platonov, Zamyatin, Grossman, Pasternak, Solzhenitsyn, Tsvetaeva and Pilnyak.

1990. Private television station YUTEL was founded to provide an all-Yugoslav perspective, and to propagate the views of the federal government of Ante Markovic. Croatia's main party the Croatian Democratic Community (CDC) requested that broadcasts cease.

1 August 1990. The Law on the Press and other Media (Soviet Union) takes effect. Censorship banned.

9 August 1990. Publication of the Albanian-language daily *Rilindja* suspended in Kosovo by Serbs.

1991. Broadcasting facilities were among the first targets of the Yugoslav People's Army (YPA). General Andrija Raseta complained that the broadcasts were bad for morale.

1991. Slovenia and Croatia saw Tanjug (the Federal News agency) as a federal mouthpiece, set up their own agencies Sta and Hina respectively. On Tanjug's editorial freedom, the editor-in-chief,

Zarko Modric said: 'There is no censorship, but there is more than just pressure.'

1991. Use of satellite TV by Croatia to influence wealthy Croatian expats. Croatia-01, Croatia-02, Croatia-03, which are linked to Intelsat, Eutelsat or Inmarsat.

25 January 1991. Television broadcast of a conspiracy allegedly plotted by Croatian Defence Minister Martin Spegelj. Shown in all republics with the exception of Croatia.

9 and 10 March 1991. Demonstrations in Belgrade. Key demands were: greater access to the pro-socialist Serbian media and the dismissal of Director of Belgrade Television, Dusan Mitevic, an associate of Serbia's President Slobodan Milosevic.

July–August 1991. Outbreak of civil war in Yugoslavia.

19 August 1991. State Committee on the Emergency Situation seizes power. Regular television programming suspended. (Soviet Union).

21 August 1991. Coup d'état fails.

29 August 1991. Croatian TV launched a 24-hour programme, 'Croatia's War for Freedom', backed up in *Vjesnik*.

7 November 1991. Tanjug News Agency purged of employees suspected of being hostile towards Milosevic.

9 November 1991. Croatia's National Assembly approved severe decree on censorship.

9 December 1991. War in Croatia ends.

27 December 1991. Russian Federation Mass Media Law (adopted). Enacted 6 February 1992.

July 1992. Hostilities erupted between staff and *Politika* when Belgrade tried to make the paper a state organ. By the summer of 1992, *Politika* had adopted a critical position on Belgrade's involvement in the Bosnian war.

January 1993. Some 1000 staff purged in Serbia Radio and Television.

1993–96. 14 journalists killed and 4 missing while covering the Chechen war.

9 July 1993. Russian Federal Law Concerning the Rights of the Author and Contiguous Rights (adopted).

21 July 1993. Russian Federal Law Concerning State Secrets (adopted).

29 July 1993. The Chechen newspaper *Marsho* shut down on the grounds that the Press and Media Law of the Chechen Republic violated. Precise conditions of the violation not cited.

15 December 1993. Serbian state authorities tried to jam Television

Studio B's live broadcast of rally attended by Vuk Draskovic.

31 December 1993. Presidential decree (Yeltsin) establishes The Judicial Chamber for Information Disputes.

Spring 1994. Bosnian Serb state TV to show a 13-part, low-budget soap called *Naked Life* in an attempt to redress domestic and international impressions of Serbs as savages.

26 May 1994. Publication of the Martin Bangemann Report, *Europe and the Global Information Society*.

23 June 1994. Journalists' Ethical Code approved by the Congress of Journalists of Russia.

10 August 1994. On the orders of Chechen President Dzhokhar Dudaev the broadcasting of Russian television in the republic stopped.

2 September 1994. Government of the Chechen republic demands that all Russian journalists leave the territory of the Chechen republic within 24 hours. Journalists from other countries permitted to remain.

17 October 1994. The military correspondent of *Moskovskiy komsomolets*, Dmitriy Kholodov, murdered in Moscow.

1 December 1994. The Russian government creates The Provisional Information Centre Attached to the Russian Federation Press Committee.

15 December 1994. Russian Federal Law Concerning the Procedure for the Reporting of the Activities of State Organs in the State Mass Media (adopted).

30 December 1994. The organization Russian National Unity calls for tighter control of the Russian mass media.

20 January 1995. Russian Federal Law Concerning Communications (adopted).

25 January 1995. Russian Federal Law Concerning Information, Informatization and the Protection of Information (adopted).

1 March 1995. Senior executive of *Ostankino*, Vladislav Listiev, murdered in Moscow.

1996. Council of Europe report recommends that the European Union adopt a version of the Clipper Chip enabling all privately-encrypted communications to be read by officials in Brussels.

28 February 1996. Russian Federation joins the Council of Europe.

30 April 1996. The Open Society Institute announces plans to spend $100 million dollars (US) over five years to establish University Internet Centres at 30 Russian universities.

5 June 1996. Russian Federal Law Concerning Participation in

International Information Exchange (adopted).

10 June 1996. Internet Centres opened at the Universities of Yaroslavl and Novosibirsk.

11 June 1996. American Civil Liberties Union challenges the American Government's Communications Decency Act 1996. Wins preliminary injunction.

November 1997. British series of *Carry On* comedy films, including *Carry on up the Khyber* and *Carry on up the Jungle* to be launched all over Eastern Europe.

Part I The Collapse of Soviet Communism

1 Information Deficit

Blocking the exchange of information is still, of course, one of their most important tasks, and a foundation stone of totalitarianism ...
Valentin Turchin, 1981

SOME CAUSES AND SYMPTOMS OF COLLAPSE

Among communism's many intellectual vices, the belief in the inevitability of a specific resolution of History was, arguably, the most far-reaching. Codified and formalized, variously as dialectical or historical materialism, or scientific communism, these sub-doctrines of Marxism-Leninism were used to justify a programme of wholesale social, moral and economic transformation. Inevitability determined that the outcome was beyond reasonable doubt. Opposition to the course of History was thus futile. History, as we know, let communism down.

If nothing else, the collapse of communism teaches us to treat the word inevitability with caution. The dangers of not doing so are both intellectual and moral. A belief in inevitability must influence the way we interpret human agency in the historical process. We either exclude human agency, or reduce its role considerably. A particular chain of events, it could be argued, ran their course. If Lenin and Stalin were inevitable, if they were the unwitting tools of History, rather than its manipulators, then we have no right to apportion blame for the Terror-Famine or Kolyma (or the Nazis' systematic murder of Europe's Jews); the resistance of individuals has no obvious moral basis; the West deserves no credit (or censure) for its actions (or inactions) during the period of East–West confrontation between 1917–91. Even worse, a belief in inevitability offers intellectual succour to the seeker after the historicist's magic stone that will, still now, it is believed, lay bare the secrets of historical change, and enable him to bring about the Golden Age.

The dismantling of the communist edifice in the 1980s, which led to its final collapse in 1991, and as a consequence, to the unravelling of the seemingly immutable, bi-polar geometry of post-Second-World-War Europe, was not inevitable. One could have argued, quite

3

reasonably, that communism would collapse at some stage. The difficulty arose when trying to estimate for how much longer the Soviet experiment would endure before it did fall apart. All the evidence tells us that the vast majority of what we would call informed observers were caught unawares. When History delivered its verdict it was swift and pitiless. Indeed, some in the West viewed the prospect with horror. An interesting question is whether the suspension of all aid might have brought about the system's collapse much sooner, and forced the Soviet leadership to pursue reform and thus avert the threat of anarchy.

For the purposes of this chapter there are two interrelated questions. First, why did the Soviet empire collapse? And second, why did it collapse when it did? Furthermore, was there anything that accelerated its final demise from the mid-1980s? Many of the reversals suffered by communism were predictable, and predicted.[1] Others grew out of the specific chemistry of totalitarian socialism and were only apparent in the final stages of its social and economic decomposition, or more accurately, were only admitted to exist after a prolonged silence. From the banal to the profound, communism was a miserable and deadly failure.

A persistent shortage of basic consumer items was one of the more noticeable consequences of communist economic practice. Entrepreneurial instincts were hemmed in and frustrated by ossified political structures, a collectivist ideology and a deeply ingrained culture of envy. Nor did Soviet industry and agriculture manage to overcome the disastrous effects stemming from the destruction of some of the most productive and energetic members of Soviet society in the 1930s. One wonders what readers of Gorbachev's book, *Perestroika: New Thinking for Our Country and the World* (1987), who had experienced first hand the effects of socialist economics, must have made of the author's startling assertion that: 'Socialism and public ownership, on which it is based, hold out virtually unlimited possibilities for progressive economic processes.'[2] Only when it was too late did the leaders of communist systems understand the folly of abandoning caution when trying to realize the theoretical certainties of ideology upon the frequently treacherous quicksands of human nature and reality. Marxist-Leninist ideology blinded the Soviet leadership to the emerging and unpredictable challenge of capitalist societies switching from labour-intensive to intellectual-intensive modes of wealth creation in the latter half of the twentieth century. Advances in information theory and information technology (IT) are the keys to this revolution in wealth creation.[3] Research, design, marketing and the service sector, indeed the whole mode of activity associated with what has been termed the post-industrial society, would be impossible without the concept, hardware and software of IT. Francis Fukuyama's observation has much to recommend it: 'One might say in fact that it was in the highly complex and dynamic "post-industrial" economic world that Marxism-Leninism as an economic system met its Waterloo.'[4]

Less publicized was the huge environmental damage resulting from communist industry. Citizens in the former peoples' republics not only received a lot less from their inefficient industries, but also paid a much greater price in terms of a heavily polluted environment, rising infant mortality rates and declining life expectancy. Insurmountable and indefensible discrepancies between the theories and promises of socialism fuelled intellectual disaffection, in turn stimulating the growth of dissident activity across Eastern Europe. Intellectually and morally, successive Soviet leaders found it ever more difficult to ignore and to defend the regime's past. Outside Russia, the revenge of the repressed posed acute problems for regimes in Czechoslovakia, Hungary, Poland and even traditionally obedient Bulgaria and East Germany. As the end approached other horrors manifested themselves: an uncontrollable black market; hyperinflation; and a near total collapse in law and order as criminal gangs fought over the corpse of the Soviet Union, a particularly gruesome affirmation of the Hobbesian nightmare.

Of course, external and internal factors worked in tandem to bring the system down. Significant among international factors were: a Western, anti-collectivist revival, heralded by the election of Ronald Reagan (1980) and Margaret Thatcher (1979); a greater willingness on the part of the West, when compared to the 1970s, to use armed force to protect its interests (Grenada and the Falklands campaigns for example, see below); a general perception that the Soviet invasion of Afghanistan was one military operation too far, even for the West;[5] the magnitude of technological change affecting the world economy; and the cumulative effects brought about by the repeated penetration of the Soviet infosphere by Western radio[6] and in some areas television (East Germany, for example).[7] Domestically important were: the Soviet leadership's lack of political will to use armed force to resolve the Cold War; the need to rejuvenate the Soviet economy; pragmatic Soviet appraisal; and the greater assertiveness of certain East European states (Hungary and Poland for example). Any one of these factors or clusters of them is insufficient to explain the end of the Cold War. Considered in their entirety the picture is somewhat different. Taken together, they created a unique opportunity. The fact that so many propitious factors converged in the 1980s is a remarkable historical occurrence, and one, it must be emphasized, that was by no means inevitable.[8]

THE DECISIVE IMPACT OF CENSORSHIP

The spectacular failures of collectivist economics with their reckless and unaccountable poisoning of the environment, the horrendous social problems and the Western revival, all help to explain why the Soviet system might eventually implode. What they do not tell us, however, is why and how such a massive fraud was successfully perpetrated for over 70 years, and why it was no longer possible to perpetuate it for another 70 years. What, in the final analysis, we are seeking, are pathologies and characteristics unique to the Soviet system which might answer these two questions.

The Baconian dictum that knowledge is power holds true for all political systems. Communist systems, however, are unique for the exceptional degree to which they have sought to interpret information on the basis of their political creed – dialectical materialism – and then impose this interpretation on all forms of intellectual endeavour. Yet, Marxist-Leninist philosophy failed to resolve the problem posed by the neutrality or objectivity of information.[9] The question unresolved, communist systems constructed an edifice of censorship, quite unprecedented in the history of human thought.[10] It is in the nature of Soviet censorship and the justification of censorship, provided for by Marxist-Leninist ideology, that we find the reason for the end of Soviet power.

Given that Soviet society was mandated on the public ownership of the means of production, then the Soviet censorship apparatus reflects a profound paradox. Information and data were categorically not subject to common ownership. Access to fairly banal information was determined by one's place in the party hierarchy. As a result, information became one of the most sought after commodities in the Soviet Union. Compare this scarcity with what obtains in the capitalist West. Despite being societies in which the private ownership of the means of production is accepted, along with property rights, vast amounts of data and information, which in the Soviet Union would have been deposited in the *spetskhran*, are freely available in the public domain. The fact that capitalist societies also tend to be liberal, open and democratic may also not be coincidental.

Under certain conditions censorship is defensible and desirable. War is an obvious example. But the restrictions of wartime censorship cannot be justified in peacetime. As a permanent feature of societal and economic policy it is counter-productive and corrosive. But Soviet society was in a permanent state of war. If the Soviet Union was not involved in a real life-and-death struggle against the Nazis, then the party demanded ceaseless vigilance in the fight against 'wreckers', 'revisionists' and other 'enemies of the people'. Endless campaigns were waged to raise production and meet the plan. Overshadowing all these campaigns was the ideological war waged against the capitalist enemy. The state of mind was one of a siege. In such conditions censorship seems quite normal, almost sensible.

Censorship in any society impedes and complicates the already considerable functions of regulating and coordinating the flow of information. In systems such as communism, by their very nature hostile to free flows of information, the task is rendered almost impossible. Similar malign effects can be observed in biological systems. For example, if a plant's access to light is restricted, say by placing it in a box with a hole on one side, the plant will grow towards the reduced light source. It may well survive, but its overall physical condition will markedly deteriorate. Censorship at even moderate levels imposes changes on the natural exchange of information. Censorship always involves some interference with the optimal flow of information. All forms of government necessarily involve censorship. The greater the censorship, the greater the risk that information is degraded and corrupted. Good government consists, therefore, in minimizing the censorship or interdiction of information and ideas. Political systems, which for whatever reasons, are unable to tolerate a trial-and-error approach towards information and ideas, believing instead in extreme prescription, are vulnerable to sudden shifts in the information environment. Like the dinosaurs, they are unable to adapt to sudden discontinuity. Even if their information environment can be insulated from the threat of external discontinuity, these systems must still cope with the consequences of internal censorship. This promotes dysfunctional behaviour, which, depending on its severity and pervasiveness, will progressively undermine all economic and political activity. The final result is systemic collapse.[11] In the case of the Soviet Union this occurred in the late 1980s, accelerated by yet another act of ideological surgery, *perestroyka* and *glasnost'*. We need not be too concerned with *perestroyka* and *glasnost'*, since the damage caused by censorship and the party's information policy was done well before these changes captured the headlines. By that time the system could not be salvaged, however photogenic the latest general secretary proved to be, or however ably he managed the Western media. The contradictions of communism were simply too contradictory. What we need to consider first is how Soviet censorship attacked economic, scientific and artistic endeavour, in short, the very sinews of culture and prosperity.

THE PROBLEM OF IDEOLOGY

There are three facets of Marxist-Leninist ideology which have great importance for our understanding of the failure of Soviet-style censorship. They are: (i) the special nature of the Soviet utopian mission, the building of the new society and the moulding of its new inhabitant, *homo sovieticus*; (ii) the influence exerted by this mission on the media, the party's indoctrinators; (iii) then there is a special problem posed by the meaning and use of the word ideology/ideological. In essence, the problem is one of a misuse of the word to include all sets, sub-sets and accretions of political and economic principles, custom and culture under the rubric of ideology. We need, I believe, to be far more selective in applying this protean word whose elasticity obscures too much. Defining our use of the word ideology more closely, and confining our use to those systems that indeed merit it, is not an empty exercise in academic hair-splitting. On the contrary, it is necessary if we are to discriminate between open societies and their dysfunctional, totalitarian rivals, and thus the causes of the latter's collapse.

Lenin, not Marx, was the architect of communist theories and models of information control. Marx laid the foundation, encapsulated in the public ownership of the means of production, but Lenin gave it form and substance, transforming it into a tool for subversion, revolution and one-party control. The very essence of this tool was thus avowedly hostile to a free flow of information and ideas. In Western societies knowledge advances through a process of testing and criticism. An idea or theory in whatever field of knowledge must fight for its survival. However elegant and cogent, it must defend itself from intellectual forces bent on destroying it. No doubt there is a degree of professional, academic jealousy involved in all of this, but the principle itself is sound and by and large works well. Lenin was a dedicated student of the West's founding fathers, so how then are we to explain Lenin's determination to expunge any 'freedom of criticism' (*svoboda kritiki*) from the ranks of the party?

Lenin's hostility to the freedom to adopt various standpoints and to disseminate various views can be explained in three ways. Firstly, there is a genuine fear on Lenin's part that ideas which he himself despises, might indeed have a much wider appeal than he is prepared openly to admit. Secondly, Lenin harboured no doubts about the scientific integrity and ethos of socialism. It was, he argued, the scientific grounding of socialism which made it superior to all other forms of political intercourse. Moreover, this scientific analysis yielded, according to Lenin, certain laws, which if interpreted and implemented correctly, would enable mankind to reach its final goal. Given that socialism was a science, and that there was no room for alternative opinions and views, socialism was the correct world view, everything else was barbarism. To give a fair hearing to other political systems would be the same thing as according the same degree of respect to the views of Newton and the Flat Earth Society: one was a scientifically correct view of the Earth, the other was false, and demonstrably so. While it is possible to demonstrate that the Flat Earth Society's view of the Earth's shape is wrong, one cannot prove with the same level of scientific and mathematical rigour that socialism, or any other 'ism' is scientifically correct or incorrect. Ultimately, it comes down to subjective factors such as experience, personality and faith. Hard-headed analyses and rebuttals of socialism by economists, such as Böhm-Bawerk and Von Mises were simply ignored. Lenin lays sole claim to the word 'scientific' on behalf of socialism. Anything which attacks socialism is simply unscientific. The scientific status of Leninist ideology arrives as a philosophical given, an immaculate conception, which only the mad will challenge. Thus any opposition to socialism – and especially Lenin – is damned from the outset. Here, too, we see one line of defence for refuting accusations of censorship levelled at the Soviet system. Since the Soviet interpretation of the world is correct, it makes no sense to give equal tolerance to views and opinions which proceed from philosophically flawed premises. Scientific rigour, not censorship, is what proscribed space for non-communist views and opinions.

Thirdly, convinced that the theory he was developing was the only possible option for the party, Lenin feared that were a forum given to ideas other than those propagated by the social democrats, then the momentum towards revolution would be dissipated and even diverted from its goals: there might not be a revolution. The movement would be guilty of the sin of 'elementalism'. Yet another reason for Lenin to pour scorn on 'the freedom of criticism': 'this pernicious freedom of criticism does not mean the replacement of one theory by another, but the freedom from any values and carefully thought out theory. It means eclecticism and lack of principles.'[12] 'Without a revolutionary theory', argues Lenin, 'there can be no revolutionary movement.'[13]

Intolerance of the freedom of criticism – as interpreted by Lenin – is entirely consistent with the interdiction of the free flow of information and ideas. Ideas and information can only flow in an unimpeded manner when some level of uncertainty and sceptical enquiry about the world is admitted. Scepticism and uncertainty are hardly the attributes of Leninism. Lenin knows where he is going. Lenin's party was no mere talking shop for disaffected intellectuals: it was an instrument for the prosecution of revolution and class war. As such, its internal culture and psychology were completely unsuited to open and informed discussion, and, naturally, a willingness to be bound by the outcome of any such discussion.

Inseparable from the free flow of information is a belief that news – processed raw data and information – should strive for objectivity, impartiality, neutrality and fairness. Here again ideology interposes itself to create two quite discrete and unbridgeable world views. Consider the criteria of objectivity and neutrality. If Leninist ideology offers the only true explanation of the world then any explanation which falls outside of its parameters is wrong. From this it follows that an objective explanation of the world is one that is entirely congenial to Leninism, otherwise it is 'objectively wrong'. Nor is neutrality a possible option.[14] The Leninist *Weltanschauung* has no room for the luxury of neutrality: those who are not for us must be against us. Precisely for that reason, neutrality threatens the claims to unique-ness made by ideology. Neutrality recognizes no special cases. For Marx and for Lenin, information and ideas can never be neutral since they either reflect their socialist or capitalist milieu. Those who claim to be neutral, they would argue, are failing to declare their bias.[15] Driven by Marxist-Leninist ideology, the rejection of neutrality is only a small part of a much more comprehensive assault on Western jour-nalism, which Lenin detested.

Under the direct control of Marxism-Leninism, Soviet journalism defined itself in accordance with a canon quite unlike anything evolved in the West. The main criteria were: *partiynost'*; *ideynost'*; *pravdivost'*; *narodnost'*; *otechestvennost'*; *massovost'*; and *kritika/samokritika*. These criteria were not intended to help the Soviet journalist, as might be understood in any Western sense. They were designed to control him and to restrict the manner in which news and information were reported in the media. To ascribe to them the function of censorship is entirely appropriate. It is also indicative of the party's attempt to censor that these criteria were central to the doctrine of socialist realism which was imposed on creative artists in 1934 (see below).

These journalistic criteria are riddled with inconsistencies and circular arguments. Take for example, *partiynost'* and *ideynost'*. *Partiynost'* signifies either membership of the party or party-minded-ness. One could cite a number of Soviet definitions, but the central thrust is that an action or an exposition of a given event must be inter-preted in a manner that is consistent with Marxist-Leninist ideology. *Partiynost'* is also the origin of the notion of political correctness, which, despite the manifest failure of communist media and other forms of lying, seems nevertheless to have achieved considerable success in the social and economic policies of many Western states. *Partiynost'* is by definition politically correct. Closely linked to *partiynost'* is *ideynost'*. A good English translation would be 'ideolog-ical correctness'.[16] Party-mindedness or party spirit is determined by its ideological interpretation and *ideynost'* is defined by the party's ideologue imbued with party-mindedness. Approaching questions of ideology from a party-minded direction is the *only* option for the ideologist. Everything else is heresy. *Partiynost'* was more than just a hint from the party to the journalist. It was an operational principle, derived from the thoughts of Lenin, and therefore sanctified, and one to be enforced in a militant and unambiguous fashion. True, the party line changed – naturally, at the party's discretion – but the effortless flexibility of *partiynost'* made it possible to obscure a multitude of sins. As far as the party's senior ideologues were concerned, its chief virtue was elasticity.

No less problematic for the Soviet journalist were the criteria of *narodnost'* and *otechestvennost'*. Marxist-Leninist ideology proclaimed the international solidarity of the working class. Yet *narodnost'* and *otechestvennost'* consciously promote the specific qualities of the Soviet people. Undeniable tension exists between the claims of ideology and the powerful pull of blood, tradition, language, history and culture. Ideology failed to resolve this tension. In theory this should not have posed a problem, since for a member of the working class there should be no conflict of loyalty between solidarity with his exploited comrades in the capitalist mills and factories, and his country, an accident of birth. Among the fraternity of socialist nations, however, the Russians were always *primus inter pares*. Matters were made still worse by the fact that many people living inside the former Soviet Union regarded Soviet citizenship as something alien. Their primary loyalty was often to a culture, history, and especially a language and literature, quite distinct from that of Russia. Obvious examples are Latvia, Estonia, the Ukraine, Georgia and the republics of Central Asia.

Superficially, the interpretation of *pravdivost'* – truthfulness or veracity – is straightforward. The journalist must be true, or perhaps it would be more accurate to say loyal, to the teachings of Lenin. Yet any scope for diverging from the accepted canon is virtually nil. Naturally, the extent to which a given issue conforms to Lenin's views is a matter for the party ideologues. Since the dissemination of ideology is two-tiered – the party élite consider theory, the masses are forced to act on it – this means that the party in its jealously-guarded capacity as the master of the keys is always able to modify its theories and explanations in response to unpleasant facts and contradictions. The leadership, unlike the masses, enjoys a remarkable degree of freedom from the content of its own ideology (as suggested by Hannah Arendt). The journalist, if he hopes to survive, must become extremely adept at reading and interpreting the latest nuances in the utterances of the leadership. Their interpretation is not set in stone, since their relative importance shifts according to the current concerns of the leadership.

The origins of *massovost'* are to be found in Lenin's call in *Chto delat'*? (*What is to be Done?* 1902) to take the message to the masses.[17] Arguments are to be simplified and generalized. However, this criterion became progressively less effective as levels of literacy and technical competence rose in the general population. It means, in effect, that the discrepancy between what the regime claims, and what takes place, was more widely perceived. The foundations of a dissenting minority are inadvertently laid. As a criterion of revolutionary journalism *massovost'* pertains more to the primitive conditions existing in many underdeveloped countries to which Marxism-Leninism has been exported, or the early years of Soviet power, than to a numerate and literate society.

Kritika (criticism) and *samokritika* (self-criticism) appear to be a belated addition to the operational principles of the Soviet media. They fulfil a number of functions: they permit information to flow from the bottom to the top; they imply self-improvement; they deflect criticism away from the leadership itself; they allow the regime to punish unsuitable behaviour; they foster the illusion that the leadership cares for the masses; and they offer a safety valve. In a society where censorship was so pervasive and fundamental *kritika* and *samokritika* offer a controlled substitute for public opinion.

The full effect of the Soviet canon emerges when we compare the Western press with its Soviet counterpart. An outsider, with only the Soviet media as his material, might be tempted to conclude that all problems can be explained and solved by application of this ideological model. The overwhelming impressions would be of order, social unity and consistency. Our outsider would reach very different conclusions about the West. First and foremost, he would be struck by the range of material available to the public. Newspapers and journals discussing natural disasters, crime, serial killers, high finance, political issues and environmental problems would represent just a small sample of what was on offer. He would note the tabloids' obsession with scandal and sensationalism, their penchant for distinctive headlines: 'One's bum year', 'Up Yours Delors', or 'John went potty and glued up his botty'. Nor could he miss the fascination with semi-naked men and women, the toe-sucking antics of certain ministers of the British Crown and the cult of violence associated with football. His survey might even lead him to the truly bizarre end of the tabloid spectrum, such as America's *The National Enquirer*, or Britain's *The Sunday Sport*. What he would make of captions along the lines of 'Woman gives birth to alien with three heads', 'Giant grasshoppers terrorize farmers in northern Nevada', or 'Hitler is my next-door neighbour', is anybody's guess. Without further detailed investigation it would be very difficult to identify what exactly made Western societies function. Lurching from one crisis to another, they seemed to be permanently on the brink of collapse, unlike the ordered and smooth-running societies east of the Berlin Wall. In short, he might conclude that the West was one giant madhouse and a very real menace to world peace and security.

On the other hand, our observer, having noticed the structure and purpose of the peoples' democracies, would note some interesting omissions: (i) There is no crime (serial killers and cannibals are only found in California, Manhattan or Yorkshire, never in the Moscow or Rostov areas). (ii) Trains and planes never crash. There are no natural disasters. (Soviet earthquakes are the most humane in the world). (iii) All Soviet and fraternal socialist industry is designed to fit in with the environment, consequently there are no environmental problems or disaster areas east of Berlin. (iv) The fraternal socialist countries never invade or make war against other countries. Socialist, fraternal armies only went to East Berlin, Hungary, Poland, Czechoslovakia and Afghanistan, because they were invited. (v) Soviet agriculture is the most advanced in the world. (vi) The Soviet people are superbly fed, fit and healthy. (vii) There are no shortages of consumer goods. (viii) There is absolutely no censorship in the Soviet Union. (ix) The Berlin Wall (read the anti-Fascist protection barrier) was erected to protect the socialist peoples of the German Democratic Republic from revanchist West Germans. People never attempt to escape from the GDR, and if they did (and it must be stressed that this is purely hypothetical), they would never be shot. (x) Jews are not persecuted in the Soviet Union. (xi) Soviet citizens are so deliriously happy with their life in the Soviet mother-land that they can hardly bear to leave. As a result, the Soviet authorities consider it to be an unnecessary expense to issue passports except for the unfortunate individuals who cannot avoid having to travel there on official business. (xii) Everybody agrees with every-body else. People are never declared insane because they disagree with officialdom. (xiii) There is absolutely no political corruption or nepotism in the Soviet Union. (xiv) The Soviet people revere their leaders.[18]

Not only are these conclusions invitingly at odds with the chaos and uncertainties of the West, but more importantly they suggest a funda-mental break with what we know about human behaviour and societies. It poses the tantalizing question: is *homo sovieticus* a reality? There is enough here to conclude that Soviet society, and by extension those societies lucky enough to have been within the Soviet 'community', represent something very special indeed. Not quite perfection perhaps, but tantalizingly close to Happiness. Professor Robert Tucker provides us with an interesting way of dealing with the omissions and accusations that we find in the Soviet media: 'whatever the Soviet press accused an enemy of was exactly what the Soviet Government was doing itself'.[19]

The idea of perfection and perfectibility was, of course, deeply rooted in Soviet ideology, so deeply rooted in fact that millions had to die in its name. This is the ineluctable conclusion of the iron logic of dialectical materialism. The grand architects of totalitarian socialism

– Lenin, Stalin, Hitler, Mao, Khieu Samphan, Pol Pot – were fanatically committed to the notion of a perfected society. Khrushchev unwisely made predictions about burying the West. The Brezhnev gerontocracy decided it would be more circumspect to encourage people to believe that for all intents and purposes paradise was here and now.

Much contemporary writing about ideology favours an inclusive rather than an exclusive application of the term; that is all political, economic and social systems are to varying degrees ideological. Neil Postman, a contemporary analyst of the media and its societal effects, offers a definition of ideology which is widely shared:

> If we define ideology as a set of assumptions of which we are barely conscious but which nonetheless directs our efforts to give shape and coherence to the world, then our most powerful ideological instrument is the technology of language itself. Language is pure ideology.[20]

For argument's sake let us accept that ideology can be applied to language in the manner in which Postman uses it. If so, we can judge the merits of various, competing languages (or pure ideologies) by the effectiveness with which they 'give shape and coherence to the world'. If, therefore, one can accept that certain languages (or pure ideologies) are better able to perform the task which Postman ascribes to them, then we can also say that the set of assumptions on which they are based are better, better that is in the sense, that they give us a clearer understanding of the world in which we live. In other words, all ideologies – as defined by Postman – are not equal. Moreover, since Postman so closely aligns language and ideology, then it seems quite reasonable to conclude that languages (and cultures as well, which are a function of language) will differ in their ability to 'give shape and coherence to the world'. Some cultures demonstrate a fitness of purpose which is superior to others.

On the other hand, if we accept Postman's definition, with its exceptionally close relationship between language and ideology, then too much coherence and shape, which we get from this relationship, may be regarded in some circumstances with suspicion. Since so much of our experience of life is beyond the grasp of language – with or without the contaminating effects of ideology, as in the case of Marxism-Leninism or National Socialism – then the greater the explanatory power of language/ideology, the more we should be on our guard. This ability, or rather the claim, to explain all the mysteries of being is perhaps the most important feature separating the genuine ideology of Marxism-Leninism from the political beliefs, prejudices and dogmas of the liberal democracies. The genuine ideologue recognizes no limits to his competence: he destroys the free-market for goods and services; he decides on the basis of ideological purity what the citizens can and cannot read, see and hear; and he determines whether the citizens should believe in God. Only when we have liberated language from ideology, can the task of finding coherence and giving shape to the world become a possibility.

Language also enables us to formulate and to coordinate tests to see whether our view of the world, as shaped by language, is accurate. The danger of self-fulfilling prophecy or the circular argument is avoided if we are ruthless in discarding ideas which fail the test of experiment. A language that is no longer able to fulfil this function, or is not allowed to, ceases to be a language. It is little more than a set of pre-programmed responses, a prison for the mind, not a vehicle for intellectual adventure and exchange.

In his recent study, *Television, the Public Sphere, and National Identity*, Monroe Price makes the following connection between broadcasting policies and ideology:

> The loyalty due to religion became the requirement of Communism; by reflex, a similar set of loyalties has become true for 'the market economies' or capitalism. Ideology, in this sense, has become an element in national identity; or, where ideology has been the justification for power, then ideology has been grafted into identity. And broadcasting, even today, is an instrument for the carriage and promotion of these competing ideas of the good.[21]

The main consequence that derives from the misuse of the word ideology is that it serves to blur the distinction between the general, and often poorly defined principles of capitalism, and the free market, and the altogether far more prescriptive, all-encompassing diktats of the genuine ideology. Further, it helps to create and to perpetuate a militantly-centrist bias, a superficial fairness, which argues that, in essence, there is no difference between the (genuine) ideology of Marxism-Leninism and the much more loosely defined and practised principles of capitalism. Once, because of the dominion of a fallacious sense of balance, we have dispensed with the notion that one political or economic set of beliefs and customs may not be deemed superior to another, then we find ourselves obliged to ignore a veritable avalanche of historical fact and testimony. The final conclusion is that the Soviet

Union was not that bad after all, and the West has not much of which it can feel proud.

From such a position it is but a short step to the conclusion that '*all news is ideological*'.[22] This view, if correct, implies something potentially very serious for those who assert profound and irreconcilable differences between the two systems; namely that an ideological framework, analogous to that of Marxism-Leninism, one as equally prescriptive and censorious, controls the Western media. In short, the comparison is not between an open and closed society, but one between two societies, which police their information spaces as jealously as one another. If a clear distinction between the two is to be made then an equally clear view of what is understood by ideology becomes even more important.

One of the most penetrating analyses of the term ideology is to be found in Hannah Arendt's seminal work, *The Origins of Totalitarianism*. Basing her conclusions on a comprehensive study of the Soviet and Nazi regimes, she argues that ideology must be understood quite literally as 'the logic of an idea'.[23] Its most distinctive feature inheres in the absence of a body of statements about what something is. Ideology is more concerned with the unfolding of a process which is in constant change:

> The ideology treats the course of events as though it followed the same 'law' as the logical exposition of its 'idea'. Ideologies pretend to know the mysteries of the whole historical process – the secrets of the past, the intricacies of the present, the uncertainties of the future – become the logic inherent in their own ideas. Ideologies are never interested in the miracle of being. They are historical, concerned with becoming and perishing, with the rise and fall of cultures ... [24]

Three specifically totalitarian elements are common to ideological thinking: (i) ideology is concerned solely with the element of movement. History is on our side was a frequently repeated boast of the Soviet era; (ii) ideology contradicts what our senses tell us, or as Hannah Arendt puts it: 'The propaganda of the totalitarian movement also serves to emancipate thought from experience and reality.'[25] (iii) since reality cannot be changed totalitarian ideology uses certain methods of demonstration:

> Ideological thinking orders facts into an absolutely logical procedure which starts from an axiomatically accepted premise, deducing everything else from it; that is, it proceeds with a consistency that exists nowhere in the realms of reality.[26]

To Arendt's classic definition of ideology we can add Edward Shils's conception of the 'ideological outlook':

> Like the politics it [ideology] supports, it is dualistic, opposing the pure 'we' to the evil 'they', proclaiming that he who is not with me is against me. It is alienative in that it distrusts, attacks, and works to undermine established political institutions. It is doctrinaire in that it claims complete and exclusive possession of political truth and abhors compromise. It is totalistic in that it aims to order the whole of social and cultural life in the image of its ideals, futuristic in that it works toward a utopian culmination of history in which such an ordering will be realized.[27]

The definition of ideology/ideological given by Arendt and Shils severely limits the extent to which news can be described as ideological: some news is ideological, but not all news is ideological. The inadequacies of the all-news-is-ideological approach are apparent when applied to the Western media (assuming that one discounts *The Morning Star*, *L'Humanité* and other exotic fare, such as *Spare Rib*). We do indeed find plenty of political commentary, deliberate bias and lies. But there is room for debate and informed discussion. The lie enjoys no monopoly. Since the Soviet media were state owned, the responsibility for bias and lies belonged to the state. Where there is evidence of biased reporting in a Western newspaper or television programme, other segments of the media and public opinion are free to expose and to criticize it. No such corrective function existed in the Soviet media. Thus a distorted picture of the world can be promulgated and constantly reinforced. By no stretch of the imagination could the sporting pages of the tabloid press, the gossip that surrounds the royal family, or the bizarre happenings reported at the extreme end of the tabloid spectrum be described as ideological. They offer a diet of trivia and sensationalism, disposable consumer items yes, mental junk food even, but not an insidious conspiracy to render the masses inert and docile.

The full dangers of such symmetrical thinking emerge even more strongly in Brian McNair's assessment of the Western and Soviet media:

> All information appearing in the news media of socialist (and capitalist) societies can be described as 'ideological' in so far as it has been selected and presented on the basis of subjective assumptions and value judgements. Soviet news is distinctive, however, in loudly

and openly proclaiming its propaganda functions of teaching and reinforcing marxist-leninist ideology, and of 'agitating' the masses.[28]

What makes genuine ideological thinking so terrifying, such as Marxism-Leninism, and the sort of behaviour it justifies, so dreadful, are not any subjective assumptions or value judgements that it brings to a problem. All thought runs that risk. No, the real danger lies in the all-embracing prescriptiveness of ideology: economics, all human behaviour and relations; customs; venerable and ancient tradition; the role of the family; religion; and the very secrets of a man's heart. Nothing is permitted to escape its clutches. Equally remarkable, as Arendt has noted, is its consistency. Such consistency is to be expected and can be demonstrated in the sciences – physics, chemistry and mathematics – but is not a feature of a pseudo-science like Marxism-Leninism. That Lenin called socialism a science and that generations of his disciples (in East and West) unquestioningly accepted the appellation, and acted accordingly, graphically demonstrates the dangers of untested subjective assumptions and value judgements transformed into ideology. But it also bears witness to the power of ideology constantly, and almost effortlessly to remould itself. Ideology has the answers to all questions for all time. To dismiss Marxism-Leninism as simply a collection of subjective assumptions and value judgements does not do justice to Lenin's prowess as a psychologist and sorcerer.

Economic liberalism, on the other hand, has no all-embracing and consistent view of itself, let alone one which can be imposed on the world. Even the fiercest advocates of capitalism do not call it a science. True, the work of Adam Smith, Ludwig Von Mises, Friedrich Hayek and Milton Friedman offers a body of ideas and principles for the capitalist economy. Yet where these ideas have been implemented they have met with considerable success; that is, they have been tested. Capitalism, unlike Marxism-Leninism, has learned to live with uncertainty and crisis.

Nor can it be said that the media in capitalist countries only report the successes of capitalism. Unemployment statistics and recession are as much part of the media's basic fare as are the undeniable successes based on the private ownership of the means of production. To survive and to prosper, capitalism needs an accurate – as accurate as possible – picture of the world. If capitalists persisted in seeing the world according to some theoretical template which disregarded empirical reality – one of the key aspects of ideological behaviour – then capitalism would be progressively discredited, as was Soviet communism: and it would not work. Neither should we be impressed by the fact that the Soviet media loudly and openly proclaimed their propaganda and agitation function. An open and strident declaration of your intended bias is exactly that, no more. Hitler and Stalin are no less mass murderers because they have earlier announced their intention to exterminate the class/race enemy. We have been warned.

Public opinion is yet another formidable obstacle separating the Western and Soviet media. To quote Barghoorn and Remington:

> If we define public opinion as uncoerced expression on matters of concern to the nation by persons outside the ruling sphere who claim a right to influence decisions through their opinions, then, as Paul Kecskemeti wrote in 1950, public opinion cannot exist in a Stalinist system, since granting the right to ordinary citizens to influence policy would contradict the political monopoly possessed by the party leadership.[29]

Views expressed in the Soviet media cannot be said, therefore, to represent the population at large. While at the same time, through a projection of monolithic unity, every attempt is made to persuade non-Soviet opinion that they represent the Soviet population, the views expressed are those of the leadership, unelected and unaccountable. The British media on the other hand draw on a huge pool of sources for their information: public opinion surveys; analyses; (official and independent) foreign press agencies including TASS and *Novosti*; and expert opinion in various fields. They may share the British government's interpretation of a given event, but they are not obliged to. In the Soviet media nothing was allowed to detract from the impression of unbreakable solidarity between people and party. Articulated public opinion in the West, and its corresponding absence from the Soviet media, renders any attempt to assess world opinion, or whether it is worth assessing – and possibly heeding – in the first place, extremely difficult. Is, for example, the fact that the British view of certain events is less representative of world opinion, cause for concern? A serious problem here is to determine what constitutes world opinion. If Britain's spin doctors and pollsters can be wrong about how Britain was going to vote on 9 April 1992, then the problems of measuring world opinion across so many cultural and linguistic barriers must be well nigh insuperable.

States whose media could be described as socialist/communist did, until the period 1989–91, exert considerable influence worldwide. Apart from the Soviet Union there were the fraternal socialist states of Central and Eastern Europe. By this time Yugoslavia and Albania had lost their fraternal status, but this did not change their media structure which remained firmly under the control of the party. Outside of Europe we find Cuba, North Vietnam, North Korea, various one-party states in Africa, and finally the other communist superpower, China. This conglomeration of states enjoyed immense political influence. Nor, indeed, is it just socialist/communist states which were hostile to an independent media voice. Military dictatorships in South America and theocracies in the Middle East are not known for their tolerance.

Bearing in mind the peculiarities of the communist media – the exclusive propagation of the Marxist-Leninist world view and the hostility towards the liberal democracies – we should not be surprised that, in any comparison, the views of the British media would be deemed to be unrepresentative of 'world opinion'. If the views of communist states are a major component of world opinion, then the British media are not likely to share the same view of the world. (It should also be pointed out that Britain's views on freedom and democracy were not shared by the political systems dominating Europe in 1940. Yet the views represented by Britain eventually triumphed). The extent to which views are shared and represented in the media of other states does not necessarily indicate whether they are good or bad. In fact, in some cases we would have to conclude that the less representative view is more in tune with the unarticulated (because of censorship and the secret police) wishes of the vast majority. This is surely confirmed by the dramatic moves in Central and Eastern Europe in 1989 to implement more open and accountable governments.

Any investigation which sought to use the conclusions of a comparative study of the British and Soviet media as the basis for determining the extent to which one or the other system was more or less representative of world opinion would have to take into account the following factors. First, what is 'world opinion', and how is it to be determined? Second, the very concept of public opinion challenges the information monopoly of the party-controlled apparatus. Third, if one bears in mind that the views expressed in the Soviet media are those of an ideological élite, then their contribution, and the contribution of other socialist states, to the formation of 'world opinion' can only be a severely distorting one. It could not claim to represent the population who are denied the basic civil right to articulate their views alongside those of the party. Moreover, the level of objectivity, balance, neutrality and impartiality with which a state permits vital issues to be discussed within its own borders is clearly a crucial consideration when assessing the value of its influence on world opinion. Consequently, the contribution made by the British media to the discussion of international issues is far less distorting than that of the Soviet media.

The treatment of dissent whether internal or external is another theme sharply dividing the Western and Soviet media, despite claims to the contrary.[30] The manner in which the activities of the British Communist Party have been traditionally reported in the Soviet media are instructive for understanding the interest in Western 'peace' movements. The overwhelming majority of the British people regarded the activities of the British Communist Party with a mixture of contempt and mild amusement. Reading the Soviet press about this extreme minority party one would get the impression that it was not only a serious contender for power, but also that its views and opinions were widely discussed and valued in British society. There existed a massive, and almost surreal, imbalance between the profile accorded the British Communist Party in the Soviet media and its irrelevance in Britain.

Similarly, 'peace' movements, certainly in Britain throughout the 1980s, did not represent British public opinion on the issues of nuclear arms and defence of the West, as tested in general elections. Throughout the eighties they were very much a minority, a vociferous one to be sure, but still a minority. The Soviet media sought to portray these movements to the Soviet people as the tip of an iceberg, to demonstrate that the British government's decision to deploy Cruise and Pershing missiles was out of step with the wishes of the majority; that it heralded an unwarranted act of aggression against the peace-loving socialist fraternity. The Soviet media omitted to discuss the fact that in three consecutive elections the British people had delivered a resounding rebuttal to the views of those of the peace movement.

Soviet media interest in these various groups was certainly not motivated by the deeper themes of individual conscience, the freedom to disagree and the freedom to attack the official government line of the day. In the distorted world of Soviet ideology there could be no dissenting voice between the party and people. By their very nature dissenting voices were 'enemies of the people'. Despite this well-attested, and thoroughly documented Soviet attitude towards dissent, the author of a study of the Soviet media, published as late as 1991, still felt able to assert that:

> [...] the traditional Western journalistic emphasis on such figures as Andrei Sakharov, Aleksandr Solzhenitsyn and Anatoly Shcharansky is echoed by Soviet coverage of Western dissidents such as Brian Wilson, Charles Heider and Leonard Peltier. In the Soviet media those names are frequently mentioned as symbols of resistance to US policy, in a manner analogous to the way in which Soviet dissidents come to represent heroic resistance to communist totalitarianism in the west. Yet Wilson, Heider and Peltier have been virtually ignored by the media of their own society and by the Western media in general.[31]

To be a dissenting voice in the Soviet Union carried immeasurably harsher penalties than it did in the Western democracies. Arrest, brutal and prolonged interrogation, many years of forced labour, incarceration in psychiatric hospitals and execution were the likely fate of those Soviet individuals brave enough to challenge the party's intellectual stranglehold. The crucial flaw in this comparison and elsewhere is that it is based on the assumption of a like-with-like comparison. Note, for example, the explanation of reciprocal media interest in dissent:

> In both Britain and the USSR the media's focus on the other side's political dissidents is best explained in terms of the ideological importance of portraying dissent in the enemy camp.[32]

Rival political systems do indeed welcome the existence of dissent in the enemy camp. It helps to vindicate their own policies. Yet there are dissenters and dissenters. Are we really to believe that someone who engages in a sit-down protest outside a US Airforce base in Britain only to be unceremoniously thrown into the back of a police van merits the same media coverage as a Solzhenitsyn or a Sakharov?

British media interest is motivated by a number of factors: intellectual, moral, social and political. All societies feel uncomfortable with dissent. Democracies are no exception. Democratic governments do abuse the human and civil rights of their people from time to time. Individuals do suffer unjustly and much can be done to make certain Western governments more accountable to their people. Nor do the Western media always focus on the issues which perhaps they ought to. Where property rights are upheld, one cannot compel a television company or a newspaper to take up the story of an individual who feels he has been wronged. It might be desirable were the media to do so, but to force them would be even less so.

Comparing the stand of individuals such as Solzhenitsyn, Bukovsky, Sakharov, Shcharansky, Plyushch, Ratushinskaya and many others from a long and honourable list with the activities of Western 'peace' movements and isolated victims of miscarriages of American justice is completely to misunderstand the nature of the system created by Lenin and fortified by Stalin. An interpretation of this type offends the memory of tens of millions of people, real and imagined dissenters, who perished in Stalin's concentration camps. Fallacious comparisons such as these have consistently bedevilled the study of things Soviet. Andrey Sakharov's verdict is worth quoting:

> How can one speak of symmetry between a normal cell and a cancerous one? With its messianic pretensions, its totalitarian suppression of dissent, and its authoritarian power structure, our regime resembles a cancer cell. The public in our country has had no control whatsoever over vital political decisions, foreign or domestic. We have lived in a closed society in which the government concealed matters of substance from own citizens. We have been closed off as well from the outside world, and our citizens have been denied the right to travel abroad or exchange information.[33]

Accepting the view that both capitalist and socialist media are ideologically biased in the way they report one another, but that the Soviet media loudly and openly proclaim their propaganda and agitation functions, must mean either that the capitalist media ignore their ideological bias, or that there is something secretive, even conspiratorial about them. The reduction of Western journalistic activity to the level of ideology turns out to be an indirect attack on the intellectual and cultural traditions from which it stems.

Consider the supposition that Lenin's principles for the Soviet media are analogous to the unwritten rules observed by the Western practice of journalism:

> … they [the principles of Lenin for the media] are to contemporary Soviet journalism what such principles as 'objectivity', 'impartiality', 'neutrality' and 'balance' are to journalists working in capitalist countries.[34]

The analogy begs as many questions as it raises. Among Western journalists there is general agreement that these criteria are desirable. But we should not be persuaded to believe that these principles are just a mask for the prescription or insinuation of capitalist thinking. Divergence from this analogy is most clearly seen in the respective origins of these principles. The Soviet media derived their authority from the work of Lenin. The truth of Lenin's teachings is self-evident. No such flawless icon towers over the Western media.

Western media derive their confidence in objectivity, impartiality, neutrality and balance from the long-standing and stunningly successful Western intellectual tradition, a cooperative venture long pre-dating the arrival of Marxism-Leninism. Such criteria are so highly valued because in the quest for knowledge, learning and the search for the new, their worth has been repeatedly demonstrated. Indeed, Marx himself owed an incalculable debt to this intellectual tradition. Without it *Das Kapital* would never have been written.

Soviet policy and attitudes towards information heralded a radical departure from an intellectual tradition going back to Classical Antiquity. Socialism reasserted the power of dogma over reason and experience. Marxist-Leninist socialism attempted to reverse the trend, reasserted at the time of the European Enlightenment. Doubters were enemies, not intellectual adventurers. If we consider the Enlightenment to be one of man's great intellectual achievements, then we are drawn to the conclusion that Marxism-Leninism is the antithesis of the Enlightenment: the former is regressive, the latter progressive (but always pregnant with the possibility of regression to barbarism, as the success of Marxism shows).

Objectivity, neutrality, balance and impartiality are anathema to the ideologues of Marxism-Leninism precisely because they are objective, neutral, impartial and balanced. Combined with a healthy scepticism, they are fatal to an ideology which claims to have all the answers to the human condition. In a climate of such utter certainty the party could argue that adherents to concepts of impartiality, objectivity, balance and neutrality are motivated by political (ideological) considerations and not unbiased intellectual enquiry. In the often unreal and paranoid world of Soviet politics they are only a short step away from being declared enemies of the people.

The search for greater understanding about the world would be a vital component in any definition of progress or progressive. The search for new forms and ideas, their unimpeded discussion, is, however, impossible in a system of information dissemination dominated by the Leninist criteria of *partiynost'*, *ideynost'* and *pravdivost'*.

For Soviet society the intellectual, moral, economic and political consequences were catastrophic. On the other hand, in states whose media practitioners set great store by objectivity, balance, impartiality and neutrality – while not always meeting these demanding standards it is true – progress in the widest sense of the word – is not only possible, but also frequently attainable.

Of direct relevance for this question are some remarks made by the Japanese Nobel Prize Winner, Susumu Tonegawa, who argued that the Japanese language was unsuitable for scientific reasoning. Neil Postman's response to Tonegawa makes the task of sorting the wheat from the chaff that much harder:

> It should be noted that he was not saying that English is better than Japanese; only that English is better than Japanese for the purposes of scientific research, which is a way of saying that English (and other Western languages) have a particular ideological bias that Japanese does not. We call that ideological bias 'the scientific outlook'. If the scientific outlook seems natural to you, as it does to me, it is because our language makes it appear so. What we think of as reasoning is determined by the character of our language. To reason in Japanese is apparently not the same thing as to reason in English or Italian or German.[35]

The scientific successes of Western culture and civilizations owe nothing to any ideological bias, be it in language or elsewhere. Quite the reverse in fact, the stronger the ideological bias – as I have tried to define it – then the weaker the scientific enterprise will be. Ideology and science are bitter enemies. Consider, for example, what happened to the scientific outlook in Nazi Germany and Soviet Russia when the results of scientific discovery challenged the state ideology (examples of where the use of ideology/ideological is appropriate). National-socialist ideology – of which the German language was just one medium of transmission – hampered Germany's search for the atomic bomb, because Hitler and other Nazis dismissed on racial grounds the consequences of Einstein's research. Likewise, in the Soviet Union scientists were forced to make public statements of allegiance to crackpot theories and charlatans. It was not the corruption of the Russian language by Marxist-Leninist ideology that impeded the scientific enterprise, though this undoubtedly did no good, but rather the violent intimidation of scientists, who knowing that a great deal of official ideology was simply wrong about the material world, were compelled, nevertheless, under pain of arrest, victimization at work (one of the milder penalties), torture, and in Stalin's day, execution, to say that they believed what they did not believe.

The scientific success of the West is a product of political, moral and societal structures – culture in a word – which made it possible for individuals (for example, Galileo) to question, to experiment and to put forward alternative views, albeit in the face of opposition and personal danger. If a language, in this case Japanese, does indeed exert some retarding influence on the ability of the Japanese scientist to reason scientifically, then the arguments made above about language and ideology hold. In the final analysis, the scientific outlook is a state of mind which can be crushed, stunted or encouraged to grow in any culture. While recognizing the importance of language for the shaping of the culture, it is the culture itself which influences the way in which scientific discovery will or will not advance, not the language.

As to whether the scientific outlook is 'natural' in the West, then this is by no means certain. If the proliferation of neo-primitivism, paganism and other cults is anything to go by, then one might conclude that for many people the scientific outlook is decidedly unnatural. It can be explained by the fact that the scientific outlook imposes a disciplining of the mind which most people find difficult to accept since this goes against the grain of what we regard as natural. From our 'natural' point of view it is quite outrageous, for example, that a large airliner should fly. Objectivity, impartiality, the respect for evidence, falsifying theories as a way of testing them (as Popper suggests), maintaining accurate records and being logically consistent are patterns of behaviour that are alien to most of us. They require a great deal of conscious effort to focus on a problem. To be aware of these natural obstacles to scientific enquiry is the scientist's first duty. He must first conquer himself. The term 'scientific bias' is either a misuse of the word bias, and/or, 'scientific', or a stylistic oxymoron, which betrays the speaker's own biases. The aim of scientific enquiry is to eliminate bias as an obstacle to the truth. If by scientific bias one means that the scientific endeavour is only one possibility of truth, of knowing the world in which we live; that scientific thinking is itself just another form of bias, inseparable from all the other biases, great and small, which afflict the human mind, then we should admit this to be so. It may even be that a superior form of reasoning and intellectual insight remain to be discovered. If that is the case, then we would also have to admit the existence of a hierarchy of bias. Some forms of bias are superior to others. This far in human history the scientific bias, judged by material results, has no obvious rivals.

Soviet information policy evolved from Marxist-Leninist ideology. This policy can be summarized as follows: (a) information and ideas reflect the class antagonisms of capitalism and socialism. (b) information is consequently never neutral. (c) propagation of ideologically correct interpretations will ensure that the masses will behave accordingly. (d) state ownership and control of the means of production will ensure the most efficient use of the state's information resources and thus strengthen the state itself. Statements (a) and (b) have already been discussed from both the Leninist and Western standpoints. Statements (c) and (d) invite us to consider the practical consequences of this information policy, to test its efficacy in the light of Soviet experience.

By 'behave accordingly' I mean that the Soviet masses were expected to function in a thoroughly predictable way. For example, if they are repeatedly given a lurid picture of capitalism in crisis, then this would undermine any residual faith in capitalism, or, if frequent assertions are made in the party-controlled media that socialist societies are in every way superior to the capitalist West, then this, too, would be believed.[36]

Yet audiences and readers do not necessarily behave in such a mechanistic fashion. Nor is this a recent discovery. Lenin was only too well aware of the dangers posed by the alternative voice, hence the reason for cutting off all non-party influences. For the success of its post-1917 experiment the party needed an infosphere that was hermetically sealed, or one that was as close to that ideal as possible. But even in this hermetically-sealed laboratory things went badly wrong. For all its efforts the party was never able to eradicate external influences and ideas. Ideological contamination proved to be a resourceful opponent, constantly mutating as new media were developed. Even more troublesome was the question of public opinion. Strictly speaking, as we have seen, there can be no such thing as public opinion in a state where policy is formulated by a party élite unanswerable to any electorate. In practical terms, however, a great deal of effort was expended to discover what people said and believed behind the façade of collective approval.

Two solutions to the problem of feedback were the criteria of *kritika* and *samokritika*. They assumed many forms. Lenin urged the press to forge and maintain close links with the people. Letters to the editors are one way in which this is done. Editors of all Soviet newspapers received huge mailbags and a separate department was given over to the reading and sorting of this information. The range of themes covered by these letters is enormous and there is no doubt that the information received offers valuable insights into public attitudes for the party. Readers' letters will often be used to initiate a campaign against hooliganism or alcohol abuse. Thus a definite link between cause (a reader's letter) and effect (a public campaign) is achieved. This lends credence to the view that the state cares about what its citizens think. At various times in Soviet history, however, letters to the editor have fulfilled a decidedly unsavoury role. They have frequently formed part of a carefully orchestrated campaign against the Soviet state's current bogeymen, in which the Soviet security organs are urged to take the harshest measures against the 'enemies of the people' (cf. The Purge Trials and the Doctors' 'Plot' 1952–53).

Unrestricted criticism was not tolerated. Criticism must always be aimed at specific shortcomings rather than at fundamentals. In practice only selected officials, those towards the bottom of the pyramid, can be targeted for criticism. The validity and absolute correctness of Marxism-Leninism remain intact. Any errors and shortcomings are not due to the leadership – which is sacrosanct – but to incompetent and corrupt officials lower down the pyramid.

THE EFFECTS OF CENSORSHIP

The Economy

All industrial economic systems generate an insatiable appetite for information. It is, however, the manner in which this information is processed, and the ensuing economic results, which separates the public ownership of the means of production from the private ownership of the means of production. Management operations in an economy based on the public ownership of the means of production ascribe exceptional importance in economic decision-making to government bureaucrats. Directives must be issued, their effectiveness monitored, results analyzed. The many layers through which information must pass is itself a major problem. Information in transit is vulnerable to corruption. If this takes place, then the change in emphasis can cause a degree of unintended decentralization.[37] Consequently, the central planner must frequently intervene to ensure that his directives are being implemented. This increases the flow of information – with the associated risk of corruption – and retards the vigour of management.

In this scenario computers confer a mixed blessing. Their speed and power impart flexibility to information processing, but this flexibility is inimical to centralized control. Even in an environment that makes use of computers the central planner must continue to intervene if his control is not to be undermined. It is this fear of losing control and the dangers of autarky (from the perspective of the central planner) which limit or negate any gains in efficiency. Limits to economic advance are set, stagnation is the result.

Despite claims of socialist solidarity, managers at various levels in the system have competing interests. Centralized control of the economy places a definite premium on telling one's superiors what they wish to hear. Moreover, information about the real state of affairs can itself be a valuable resource to be withheld or shared according to the needs of a manager at any level in the system. Initiative is penalized and promotion and rewards accrue to a type of individual who will always follow orders even when it is absurd to do so. One of the more serious long-term effects of this policy is to shield the central planners and the leadership from the structural and operational failures of the system to the extent that remedial action is carried out when it is too late, and is, therefore, largely ineffective. As Vladimir Bukovsky has noted:

> From the standpoints of cybernetics the system was very foolishly organised, it did not have a feedback. You had the single instrument, the party, and it was enforcer as well as controller. Since their feedback was inaccurate, they waited for too long, by which time there was no cure.[38]

When all is said and done this was the crucial flaw inherent in *perestroyka*: too little, too late.

Marxist-Leninist economic theory exists with a far greater degree of certainty than its capitalist counterpart. Policies are determined by the party and implemented in accordance with the latest plan. Confidence in the iron certainty of the plan derives from the analysis of socio-economic conditions made possible by Marxist-Leninist ideology. This has profound implications for macroeconomic modelling and econometrics.

Econometrics studies economic theory in its relations to statistics and mathematics. It is a valuable, though by no means foolproof, tool for identifying discrepancies between theory and practice. An effective econometric model consists of three basic elements: (a) a sound model; (b) a reliable data base of time-series data; (c) and the necessary computing capability.[39] A model, sound or otherwise, is always an attempt to explore an unknown situation, to ask the question, what will happen, if ...?

Certainties about the economy's future inhibit the exploration of alternatives: if you know what is going to happen, there exists no need to enquire about the future. Where alternatives can be modelled and explored there exists no guarantee that the conclusions will be implemented. Ideology, vested bureaucratic interests and sloth are formidable obstacles to the innovator in any discipline. Apologists for the Soviet system might argue that econometric modelling is unnecessary for a centralized economy. However, the political or ideological use of computer modelling should not be underestimated. A high correlation between Soviet theory and practice would hardly have been unwelcome in the battle to convince an uncommitted audience of the intrinsic superiority of the Soviet economic system.

For example, a study of economic computer modelling in America noted many overtly political uses for the results: decision-making was delayed or confused; symbolic attention was given to a particular policy; attention could be focused on only one side of an argument when it was quite possible to consider all sides; a model could be used to justify a decision already taken; and the status of the computer could be exploited to confer a sheen of sophistication or expertise on the decision-maker.[40] These options are not the sole prerogative of competing organizations in a free-market economy.

Effective Soviet modelling also suffered from a crippling shortage of reliable time-series data. Where ideology rather than reliable data is regarded as more important for the running of the economy, there will be no need to collect time-series data and maintain accurate records (or accurate records will be maintained, but access will be severely limited). No matter whether the modeller enjoys access to state-of-the-art computing technology any attempt to model a scenario will inevitably run foul of the first law of computer modelling: trash in, trash out (TITO).

Pioneered by independent organizations such as Data Resources Incorporated (DRI), the growth and increasing sophistication of econometric modelling in the United States gave a massive boost to the collection and refinement of economic data.[41] This undoubtedly led to greater predictive power, and at least offered the potential for sounder economic policy. Econometrics is by no means a panacea for poor decisions, but it can be used to highlight failures in policy before too much damage is wrought. More important than econometrics are the conditions that make it possible: flexible assumptions about the nature of economic reality and accurate data. Denied these conditions, the socialist-command economy could not respond to change. It was, to quote James Davidson and Lord Rees-Mogg, 'like a blind, one-legged centenarian on the centre court at Wimbledon'.[42]

The shortcomings discussed so far are, in fact, minor when compared to the one insurmountable obstacle facing Soviet economic planners. It was one of the great ironies of Soviet-style economics, with its huge emphasis on rational planning, that the planners were denied the most important aspect of all economic planning: economic calculation based on prices set by a market. As early as 1922, the Austrian economist Ludwig von Mises first identified this as the single most important weakness of all economic behaviour under conditions of public ownership of the means of production. In *Socialism*, one of the most far-sighted and penetrating analyses of socialist economies and socialism, ever written, and whose conclusions have been stunningly vindicated, Ludwig von Mises demonstrated that the basis of economic calculation is the market: 'Where there is no market there is no price system, and where there is no price system there can be no economic calculation'.[43] Under market conditions the price system provides information about supply and demand. In the absence of such conditions economic calculation, that is capital calculation, becomes guesswork. Prices for goods and services reflect the opinions of bureaucrats and planners, that is they are established arbitrarily. Prices in conditions of a free market function as information. Planners in the Soviet economy did not, indeed, could not have that information. Consequently, their economic planning could not be rational. To quote von Mises: '[...] we have a socialist community which must cross the whole ocean of possible and imaginable economic permutations without the compass of economic calculation'.[44] It is also to von Mises that we owe the observation that, in the absence of economic calculation, the socialist planners can turn to the workings and prices set under conditions of capitalism for information. The workings of capitalism, in other words, are a standard of efficiency and success, which though vilified in countless propaganda tracts, are watched closely for the guidance they provide.[45] Prices under conditions of socialism are essentially an extension of *agitprop*, not rational economic calculation.

Science

Censorship and excessive secrecy impose a massive burden on all forms of intellectual endeavour. Yet it was from among the ranks of scientists – and writers – that the most effective opposition to communist rule arose. Once again it is pertinent to consider the influence of Marxist-Leninist ideology in order to identify the origins of this collision.

If ideology has all the correct answers, it must, logically, have formulated all the correct questions. If all the correct questions have been formulated, then no further questions remain to be formulated. At this juncture scientific enquiry comes to a grinding halt: it is the end of history. The problem is by no means unique to the twentieth century. Giordano Bruno (1548–1600) was burnt at the stake for his publicly-stated conjectures, and his illustrious fellow-countryman Galileo was threatened with a similar fate. Whether in Italy at the dawn of the Enlightenment, or in Soviet Russia, the conflict between science and dogma remains essentially the same. In the twentieth century there is, however, a new, far more virulent dimension brought about by Marxism-Leninism.

Backed by the militant materialism of the Soviet state, the scientist was regarded as one of the key figures in the construction of socialism. But the Soviet leadership's attitude was one of ambivalence. Scientific advances depend on chance and on the scientist who against all the received wisdom of his time will think the unthinkable. Like the economic modeller the scientist must ask what will happen if ...?, if he hopes to progress beyond the known. Discoveries in twentieth-century physics have proved particularly troublesome for Marxist-Leninist ideology. Relativity theory, quantum mechanics, indeterminacy theory and cybernetics have all struck blows at the simplistic reductionist world view of the party. Consequently, every effort was made to bring scientific research under control. In addition to their chosen fields of physics, chemistry and mathematics, Soviet students were obliged to take courses in dialectical materialism, historical materialism, the history of the party and scientific communism. But even if a quarter of a student's time is taken up with party indoctrination, the bulk will have to recognize such scientific principles as evidence, the burden of proof and the necessity for accurate data. In short, scientific progress will only be possible where the scientist casts off the straitjacket of Marxist-Leninist ideology. The party now finds itself on the horns of an unpleasant dilemma: the scientist cannot be permitted to publish his objections or the observed contradictions between ideological prediction and result; but the party cannot afford to ignore scientific research which will enhance the prestige of the regime, or which will have a military application. Such schizophrenia offers ample opportunity for the charlatan and careerist, as can be seen from the meteoric rise of Trofim Lysenko.

The search for extra-terrestrial intelligence is one area of space research, which would, one might think, be beyond the reach of Marxism-Leninism. Not a bit of it. In 1966 the American astronomer, Carl Sagan, and the Soviet astrophysicist, Iosef Shklovskii, co-published *Intelligent Life in the Universe*.[46] In the preface Sagan points out that some members of the former Soviet Institute of Astrobotany, argued that the existence of extra-terrestrial life was required by dialectical materialism. Consequently, its absence on Mars and even Jupiter would have unpleasant intellectual consequences for dialectical materialism.[47] Later in the book, Shklovskii expresses objections to the pulsating model of the universe. 'The simple repetition of cycles', asserts Shklovskii, 'in essence excludes the development of the universe as a whole; it therefore seems philosophically inadmissible.'[48] Shklovskii is, of course, quite right to challenge this view from a strictly scientific point of view, which he does when he asks: '[...] if the universe at some time exploded and began to expand, would it not be simpler to believe that process occurred just once?'[49] 'Philosophically inadmissible' is a euphemism for 'unacceptable to Marxism-Leninism', which with its total insistence on a linear, progressive teleology, cannot accommodate any possibility that the universe is locked into a cycle of endless repetitions and rebirths. Human societies that were doomed to relive their successes and failures in a series of eternal recurrences, even if they did not, as it were, to paraphrase Heraclitus, step into the same river twice, would not move or progress in any way that could be predicted by dialectical materialism or scientific communism. The classless, conflict-free society would have little chance of being realized. Human societies evolve in unexpected and unforeseen ways, and it is this inescapable and demonstrable fact that renders dialectical materialism worthless. According to Shklovskii:

> Dialectical materialism states that among the basic attributes of the universe are its objective reality and its knowability. Therefore the laws of nature do not depend on the preconceived opinions of

various individuals who do not comprehend the underlying spirit of dialectical materialism.[50]

The intellectual danger for the uninformed Western reader resides in Shklovskii's particular, and not immediately obvious, use of 'objective'. In Soviet-speak the meaning of objective can only be derived from Marxist-Leninist philosophy. An idea or fact that contradicts a tenet of Marxist-Leninist thought, however well-formulated, and irrespective of any degree and success of independent verification, is, *ab ovo*, not objective, and can therefore be dismissed as '*burzhuaznyy ob"ektivizm*' (bourgeois objectivism).[51] This explains why the party conducted such vicious campaigns against the biologist, Vavilov, why cybernetics and Relativity theory were ridiculed, and why at the time of publication of the Sagan–Shklovskii book, 1966, Lysenko had still not been totally discredited.[52]

Had Shklovskii's second sentence terminated at 'individuals', one could merely add that many, possibly not all, scientists accept the idea of objective reality and the knowability of the universe, or some considerable degree thereof. Shklovskii goes on to tell us that comprehension of the 'underlying spirit of dialectical materialism' is necessary if we are to understand the laws of nature. Such question-begging leads us back to the point already made that objective reality when used in Marxism-Leninism does not mean a reality which exists independently of, and is not contingent on, our political or, rather here, our 'class' prejudices. On the contrary. When he looks into the night sky, pondering the mysteries of the universe, the Soviet astronomer must accept that the light which passes through his telescope is refracted through the lens of Marxism-Leninism. It is not Snell, but Lenin who is the final authority. And we can take it for granted that in the Soviet version of Spielberg's *ET*, the class-conscious and ideologically-vigilant extra-terrestrial denounces Sakharov for his criticisms of Stalin.

The violent nationalization of intellectual life, the fact that the physicist, for example, cannot function without a laboratory, means that the state is able to construct a system of rewards and punishments based on censorship. The simple act of denying the chemist access to laboratory facilities is sufficient in itself to blight the recalcitrant scientist's career. This is an effective form of censorship, and again made possible where the state enjoys a total and violent monopoly. On the system of rewards, one wonders why travel abroad be deemed a reward. If the regime recognized it as such, and all the indications are that it did, then does this recognition not underline the system's failure. Service to the Soviet state should be its own reward. Why reward people in a way which exposes them to 'ideological contamination'?

Just how much of a pivotal problem for the Soviet scientist censorship was, emerges very clearly in the experience of Valentin Turchin and Andrei Sakharov. In his manifesto, *Progress, Coexistence, and Intellectual Freedom*, first published in 1968, Sakharov had argued for a press law and the elimination of the system of censorship.[53] Sakharov identified censorship as the factor common to many, if not all the ills, afflicting Soviet society. As he argued: 'Today the key to a progressive restructuring of the system of government in the interests of mankind lies in intellectual freedom.'[54] Abolition of GLAVLIT, or at the very least, 'major organizational and legislative measures' were required.[55]

Sakharov's *Memoirs* provide a great deal of further insight into how the ideological bureaucracy impeded scientific research. Elena Bonner's insistence that her husband is a *'physicist, not a dissident'* makes a serious point.[56] It forces us to consider Sakharov's profound analysis of Soviet society and the world at large from the standpoint of his being first and foremost a physicist. Sakharov's analysis is scientific, not political or ideological. That his scientific analysis has political and ideological consequences is another matter. Indeed, the very fact that Sakharov's scientific analysis is condemned by the Soviet state as being anti-Soviet and anti-ideological demonstrates the stance required of the Soviet scientist. To be anti-Soviet is to be anti-ideological. To be anti-ideological is to be anti-scientific. Sakharov's crime was that he broke the spell of the magic circle.

Elena Bonner's distinction underlines why the conflict between science and Soviet ideology is inevitable, why the two modes of thinking are mutually incompatible, and it is this realization which made Sakharov (and many other Soviet scientists) so dangerous to the party's world view. Dissident has a pejorative ring, the suggestion that the addressee is some kind of social malcontent or psychological misfit who should be placed at the tender mercies of Soviet psychiatrists. In short, the dissident should not be taken too seriously. A physicist, on the other hand, and especially one of Sakharov's stature and achievements, cannot be dismissed as easily.

Sakharov cites two reasons which help to explain the success of Lysenko after the denunciation technique lost its effectiveness: he always came up with new quack solutions; and the party's agricultural establishment could not afford to see Lysenko discredited otherwise it, too, would be brought down with him.[57] When Nikolai Nuzhdin, one of Lysenko's protégés, was put forward for promotion to a full member of the Academy of Sciences, Sakharov spoke out against him. Lysenko's response was not unexpected: 'People like Sakharov should be locked up and put on trial.'[58] Every effort was indeed made by the Soviet security services to silence Sakharov and his entourage of supporters. After he had given an interview with the correspondent Olle Stenholm, he was subjected to a sustained campaign of vilification in the Soviet press. Exile to Gorky eventually followed accompanied by another disgraceful attack of state-sponsored vilification in Nikolai Yakovlev's book, *CIA Target – the USSR* (1983). Throughout the exile period in Gorky – and indeed before – personal harassment by the KGB was routine. This varied from the standard telephone bugging to overt, physical surveillance and intimidation and the repeated seizure and theft of manuscripts, diaries, letters, notes, scientific papers and even his Nobel Prize certificate. In a letter dated 17 March 1978 Sakharov notes: 'In their latest theft the KGB make it clear that they are determined to deprive me of my memories, records of my ideas, and the possibility of any intellectual life, even in solitude.'[59]

For Valentin Turchin the main flaw in Marxism-Leninism, and one which divides it sharply from physics, is that it 'does not have the power to predict events, yet it imposes a conceptual apparatus that is dead and incapable of development'.[60] In the aftermath of the Stalinist phase of Soviet development the problem for the party is how to ensure, what Valentin Turchin calls, a 'steady state'.[61] The aim of this steady state is to be able to reproduce the system from one generation to another. Control of the infosphere is vital if this aim is to be achieved. In such circumstances ideas are a serious threat to stasis since they can generate demands for change, one of the threats posed by the dissident movement. As a result, 'The struggle among ideas gives way to the struggle against ideas by means of physical force.'[62] Turchin's approach to the problems and consequences of Soviet society's information deficit, as with Sakharov's, is a direct consequence of his profession. Steady-state totalitarianism requires absolutely steady conditions. Any change in these conditions is fraught with danger (a problem foreseen by Plato in the design of his utopia in both *The Republic* and *The Laws*, and one which must confront Soviet ideology when the end of History is reached). The party apparat, argues Turchin, does not understand this, believing that 'a society which has banned freedom of thought can go on indefinitely, "meeting the constantly growing demand"'.[63] Also, the party failed to understand that any significant change in the free world would have an impact on the totalitarian society's attempts to maintain a steady state.

The communications revolution brought about by IT is the case in point. In a letter to the Soviet leadership in the spring of 1970, which was co-written with Roy Medvedev and Andrei Sakharov, Turchin and his fellow authors paint a grim picture of stagnation. In particular, the authors noted the state of research in computer technology, which was 'immeasurably behind' America.[64] They continued:

> The last is especially essential, for the introduction of the computer in the economy is a factor of decisive importance, radically changing the character of the system of production and all culture. The phenomenon is justly called the second industrial revolution. Yet the capacity of our computers is hundreds of times less than that of the United States, and as regards utilizing computers in the economy the disparity is so great that it is impossible even to measure it. We simply live in a different epoch.[65]

Some fifteen years later the full impact of the computer revolution in America and the West would be a decisive factor in the unravelling of the Soviet Union both indirectly, in its economic and military applications, and directly in its ability to shift news and information.

In Stalin's time terror and the threat of terror were regarded as proper weapons for inducing ideological conformity among scientists, and the population at large.[66] The use of terror did not cease after 1953, but was used more selectively, against specific individuals rather than whole groups. The Khrushchev 'thaw' stimulated certain elements in Soviet society – overwhelmingly intellectuals – to demand, indirectly, greater freedoms for themselves. Andrei Amalrik has termed these groups and isolated individuals the 'cultural opposition'.[67] Central to these freedoms was a demand for greater information about Soviet society. Access to adequate and accurate information about the world was seen – quite rightly – as the absolute precondition of responsible citizenship. For its part the regime was determined to maintain its information monopoly. These two mutually opposing trends gave birth to *samizdat* or self-publishing. *Samizdat* enabled individuals to circulate manuscripts, which in the 'normal' course of events would have been rejected out of hand by the censor. Not surprisingly, the party reacted with vigour against what it regarded as a serious challenge to its monopoly in the dissemination of information.

The historical parallels must have seemed uncomfortable too. Here was a stratum of Soviet society circulating manuscripts and ideas critical of the regime in a manner that bore an uncanny resemblance to the activities of the Bolshevik underground press before 1917. The growth of *samizdat* and other informal, non-party channels of intellectual exchange, demonstrates that where the state fails for whatever reason to meet a demand for information, new media of exchange will be created. In a democracy this is perfectly acceptable and desirable. In a totalitarian state, however, such a manifestation is subversive and destabilizing. Unchecked, it will unleash forces that threaten the very existence of the state.

In *The Human Use of Human Beings* Norbert Wiener identified two types of discourse: communicative and forensic.[68] Communicative discourse seeks meaning from the world of nature, which while subtle, does not strive actively to pervert attempts to understand it. The scientist is familiar with this problem. Once a pattern has been observed, a law deduced or a general principle established, then it becomes possible to resolve questions of increasing complexity. Were the laws and principles on which scientific endeavour is based to change with every passing wind, then it would prove impossible to make anything but the most superficial statements about the world.

Forensic discourse on the other hand between human agents involves deliberate attempts to deceive and to pervert meaning with the aim of seeking some advantage. This might almost be a definition of politics. Given the differences between these types of discourse, we would expect the scientist to be at a severe disadvantage in his dealings with the professional politician, and indeed this might account for the air of naïveté that tends to be associated with scientists. But what passed as the real world in the Soviet Union was a bizarre picture created by the party's propagandists.

Literature and Language

The growth of *samizdat* and the subsequent confrontation between intellectuals and the party marked the beginnings of an attempt to restore the authority and integrity of communicative discourse.

Lenin and subsequent designers of the Soviet experiment envisaged literature as an extension of propaganda to be based on, and controlled by, the same criteria as journalism.[69] Consequently, a discussion of literature is not tangential to the task in hand. If, in the words of Norbert Wiener, 'information is a name for the content of what is exchanged with the outer world as we adjust to it, and make our adjustment felt upon it',[70] then it is quite logical to regard literature as a massive and rich fund of information. If this seems to be stretching Wiener's definition too far, then consider how valuable literature can be in informing us of worlds long gone and of societies we have not visited. Plato's dialogues, Shakespeare's plays or the novels of Dickens offer a record, which for all its lacunae and imperfections, does indeed relate man's attempt to adjust to his world and to make his adjustment felt upon it.

This basic drive was denied the Soviet writer, his individual mark on the world disregarded, since he was compelled to write according to the doctrine of socialist realism. He was in effect reduced to a party loudspeaker. Yet even the most vicious censorship and repression could not eradicate the individual writer's creative impulses. Here the roles between scientist and writer in the struggle for professional integrity were reversed even though both were seeking the same ends.

In the duel between scientist and ideology, the scientist found himself defending a long-established tradition of intellectual discourse (communicative) from a subversive agent which would not acknowledge its failures. When we examine the writer's lot things are slightly different. Forensic discourse, in the sense indicated by Wiener, is intended to subvert meaning, to deceive, to misinform, sometimes to lie. These techniques lend themselves particularly well to a group hoping to undermine an established order, the aim for example of the Bolsheviks in their underground opposition to tsarist autocracy. In power, the Bolsheviks were able to use these same techniques to manipulate the flow of news and information received by the population through the means of mass communication. Once the foundations of this new order had been laid the Bolsheviks found themselves as defender of the status quo, not its enemy. The techniques of subversive discourse could now be used against them. By virtue of a unique tradition, the nature of his calling and the medium with which he worked, the Russian writer was perfectly suited to the role of intellectual saboteur of the party's ideas. Of course the party recognized the dangers, hence why it sought to impose the doctrine of socialist realism. But in the duel between Soviet writer and state, socialist realism was essentially a defensive measure against an enemy enormously skilled in the techniques of manipulating language.

The writer adds value – in the term of the information industry – to the unarticulated, raw experience of his society. The finished product, a highly personal, often idiosyncratic view to be sure, provides the social mechanism from which it is drawn with feedback. If the feedback is accurate, it can have enormous social and economic repercussions. Two examples will make the point. Turgenev's devastating sketches of the iniquities of serfdom in Russia, and Dickens's grim accounts of children in Victorian factories, exerted a profound influence on the legislators of their time. Not for nothing do we refer to writers as our moral conscience. A society that for religious or ideological reasons denies itself this feedback, or creates artificial feedback about reality (cf. socialist realism) for internal and external consumption, cannot learn about itself. If it cannot learn about itself, then it must run the risk of moral and social stagnation, and decline. Now it might be argued that in a society where public ownership of the means of production is seen as the key to resolving all moral and social problems there would be no role for the independent, moral conscience. If anything the need is overwhelming. When a nation suffers, the way the Russian people have suffered, it must grieve. To grieve, to share the burden and to understand, a nation must talk to itself. Literature is one way in which a nation talks to itself. Denied the opportunity, a nation cannot heal its wounds and become whole again.

If literary censorship and the use and threat of terror were intended to silence the lone voice, then they must be judged a failure. How else are we to account for the emergence of Solzhenitsyn, Sakharov, Pasternak and Grossman? I am tempted to conclude that a law analogous to Newton's third law of motion applies to the relationship between ruler and ruled in the totalitarian state: every twist of the screw invites a counter-reaction. In Newtonian mechanics it is possible to describe the precise nature of this reaction. In something as complex as a human society, even a totalitarian one, this is not possible. But the results can be identified: the growth of the dissident movement, culminating in Solzhenitsyn's much publicized – and for the Soviet Union highly damaging – exile.

'Language as pure ideology' reached the greatest perfection in the Soviet Union, in some ways becoming the ultimate form of censorship. Any possibility of transforming base human beings into the gold standard of *homo sovieticus* was crucially dependent on the manipulation and control of language. A new language would fulfil two distinct, but mutually linked functions: it would serve as a conduit for the ideology of the new state; and would help to censor ideas and information which may be harmful or destabilizing. Alternative ways of thinking become increasingly difficult, and dangerous.[71] As Leonard Schapiro noted, [...] 'the first trace of unorthodox thought immediately reveals itself as a jarring dissonance'.[72]

In the Soviet language the word takes on a special function. Meaning is subject to constant and arbitrary replacement and modification according to the Party's latest plans. Words are empty shells whose meaning has to be supplied. Naturally, the party is the master of lexical change. One consequence of this policy is that meaning cannot be independent of party authority. Words mean what the Party wish them to mean, which confers a formidable advantage in the battle with ideological opponents.

Lenin's writings are very revealing for the changes which were to become a permanent feature of the Soviet language. Lenin devoted considerable effort to destroying and undermining respect for ideas that stood in the way of the Revolution, such as 'freedom', 'civil society', 'the rule of law', 'freedom of the press', 'democracy', 'free elections' and 'parliaments'. These words had to be attacked because they carried ideas and concepts that were effective – and as history has shown – deadly rivals to the world Lenin wished to build. Once destroyed and discredited, they could be replaced by the linguistic, ideological baggage that Lenin had created. Lenin attacks the idea of a free press, among other reasons, because its existence raises awkward questions for a leader who has no intention of permitting one. According to Lenin, the notion of a free press is a trick. Likewise, because Lenin has no intention of permitting free elections the notion of democracy has to be attacked, and replaced with 'democratic centralism', and so on until the differences between capitalism and socialism have been rendered harmless, or ridiculed beyond redemption. Lenin was a master of this 'dissuasive speech', the technique of undermining the opponent's language and replacing it with another set of ideas.[73]

In common with many demagogues Lenin exploits the carefully structured use of repetition, the creation of slogans and set-piece responses to complex situations. The aim is not reasoned discourse, that convinces by force of argument and logical persuasion, but to produce an effect that appeals to the irrational and to the ease with which many people can be won over by verbal formulas. The eventual aim is to eliminate or to reduce the critical, thinking faculty. Lenin narrowed down the alternative possibilities to his argument, forcing the reader to one conclusion. A favoured technique was the use of verbs in three tenses: 'there was, there is, there will be'. Repetitions such as this mimic the structure of a logical argument, a syllogism for example, which is based on three elements: major premise, minor premise, and a conclusion.

One of the most effective ways to bring ideological influences to bear is in the dictionary. In the words of Grigory Vinokur [...] 'the rationalization of phraseology is the first problem of linguistic policy.'[74] 'Rationalization of phraseology' meant stripping the language of terms deemed superfluous, narrowing the range of linguistic expression. Slogans were the natural and ideal solution to the problem. The real danger of the 'rationalization of phraseology' was the threat it posed to unorthodox thinking. 'Beyond the limits of that phraseology', observed Vinokur, 'it is impossible to think in a revolutionary way or about revolution'.[75]

The effects of this policy can be demonstrated quite easily by examining the results. One example will make the point. In the 18th edition of the Ozhegov Russian dictionary (1987) militarism is defined as follows: 'A reactionary policy of the strengthening of military might conducted by capitalist states with the aim of preparing new aggressive wars.'[76] The definition relies on key words such as 'reaction', 'policy', 'class', 'capitalism', 'state' and 'aggressive'. Some of the definitions conclude with illustrative examples of how the word is to be used. Under the entry for *kapitalizm* we find '*Gibel' kapitalizma neizbezhna'*.[77] For *agressivnyy* we find '*agressivnaya politika imperialistov'*.[78] The striking feature about these component-words is that they achieve a remarkable degree of consistency with party ideology. Militarism, it emerges, is a vice found only in capitalist states. Moreover, diverging from the definition given in *Ozhegov* is excluded because the key elements in militarism are also narrowly defined in accordance with Marxist-Leninist ideology. Definitions are circular. The Soviet writer or speaker is trapped in a huge magic circle from which there is no exit.

George Orwell's Newspeak identifies the full effects of ideology on language. Similarly, Stefan Amsterdamski's comments on *nowamowa* (the Polish version of Newspeak) are as relevant to German, Rumanian, Czech, Bulgarian, Korean (North), Chinese and Vietnamese as they are to Polish.[79] This is one reason why the legacy of Marxism-Leninism has proved to be far more insidious than that of National Socialism. Utopia based on class can infiltrate just about any society. It has a universal appeal that the exclusive racial policy of National Socialism cannot match. Grafted onto the living tissue of human language, Marxist-Leninist Newspeak renders it inert, turning it into a series of ritualistic utterances. This is the beginning of the death of language, and thus the death of thought and intellectual progress.

GORBACHEV, *GLASNOST'*, COLLAPSE

Gorbachev's decision to seek a rapprochement with the West was, we can assume, the result of some hard-headed calculation. There most certainly were options other than the reform process, which came to be associated with *perestroyka* and *glasnost'*, and ensured the Nobel Peace Prize for Gorbachev. The first was whether to take up the challenge of the American Strategic Defense Initiative (SDI) and to allocate the necessary resources for its research and development, in effect, taking part in another technological challenge along the lines of the race to carry out a manned landing on the moon. The potential success of the SDI challenge struck at the Soviet Union in two ways. Were it to be successfully tested and deployed, SDI would negate the Soviet retaliatory response.[80] Well before this situation arrived, the Soviet Union would have to consider whether it could match the American programme, and if so, at what cost. The secondary, possibly the main, threat posed by SDI was thus economic. It seems highly unlikely that the sclerotic Soviet economy could have handled the demands of another massive bout of technological competition with the West.

The second option was war. It is possible that the Soviet leadership and its advisers did not believe in the successful outcome of SDI. Could they, however, in the event that the USA went ahead with this project, ignore the prospect of an American success? Lagging behind the Soviet Union in the initial phase of the race for the moon, the Americans had, nevertheless, risen magnificently to the challenge. In short, our Soviet advisers might have argued, the Americans might just do it. What then?[81] Could the Soviet leadership allow a situation to develop in which their ability to retaliate had effectively been neutralized? A high premium would be placed on a pre-emptive strike, or the threat of one, before the American system was fully operational. History provides us with plenty of examples of states which have resorted to war in an attempt to resolve, or to divert attention away from, internal problems. The risk of war heightens as political power in states becomes isolated from the ruled, or when economically there is a perception that nothing is to be lost by waging war. Such a situation undoubtedly informed the background to General Galtieri's decision to invade the Falkland Islands in April 1982, the outcome of which had, I believe, ramifications for the manner in which the Cold War itself was resolved.

Imperial decline, with or without the threat of SDI, also had its special appeal for the Soviet military and political leadership for purely ideological considerations. At various times after 1945 a Soviet military *Blitzkrieg* against Western Europe was always a real possibility. Soviet training, preparation and doctrine were overwhelmingly offensive. Ideologically, these preparations could be justified as being part of the final act of the 'decisive struggle' (*reshayushchaya bor'ba*) between capitalism and socialism. War waged on behalf of the socialist utopia was a just war (*spravedlivaya voyna*). For such a *Blitzkrieg* to succeed there were two absolute preconditions: massive and overwhelming military superiority had to be guaranteed within the crucial field of operations (Central Europe, Berlin, west to the French coast); and, crucially, the West's will to resist had to be undermined.

Despite having achieved the necessary quantitative superiority, the Soviet Union lagged a long way behind in some of the vital technical areas of modern war. And even where parity could be achieved, or the gap was not too great, the quality of soldiers, non-commissioned officers and officers proved to be a grave weakness. Witness the Soviet performance in Afghanistan and more recently that of the post-Soviet army in Chechnya. As more and more sophisticated weapons were developed and became available to NATO's high command, so the purely quantitative advantage enjoyed by the Soviet Union was reduced. Here again, we see another impact of information technology (IT).[82] Thus the campaign(s) to weaken the West's resolve to go to war assumed much greater importance as the military option became less viable. As a consequence of this, the role of the Soviet and East European media assumed greater importance in the communist twilight. Against this background, the decisive battle between capitalism and communism, as it turned out, was not fought on the North German plains but in the hearts and minds of Western democracies.[83]

In the context of the late Cold War the British victory in the Falklands assumed a significance, which in the 1960s or 1970s would not have been the case. It underlined in a way, in which no amount of diplomatic posturing ever could have done, that Great Britain, under the leadership of Prime Minister Thatcher, would defend its vital interests. There could be no doubt among the Soviet gerontocracy that any military adventurism in Central Europe, say a move against Berlin, or even a limited war confined to the territory of West Germany, would be firmly resisted.[84]

Had Britain failed to recapture the islands or indeed been defeated, then the consequences would have been considerable both domestically and internationally. Would Mrs Thatcher have won the general election in 1983, had she been humiliated in 1982? Would she and her government have survived a military defeat? And if not, what kind of Tory party would have emerged, had it survived in power, from the leadership struggle? It would, one suspects, have been a lot less adventurous in all kinds of ways. We would have seen a return to the kind of Heathite consensus which did so much to consolidate union power. Privatization – one of the great successes of the Thatcher years – might not have taken off. And would a government that had been so badly mauled in a foreign war have had the confidence to take on the National Union of Mineworkers (NUM) and to see the strike through to the end?

The other side of the British victory that had significant consequences in the battle of ideas in the 1980s was the effect on the political situation in Argentina and later on, South America. The military junta was thrown out and Argentine politics took a different course. Free-market economics were given a try. Again, if the junta had managed to hold on to the islands, then this would have strengthened the hand of the military dictatorship. Atrocious human rights abuses would have continued. Pressures for any kind of reform would have abated. When one takes all these consequences into account – actual, likely, direct and indirect – then it seems that the British victory was an important circumstance in the final phase of the Cold War.[85]

The above analysis of the military options, somewhat speculative, but not outrageously so, suggests why the Soviet leadership decided to follow the path of reform, when it did, why war was rejected as a final solution of the capitalist question. But other dangers loomed, unforeseen by the Soviet leadership. What made the reform process in the period 1985–91 so markedly different – and highly dangerous – when compared with earlier reform attempts was the fact that it was played out to a global television audience, whose ability to receive and to consume news and information had been transformed and enhanced by satellite. Other media, – fax, video, camcorders, electronic mail and the personal computer, the harbingers of the IT revolution – were also making their mark. Future historians may well judge the digitalization of data to have been one of the important technological breakthroughs of the twentieth century. This far in human history, these media are indeed, in de Sola Pool's expression, 'technologies of freedom'.[86]

Gorbachev's analysis of the plethora of ills facing the Soviet Union, his justification for reform and the direction that reform should take, is laid out in his book, *Perestroika: New Thinking for Our Country and the World* (1987). Unfortunately, it is not so much an analysis, but rather a half-hearted attempt on the part of the last Soviet leader to maintain the status of the Soviet Union even as the foundations were crumbling and the walls were starting to tremble. The promise of some 'new thinking' remains unfulfilled. As late as 1987 there was something unreal about Gorbachev's many appeals to Lenin's legacy, how Lenin could inspire the reconstruction and renewal of the Soviet Union. In the 1990s *Perestroika* and Gorbachev's remedies suggest a script written for the *X-Files*. Nevertheless for all its vagueness, ideological clichés and uninspired solutions – precisely because of them – *Perestroika* supports the view that Gorbachev and his reform-minded peers, by virtue of their isolation, failed to understand not merely the hopeless state of the Soviet economy (and all the problems that came with it), but also the real threat posed by technological change in the West.

The strength of the ideological straitjacket binding the Soviet leader is evident in all his analyses and solutions. Typically, the widening gap in economic performance between the West and the Soviet Union is attributed to 'stagnation and other phenomena alien to socialism'.[87] The problems that beset the Soviet economy were problems of excessive planning, inaccurate data, and interference by government bureaucrats. Consumer needs determined by bureaucrats led to over-production in some areas and under-production, and often poor quality, in others (and frequently in those areas where the potential consumer demand was greatest). Gorbachev's assessment of the ideological malaise serves the purposes of this chapter quite well:

> Propaganda of success – real or imagined – was gaining the upper hand. Eulogizing and servility were encouraged [...] In the social sciences scholastic theorization was encouraged and developed, but creative thinking was driven out from the social sciences, and superfluous and voluntarist assessments and judgements were declared indisputable truths.[88]

No amount of exhortations to ideological renewal can remedy the situation, a point which seems to be lost on Gorbachev. Once social and personal advantage is perceived to exist in the endless analysis and interpretation of Marxist-Leninist ideology; that it offers excellent career opportunities for the charlatan, then the stage is set for the growth of an ideological priesthood. Its rise and consolidation were deadly to serious intellectual enquiry. The penetration and ubiquity of Marxist-Leninist ideology in Soviet society was part of the problem, not the cure. That Gorbachev failed to realize this can only be explained, I think, by the ideological influences of the very machine he was trying, without success to reform, and that he had no intention of dispensing with ideology. He was after all one of its privileged sons, who, through diligence and loyalty had risen to the highest post in the land, his formative years coinciding with the last ten years or so of Stalin's rule.

Gorbachev's sweep of Soviet history shows him to be a communist with fairly conventional views. His assessment of history rests on the Stalin-was-a-bad-man evasion. According to this view, Stalin and Stalinism were aberrations, hence the appeals to Leninist purity and orthodoxy, the need to return to some mythical, ideologically-pristine past, which can be made to serve the present. In Gorbachev's own words:

> The works of Lenin and his ideals of socialism remained for us an inexhaustible source of dialectical creative thought, theoretical wealth and political sagacity. His very image is an undying example of lofty moral strength, all-round spiritual culture and selfless devotion to the cause of the people and to socialism. Lenin lives on in the minds and hearts of millions of people.[89]

That Gorbachev turns to Lenin as 'an ideological source of *perestroika*'[90] should, in view of what we have seen of Lenin's own position and behaviour towards questions of information, censorship and the press, be enough to dispel any doubts as to Gorbachev's intentions. *Perestroyka* was intended to rescue the system. And once again Lenin, whose curious mix of ideological fervour and pragmatism Gorbachev defends and admires, provides some inspiration. The ideological stranglehold is quite apparent in Gorbachev's language. All the standard Leninist jargon can be found: 'democratic centralism'; 'criticism', 'self-criticism'; and the repeated use and appeal to 'objective conditions'; and the use of the euphemism for Stalin's terror the 'personality cult'. A telling revelation is Gorbachev's defence of collectivization, of which he notes:

I know how much fiction, speculation and malicious criticism of us go with this term, let alone the process itself. But even many of the objective students of this period of our history do not seem to be able to grasp the importance, need and inevitability of collectivization in our country. [...] Collectivization changed, perhaps not easily and not immediately, the entire way of life of the peasantry, making it possible for them to become a modern, civilized class of society.[91]

Such an assessment beggars belief.[92] In numbers alone it was the greatest act of mass murder ever to have taken place on the European continent. Henceforth, the Soviet Union was unable to feed itself. The extent to which Gorbachev attempts to evade the whole dreadful episode can be best understood by imagining Hitler's arguing that Europe's Jews had benefited from the Holocaust. Or we might place it alongside the many Holocaust-denial stories that have circulated since 1945. It tells us, however, a great deal about Gorbachev himself and his plans. A Soviet leader who can defend the Terror-Famine (Conquest), and, in the same breath, talk of reform and *glasnost'* is one whose motives deserve the closest scrutiny.

Gorbachev's ambitions for *glasnost'* seemed to have been based on the assumption that by allowing discussion of Stalinism all the pent-up frustration and disgust would be channelled into something that the party could control. One of the more obvious omissions in Gorbachev's book is any reference to the censorship apparatus and its degrading social and economic effects. Omission and some tortuous circumlocution are evident in Gorbachev's expectation of *glasnost'*: 'Criticism can be an effective instrument of *perestroika* only if it is based on absolute truth and scrupulous concern for justice.'[93] The hidden or less than obvious danger for the reconstructed Soviet journalist lies in Gorbachev's devotion to Lenin's 'creative thought and sagacity'. It was Leninist-media policy, with censorship and the banning of all hostile publications, that paved the way for Stalin with his enforced homonoia after Lenin's death. *Glasnost'* is not to be a genuine, uncontrolled, spontaneous debate, but one that takes place under the auspices of the Party. The terms of the debate are to be set by Lenin with Gorbachev, for the benefit of doubters and sceptics, as his interpreter and final arbiter. In other words, Gorbachev was trying to set limits to the policy of *glasnost'*. All argument and discussion must stay within the realm of Leninist feasibility or else they fail the touchstone of truth, and can be ignored. If we accept this outcome then we must recognize that the type of polity which Gorbachev envisaged for the Soviet Union was not a democracy but an anaemic shade of totalitarian red. We see this desire to set the terms of discussion in Gorbachev's belief that this time things will be different: *'Glasnost'*, criticism and self-criticism are not just a new campaign. They have been proclaimed and must become a norm in the Soviet way of life. No radical change is possible without it.'[94] One does not have to look too far to discern the traditional patterns of behaviour of the Soviet leadership. A *glasnost'* that is proclaimed and which 'must become a norm' is yet another attempt by the party to dictate the terms of social and economic change. More importantly, it challenges Gorbachev's insistence, made later in the book,[95] that the rule of law is of great importance. Arbitrary and *ad hoc* laws and decrees of the kind which proclaim *glasnost'* are not the same thing as the rule of law.

At the same time as Gorbachev was receiving world-wide publicity and acclaim as the architect of a more open Soviet Union, the KGB was doggedly pursuing dissidents and trying to analyze their activities for the benefit of its masters. A top secret report, entitled 'Results of the Work of the KGB in Investigating Authors of Anonymous Materials of a Hostile Nature', circulated to the Party's Central Committee on 21 March 1988, at the height of *glasnost'*, gives some idea as to just how vulnerable the experiment was. KGB chairman, Viktor Chebrikov, noted that *glasnost'* has resulted in 'a 29.5% reduction in the distribution of anonymous materials of an anti-Soviet, nationalistic, and politically injurious content as compared with the previous year' [1986].[96] Any sense of irony or perception of inconsistency in the fact that the state should declare its support for *glasnost'* on the one hand, and yet monitor so closely the dissemination statistics of 'anonymous materials' in a top secret report, is entirely absent.

Various political and non-political reasons are cited in the report for the dissemination of anonymous materials, ranging from nationalist sentiments to difficulties with housing and household needs. From the KGB's point of view the main concern is the desire of the authors to protect their identity. The report's author seems sublimely unaware that the traditional Soviet manner of dealing with any form of dissent might just have something to do with a desire for anonymity. Nor does the KGB's follow-up to this situation promise any good for *glasnost'*. In his conclusion Chebrikov sounds an ominous note, and one which speaks volumes about the deep-rooted inertia paralyzing Soviet institutions. 'The KGB', he writes, 'is implementing measures to prevent and suppress in a timely fashion negative incidents connected with the distribution of anonymous materials'.[97]

It is of course quite legitimate that a state or private body should mount an investigation into what people think on certain issues. After all, this is the aim of market research, but the data are gathered in an open manner, are made available and are attributable. That this task should be entrusted to the state's leading security agency, and that the report should be designated top secret as late as 1988, says much about the paranoid world inhabited by the Soviet leadership. The report hints at the enormous and costly effort expended to monitor utterly trivial issues, when measured against the really serious ones facing the Soviet Union in the late 1980s. It highlights, too, the limitations of intelligence services, no matter how efficient and ruthless, if the intellectual courage to draw the necessary conclusions, and the political will to act on these conclusions, is absent.

Glasnost' was concerned with both the past and present and especially with the way the two relate to one another. When we talk of *glasnost'* we could easily use the German term *Vergangenheitsbewältigung*. For that is essentially what it was. Censorship destroyed the collective memory. Huge numbers of writers, musicians, playwrights and other intellectuals were rehabilitated. It represented an information explosion of blinding brilliance. In other respects, the Soviet experience of coming to terms with the past differed quite dramatically from that of Germany. Germany's rebuilding – in all kinds of ways – coincided with its military defeat. The destruction of the Soviet information status quo came after some seventy years of utterly determined denial, and one, in marked contrast to the Nazis, which was supported by a great many Western intellectuals, social scientists, politicians and journalists. The reconciliation with the past came suddenly and unexpectedly (to all but a few). The sudden release of so much suppressed information overwhelmed the Soviet state, with scarcely any time to ponder the collapse of the empire. The danger was not that all news was ideological, it was the sheer volume of what was being transmitted. Revelations about Lenin and Stalin competed with an emerging consumer culture. The Katyn executioners drowned in Pepsi Cola or were trampled in the rush for Levis.

Gorbachev believed that this explosion could be controlled for specific ends. He believed that the intellectual ferment would make the position of the apparatchiks, one of the main obstacles to reform, untenable. In return, the leading and guiding role of the CPSU would be retained. In one sense, therefore, *glasnost'* was a calculated risk; a means to an end. Many of Gorbachev's statements on the purpose of *glasnost'* leave us in no doubt that this was his aim. The gambit failed for precisely the reasons it was necessary: it was necessary because the Soviet Union, were it not to become relegated to permanent Third-World status, needed to join the global exchange of information, the key to increased prosperity; it failed because Gorbachev, having abrogated the Party's right to be the sole purveyor of knowledge – already a *fait accompli* – was not able (neither were the hard-liners who ousted him) to control the information explosion. *Glasnost'* merely accelerated the onset of critical mass.

CONCLUSION

I recognize that some will not accept the general reasons which I put forward to explain the collapse of communism. Many Western scholars, intellectuals, journalists and politicians who nevertheless enjoy the freedoms of the West still – it is quite clear – regret the passing of the Soviet empire and all it stood for. These residual sympathies are very much in evidence in publications trying to account for the Soviet collapse.[98] Some of their explanations, such as they are, are worth a brief examination since they deal directly and indirectly with the main thrust of this section.

The literature of justification and evasion appeared as soon as the corpses started to pile up after 1917 and there is no reason to suppose that any addition to the massive evidence against Soviet totalitarianism which was available well before Gorbachev – and the fall of Honecker, Zhivkov, Ceauşescu and Jaruzelski – will significantly change the minds of those who are wedded to the socialist project in one form or another.

There is a marked tendency, one suspects a leftover from the substantial writings of convergence theory, to see the differences in economic success separating West and East, as being one of degree rather than reflecting the far more profound and irreconcilable differences between capitalism and socialism. For example, Charles Maier asserts: 'The Communist collapse was a reaction to forces for transformation that have gripped West and East alike, but which Western Europeans (and North Americans) had responded to earlier and thus with less cataclysmic an upheaval. The most compelling pressure was economic.'[99] Some crucial questions remain unanswered here. Why was the West able to respond to the problems in a way in which the East was not? What pathologies or insuperable obstacles can we find in the East which were not present in the West? Marxist-Leninist ideology and censorship are the factors which explain the difference in performances. Marxist-Leninist ideology justified censorship and censorship isolated the East's leadership from the grim realities which dominated the lives of their citizens. Moreover, reform of any kind was dangerous because it involved change and that (as Khrushchev and Gorbachev found out) could have unforeseen consequences. The West was able to react to the changes in the economy in good time because even if governments or certain segments of governments (and during the period to which Maier refers left-leaning governments held power in Britain and America) ignored the danger signs, institutions, think-tanks, opposition parties and non-government experts, did not. Finally, there is the sanction of the ballot box which did not exist in the 'peoples' democracies'. The longer the delay in facing up to the real nature of the problem, the less likely that reforms would have any effect, at least not that intended by the reformers. Nor should we ignore the nature of the changes themselves which convinced certain politicians in the West that the collectivist economics and social policies which had commanded near universal consensus in the West after 1945, could no longer be sustained. As long as productivity and wealth were measured in terms of the tonnage of coal, steel and tractors, then the East had some chance of not falling too far behind the West (quality was of course another matter entirely). Wealth creation that switches emphasis from heavy industry – the traditional home of unionized labour – to industries and services which exploit information technology, posed a severe challenge for the Soviet bloc's dependence on heavy industry. Furthermore, it is pertinent to seek an explanation for Western dominance in the field of computers and software. The IT revolutions have indeed brought considerable hardship to certain segments of the population, but there are opportunities. The West was able to respond better and sooner to them than the Soviet empire for three reasons: (i) sufficient numbers of decision-makers both private and official in the West were not burdened by an all-encompassing ideology and the intellectual censorship that came with it; (ii) capitalism is essentially pragmatic, empirical, opportunistic and highly adaptable and flexible (communism was not); (iii) the IT revolution was essentially Western-driven and gave enormous power to small businesses and individuals. One result was that the monopoly of organized labour could be broken.[100]

Again, the following assessment must be challenged. Maier argues that: 'The need for restructuring was a challenge that gripped West and East. It was not originally system-specific; but by the 1980s, the continuing afflictions in the East testified to the pathology of communism, just as those in the 1970s reflected the deformations of capitalism.'[101] The nature of the restructuring that took place in the West was of different order and cause from that which had to take place in the Soviet empire. The 'deformations of capitalism' were the ruthless exploitation by unionized labour of strikes and the spiralling costs of the welfare state combined with confiscatory levels of taxation. These were the responsibility of the Labour party in Britain and most certainly did represent the 'deformations of capitalism'. For the reasons given above corrective measures could be taken and collectivist failure and corporatism could be abandoned. The damage done to Western economies by high public spending and inflation did not reflect any intrinsic systemic failure. Rather, it was the failure of the welfare economics favoured by one particular political party whose policies could be legally challenged. No such challenge was possible in the Soviet Union (it would be regarded as counter-revolutionary activity) and so alarm signals, which in any open, free and politically-pluralist system would have been heeded, were not. As a result, the suggestion that the problems besetting the Soviet empire were not 'system-specific' is false.

The pervasive and insidious symmetrical approach also blinds Maier to what took place in the societies of 'real existing socialism'. Thus, he argues: 'both East and West have undergone a crisis of bureaucratic control, which rendered it supremely difficult for authoritarian rulers to manage the pressures emanating from civil society'.[102] There was, of course, no such thing as a civil society east of the Berlin Wall. One should also object to the use of a half-way-house word such as 'authoritarian'. Totalitarian applies to the East and while Western leaders can have authoritarian ideas they are subject, once again to the sanction of the ballot box. We should also bear in mind that the structures and associations of a civil society can survive quite well in an authoritarian society, whereas in a totalitarian state they are either crushed or subverted and then remoulded into a grotesque parody of the original. Soviet leaders who habitually polled 99.9 per cent of the vote is just one example. One reason, why Portugal and Spain have been able to overcome their historically-recent authoritarian legacies is precisely because a civil society in both states was not crushed.[103]

For his part, Eric Hobsbawm informs us that socialism 'did not "fail" in any absolute sense'.[104] He cites three reasons for socialism's non-failure in any absolute sense:

First, socialism was incapable of moving fully into, let alone generating, the new hi-tech economy, and was therefore destined to fall even further behind. To have constructed the economy of Andrew Carnegie was no good unless one could also advance further into the economy of IBM – or even of Henry Ford, for socialism signally failed to achieve the mass production of consumer goods.[105]

Second, in the society of global communications, media, travel and transnational economy, it was no longer possible to insulate socialist populations from information about the non-socialist world, that is, from knowing just how much worse off they were in material terms and in freedom of choice.[106]

Third, with the slowing down of its rate of growth and its increasing relative backwardness, the USSR became economically too weak to sustain its role as a superpower, that is, its control over Eastern Europe. In short Soviet-type socialism became increasingly uncompetitive and paid the price.[107]

All three reasons cited by Hobsbawm are permeated by considerations of information and data-deficit.[108] We must ask why it was that socialism proved to be quite incapable of generating the new hi-tech economies, which meant, above all else, computer software and hardware industries. Agreed, it no longer became possible for the Soviet empire to insulate itself from its capitalist rivals, but one would like to know why the party ever wished to insulate its populations in the first place. Of what was the party fearful? And why? And why did the party treat with the utmost brutality any individual who tried to overcome the party's information monopoly? Why was it that in National-socialist Germany people were allowed to retain their radios even during the war, whereas in Soviet-socialist Russia, a decree demanded they be handed in? Why were the citizens of the 'peoples' democracies' denied the basic right to travel freely? Socialism, even Soviet socialism, could mass-produce consumer goods, just, but that was not the problem. Hobsbawm misses the point: consumer goods are for consumers and in any system where the means of production are in private hands then a great deal of time and trouble is expended to discover what consumers require (the role of information and data once again is clearly vital in this market research process and this in turn stimulates the use, refinement and proliferation of computing). Where the state is the owner of the means of production and distribution then party bureaucrats decide what the priorities for consumption are, not the consumer: the consumer gets what he is given. Since the consumers' wishes can be ignored, for the consumer in any Western understanding of the word does not exist, then there is no pressure on party economists to worry about quality or quality control. The result is that a vast amount of shoddy goods are produced that nobody wants to buy, or if they do buy them, they do so grudgingly out of a total lack of any alternative. Even had the Soviet economy been able to match Western standards of quality, quality control, as well as storage, distribution – and such capabilities would have implied a totally different Soviet Union from the one that 'actually' existed and then actually collapsed – then this would not have been enough to avoid profound structural economic change. Nor would emulating IBM or Henry Ford have been a sufficient achievement for the economies of the Soviet empire, even if they were capable of it. Modern methods of mass production are not labour-intensive. There is no place for an industrial proletariat where goods can be designed and produced by computers, where adding value does not require vast amounts of plant, and the presence of unionized labour that frequently went with it. The failure to develop a computer industry that could rival the West's hurt the Soviet Union especially badly in the field of military research. Once again, it was not enough to mass-produce Kalashnikov assault rifles[109] for use by the Red Army and terrorist groups. Parity with the West required smart weapons which were not possible without strengths in computers and software.

This failure to produce effective computers and software has not deterred Hobsbawm from asserting that the Soviet system was better 'than capitalism at providing mass education'.[110] Yet what can be said of the quality? If the aim of mass education is to produce a people who unquestioningly obey the decrees of the communist party, who accept that in all areas of intellectual endeavour the judgement of the ideologues of the CPSU is final, who accept that to ask awkward questions about the past is justifiably to incur the wrath of 'the people', guided naturally by the party, then yes, one could say that the provision of Soviet mass education was infinitely superior to anything available in the West. Soviet mass education sought to provide obedient managers and technocrats, cogs in the Soviet machine, precisely the sort of people who would impede the growth of IT. Its aim was most emphatically not intended to provide thinkers, visionaries, heretics and sceptics, our intellectual movers and shakers. That from such an educational system so destructive of genuine moral and intellectual attainment, individuals of the stature of Sakharov, Solzhenitsyn, Bukovsky, Shcharansky and Ratushinskaya did emerge, is all the more remarkable and inspiring. Hobsbawm's observation demonstrates a truly appalling lack of awareness of what Soviet mass education entailed, with its huge emphasis on Marxist-Leninist agitation and propaganda, a curriculum that was subject at all levels to ferocious censorship as was the rest of Soviet society, and one that squeezed out anything remotely at odds with the party.

Both Maier and Hobsbawm acknowledge the failure of the socialist economies in the all-important realm of IT and computers. Unfortunately, they offer no explanation. It seems to me that this Western dominance is to be expected and is a natural outcome of the differences between capitalism and socialism, of which education is just one difference.

Many scientific discoveries and business applications occur by accident. The incremental steps that lead to a marketable consumer product such as the personal computer are often the outcome of a strange cooperative venture; strange because those involved are not consciously working towards any finished product but are driven by the intellectual or egotistical need to solve some problem. That their solution could have an application in other areas is not important, at least for them. Nor is it always immediately obvious. Such an apparently haphazard approach is completely at odds with the idea that economic growth can be planned.

A striking feature of the development of the computer industry in the United States has been the enormous role played by individuals with no institutional affiliation, whose interest was essentially that of the obsessed amateur. Now highly successful businessmen, individuals such as Steve Wozniak (builder of the first Apple computer), Steve Jobs, Paul Allen and Bill Gates (Microsoft) would have been regarded as people with an interesting but unusual hobby in the 1970s. Jobs, Wozniak, Gates and the many others who made the personal-computer industry were pioneers. To quote Robert Cringely: 'Like any other true pioneers, they don't care about what is possible or not possible; they are dissatisfied with the present and excited about the future. They are anti-establishment and rightly see this as a prerequisite for success.'[111]

America's ability to accommodate this restless energy, this sense that new ways have to be found of doing things confers enormous advantages. Consider what would have befallen Wozniak *et al* in the former Soviet Union. Dropping out of college to pursue their obsessions, they would have been regarded as 'socially dangerous elements', and quickly attracted the attention of the KGB. Any incipient computer revolution would have finished at the very outset. The visceral fear that characterized Soviet attitudes towards computers stemmed from the party's total monopoly in the collection and dissemination of information. A society that until the middle of the 1980s outlawed the private ownership of photocopiers and faxes, if they could be found, was simply not geared to understanding the nature of technological change taking place. Add to this the state ownership of the means of production and we can see that even if by some miracle those fictional Soviet PC hobbyists had avoided arrest and incarceration, the market conditions for success were non-existent. At the most fundamental level, however, it was the party's deep-rooted hostility to all forms of individual initiative and achievement that proved such a crippling handicap. Innovation and the sort of risk-taking responsible for the personal-computer industry cannot be driven by Soviet-style collectives and centralized economic planning.

We should also consider the speed and magnitude of change. Long-term planning is possible when you can assume some sort of product stability over the middle term, when, in other words, the world remains more or less the same. In an industry such as personal computers, however, where the product and its capabilities are constantly being improved, it is a question of permanent revolution.[112] Chaos and instability are the norms.

The battle between the computer giant IBM, whose money was made with mainframe computers, and the would-be, personal-computer manufacturers began the moment the microprocessor was invented by Intel. Personal computers threatened the monopoly position enjoyed by IBM. IBM executives rejected the personal-computer concept, one can assume, because they could not conceive of anything other than the mainframe computer. To IBM's corporate planners computers were mainframes. Anything else was not taken seriously. To quote Bill Gates: 'Computer manufacturers, however, didn't see the microprocessor as a threat. They just couldn't imagine a puny chip taking on a 'real' computer. Not even the scientists at Intel saw its full potential.'[113] Gates highlights the important link between invention and application. Frequently, the inventor will not see the opportunities created by the invention. Once again, the stimulus for any application is profit, in a word the market. Yet, there is another aspect to IBM's failure to take the personal computer seriously, as suggested by Robert Cringely's summing up of the IBM ethos:

> IBM executives don't design products and write software; they *manage* the design and writing of software. They go to meetings. So much effort, in fact, is put into managing all the managers who are managing things that hardly anyone is left over to do the real work. This means that most IBM hardware and nearly all IBM software is written or designed by the lowest level of people in the company – trainees. Everyone else is too busy going to meetings, managing or learning to be a manager, so there is little chance to include any of their technical expertise in IBM products. [...] IBM has layers and layers of management to check and verify each decision as it is made and amended. The safety net is so big at IBM that it is hard to make a bad decision. In fact, it is hard to make any decision at all, which turns out to be the company's greatest problem and the source of its ultimate downfall.[114]

Endless meetings, an obsession with management at the expense of design and an alarming ignorance at the higher levels concerning the products created, reinforces the view of a company that was not able to grasp the significance of the emerging personal-computer revolution.

Imagine a state run along these lines. Instead of management there is strict ideological control. Ideological conformity rather than hands-on competence in any field is the highest virtue for any ambitious official. Because of a massive system of censorship, state officials have no idea about what is happening beyond the state's borders. Orthodoxy is monitored and enforced by concentration camps and a massive network of secret police and informers. This is, of course, the Soviet Union, or anywhere east of the old Berlin Wall.

I must stress that I am not a convert to the view that differences between large Western corporations, such as IBM or multinationals, and something as odious as the former Soviet Union, are only superficial. Rather, the comparison is intended to illustrate that even for a Western company operating in a free and open society the consequences of a loss of operational flexibility and innovation, especially when competition is fierce, and still worse, only dimly recognized owing to complacency, can seriously damage profits.

In the case of IBM that complacency was born of the success generated by mainframe computing. Such success blinded IBM to the possibility that this mainframe monopoly might be challenged. Of the opinion that its monopoly would endure indefinitely, IBM executives were caught unawares by the PC industry. IBM's total collapse would not be good for IBM employees, shareholders or the coffers of the American government but it would hardly bring about the collapse of America. IBM would enter the history books as a company that became too rigid, was unable to adapt and suffered the ultimate failure of companies that failed to heed warning signs in good time, and was liquidated.

Based on extreme ideological prescription, and, as a result, appalling ignorance about what was taking place, the nature of Soviet complacency was altogether more profound and far-reaching, the consequences more devastating. If American IBM executives were taken by surprise, then we can see how little the chance was that the Soviet Union, with one or two marginalized and persecuted exceptions, would ever be able to recognize the problem in time and act.

The history of the development of the computer underlines the powerful relationship between technological innovation, invention and the private ownership of the means of production. On the other hand, the conspicuous failure of the Soviet Union or any of its satellites to develop computer hardware and software industries capable of rivalling those in America must be seen as both an intellectual and economic failure: an intellectual failure because of the party's unjustified belief in its own omniscience; economic because without buy-outs, start-ups and venture capital, without, in other words, the economic infrastructure which capitalism and the private ownership of the means of production make possible, none of the small businesses that went on to become the big software and hardware names would ever have started. We can see the development and staggering growth of the personal-computer industry as one of a number of allegories of capitalist success, and equally, an illustrative, single example of what went so badly wrong in the Soviet Union.

The retarding effects of censorship, which in the Soviet case, Gorbachev hoped to overcome by *glasnost'* and *perestroyka*, were by no means unique to the former-Soviet system of Central and Eastern Europe. Throughout history societies and cultures have attempted to prevent the inflow of ideas and information. In a pre-electronic age the impact of new ideas and potentially hostile information was delayed by the speed with which they travelled. Time and distance aided and abetted the censor. Sea power, trade, telegraph, then radio and finally satellite communications in conjunction with personal computers, fax and electronic mail, have negated the advantages of time and distance. In the aftermath of the dramatic role played by the electronic media in the 1989 revolutions and especially in weakening the Soviet coup of August 1991, few would dispute Ronald Reagan's observation that: 'Technology will make it increasingly difficult for the state to control the information its people receive [...] The Goliath of totalitarianism will be brought down by the David of the microchip.'[115]

If information technology helped to undermine the Soviet model of censorship, it also cruelly exposed the deficiencies of an economy lacking in such technology. Where the West itself did not possess the quantitative and qualitative advantages of IT across the whole spectrum of economic and media services and products then the Soviet Union could afford to view the supposed benefits of the personal computer with scepticism, even indifference. As, however, the computer revolution started to take off in the West, so the advantages, especially in the dissemination of news and information, moved inexorably in the West's favour. IT enhanced the already superior empirical and flexible practices of the Western media. Add to this the increased volume of data and information that could now be processed and transmitted and the advantages start to look overwhelming. As I have argued elsewhere:

> Unable to cope, Soviet delivery systems, domestic and international (TASS and APN), lost the initiative and found themselves on the defensive. The ability of the new electronic media to seep through just about any barrier, and as important, their ability to impose a new *modus operandi*, on the dissemination of news, meant that the Soviet Union had, whether the party liked it or not, been drawn into a global media structure, in which the West – to use the current phrase – was setting the agenda. This situation marks the prelude to the Gorbachev reforms and the policy of *glasnost'*.[116]

And here we come to yet another of those errors which history so often conspires to lay before the well-meaning politician: in this case timing. Gorbachev hoped to play midwife to a new, reformed Soviet Union. Instead, he unwittingly administered the *coup de grâce*. It was his great misfortune that he initiated *perestroyka* and *glasnost'* at a time when these new media were already starting to change patterns of news and information use and consumption.[117] The computer and IT revolutions of the 1980s accelerated the penetration and invasion of the Soviet infosphere at the worst possible moment for those who wished to salvage something from the system. Profound structural weakness was revealed both internally and externally, and moreover at a time when the penetrative power of the new media, boosted by the digitalization of data, was greater than ever before; and when the historical and contemporary ills and failings of Soviet society were being exposed to unprecedented national and international scrutiny.

IT used by Russians played an important role in breaking the conventional media blackout imposed during the August coup of 1991. In a subsequent survey of computing networks in Russia, Bob Travica and Matthew Hogan noted the use of these networks by those opposed to the coup leaders. They posed an interesting question, namely whether: 'the coup leaders failed to grasp the powerful broadcasting potential and informing abilities of telecommunications systems and computer networks?'[118] The authors also noted that: 'While the coup leaders initially closed down independent television and radio stations, they ignored dedicated and public telephone lines, packet switches and satellite links.'[119] The answer to the first question is a resounding affirmative: the coup leaders did indeed fail to grasp the enormous potential of computer networks. But this comes as no surprise. For this same generation of party apparatchiks – Gorbachev's peers – also fatally misunderstood the changes which had occurred in IT. The same developments which had forced *perestroyka* on the Soviet Union were in 1991 able to undermine attempts to reverse it.

One of the great ifs of the Soviet collapse is whether the Soviet Union might have survived in some form had *perestroyka* and *glasnost'* been introduced in the 1960s or early 1970s, that is before irreversible weakness was apparent and before the computer and IT revolutions of the mid-1980s.

'There exists', argues the historian Paul Kennedy, 'a dynamic for change, driven chiefly by economic and technological developments, which then impact upon social structures, political systems, military power, and the position of individual states and empires.'[120] The lesson was certainly not lost on Soviet leaders, but they failed to understand that economic and technological developments are driven by learning and knowledge.

Censorship of the kind practised in the Soviet empire attacks the basis on which economic and military might rest. In the economic sphere, too many layers of bureaucracy imposed debilitating constraints on information flows, an effect exacerbated by the general unavailability of accurate data. As a result an industrial culture was created in which Soviet managers were either unable to adapt to, or simply failed to understand, the impact of cheap, powerful and ubiquitous computers on industrial, social and economic behaviour.

In its attempts to catch up with the West in the 1930s Soviet planners could afford to use the most brutal and wasteful methods to achieve results. In the post-industrial era limitless muscle power and natural resources are not enough. Nor, as we have seen, were the damaging effects of censorship just confined to the economy. Scientific endeavour, law, literature and the arts, the writing of history, the collection and dissemination of statistical data, the broadcast and print media, even the language itself were systematically undermined. Thus, even if economic and military parity could at some stage be achieved, they could not be maintained. Censorship (of the Soviet kind) and education for the knowledge-based industries emerging in the latter half of the twentieth century proved to be a contradiction that could not be sustained indefinitely.

Part II Liberty:
The Nurse of All Great Wits

2 Mass Media Legislation of the Russian Federation

> If we think to regulate printing, thereby to rectify manners, we must regulate all recreations and pastimes, all that is delightful to man.
>
> John Milton

INTRODUCTION

Sifting through the mountain of decrees and laws dealing with the mass media, analyzing and cross-referencing the various shifts in emphasis and import, is a task for the legal scholar. Since, however, the legal status quo affects the Russian mass media in so many ways, guaranteeing above all the rights of Russian journalists to practise their profession without the restraints of the past, then discussion of these changes serves as a prelude to our understanding the practical problems and consequences of media privatization, investigative journalism and journalistic ethics. Indeed, many of these problems arise from disputes over interpretation of media legislation.

Nor are potential legal problems and obligations confined to the plethora of media and non-media legislation of the Russian Federation itself. As Russia moves towards the rule of law so international laws and conventions, which in the past were routinely and brazenly flouted, will have an impact. Apart from Article 19, for example, there are at least six other articles of the United Nations Declaration of Human Rights (UNDHR), which are relevant for the Russian mass media.[1]

Proclaimed by the General Assembly on 10 December 1948, the UNDHR imposed no obligation to implement its principles. It was only as late as 1976 that two additional pieces of legislation, The International Covenant on Economic, Social and Cultural Rights (adopted 1966) and the International Covenant on Civil and Political Rights (adopted 1966), imposed legally binding commitments on their signatories. Article 19 of the International Covenant on Civil and Political Rights (ICCPR), while clearly based on Article 19 of UNDHR, draws attention to the need for responsibility in the exercise of freedom of expression, a matter which is currently of great concern for the Russian media. Given, moreover, that the Russian Federation is now a member of the Council of Europe, then decisions of the European Court are going to have an impact on Russian legislation at some stage. Future legislation on the use of the Internet, especially for business purposes, will not leave the Russian Federation untouched either.

TOWARDS THE 1990 PRESS LAW

The dissident movement or 'cultural opposition' to use Amalrik's term, was not just content to fill the many gaps left by the official Soviet mass media. Its members recognized that certain basic freedoms, protected and enforced by law, were the best guarantor of human and civil rights.[2] An indication of the crucial awareness of the importance of the freedom to disseminate information and ideas – the basis for so many other freedoms – can be seen in the fact that the *samizdat* publication, *The Chronicle of Current Events*, adopted Article 19 of the United Nations Universal Declaration of Human Rights as its motto.[3] One of Andrei Sakharov's key demands in *Progress, Coexistence, and Intellectual Freedom* was the introduction of a press law to set limits to state intervention and thus protect the freedom of intellectual exchange.[4] But these ideas were ahead of their time. It was not until 1986 that there existed a real possibility of drafting a press law.[5]

Yuriy Baturin, Vladimir Entin and Mikhail Fedotov, who went on to draft the 'Zakon o pechati i drugikh sredstvakh massovoy informatsii' (The Law on the Press and Other Mass Media) have provided a lot of information on the behind-the-scenes struggle to get this legislation passed into law. By April of 1989, note the authors, the draft text of this law had been circulated to the editorial boards of the major Soviet periodicals and the Ideological Commission of the CPSU's Central Committee. By then it had also received the approval of the Politburo.

The draft favoured by the party included a list of provisions designed to protect its own interests rather than those of journalists and society at large. For example, only officially registered organizations would be allowed to found periodicals, and, strikingly indicative of the limited mental horizons in which the party apparat locked itself, individuals would not be allowed to own copying machines and duplicating equipment. There was a long list of reasons which might preclude registration, and an equally long list of subjects that could not be discussed publicly. As Baturin and his co-authors noted: 'In short, the official draft was a great step backward, even in comparison to the situation that existed under Brezhnev.'[6]

In response to this interference from vested official interests, the authors prepared and published their own draft which was circulated to deputies, legal scholars and journalists. As a result, the People's Deputies rejected the official draft, and the private initiative was accepted as the basis for the new Press Law. Despite this considerable success every attempt was made to include the provision of clauses and articles justifying prior censorship. On 23 November 1989, a mere twenty-four hours before the final discussion of the law was scheduled, and two weeks after the Berlin Wall had been breached, an anonymous version, differing substantially from the one already examined by the various committees, was circulated. 'It was', observed the authors, 'more sad than funny that a draft law which proclaimed the abolition of censorship was itself subjected to censorship.'[7] The provisions in the pre-emptive draft, which sanctioned official interference, arbitrariness and failed to recognize the impermissibility of censorship, amounted to a negation of the entire project. Fortunately, the last-minute ploy failed.

'The Law on the Press and other Media' signed by Gorbachev on 12 June 1990 (hereinafter the 1990 Press Law), and taking effect on 1 August 1990, formally removed the party's grip on the media, in place since immediately after the 1917 revolution. Given what we have seen of Gorbachev's hopes and fears for the reform process, then one might argue that the enactment of this law formally acknowledged that the reform process was dead; that the communist system could not be reformed or refashioned, only replaced. The 1990 Press Law represented an undoubted triumph for the many reformers of various political hues who had helped to create and to exploit the opportunities of *glasnost'*. The importance of this draft's becoming law cannot be overstated: 'The adopted law created a precedent. For the first time in the history of the Soviet state and law, a legal proposal, worked out by private individuals as a citizens' initiative, ousted the text of law that was worked out in the corridors of power ... '[8]

Yet, as one might expect, the drafters' assumptions and expectations encountered practical obstacles, and the bewildering pace of change and the dismantling of the Soviet edifice a year later, posed problems which could not have been foreseen.

The 1990 Press Law consists of a total of 39 articles organized in seven chapters.[9] For the first time in Soviet history press freedom is recognized and censorship outlawed (Article 1), without, unfortunately, defining what constituted censorship.[10] Likewise, the Law sought to protect state secrets without defining the range and significance of a state secret (Article 5). In view of the brutal and all-encompassing nature of Soviet censorship, legal precision might be considered superfluous.

The abolition of censorship removed the intellectual monopoly of Marxism-Leninism, and thus the ideological basis (as understood in the previous chapter) for the dissemination and interpretation of news. Henceforth, Marxism-Leninism was just another '-ism' competing for its market share of political allegiance. News was no longer the special prerogative of one party. According to the 1990 Press Law, '[news] is understood as publicly disseminated printed, audio and audiovisual reports and materials' (Article 1).[11] Another consequence of the abolition of censorship was that the educational, guiding role of the mass media – a function imposed by the communist party – fell by the wayside.[12] The question of censorship was a major battleground throughout the Cold War. The full historical importance of Article 1 is therefore considerable. For, it formally and publicly exposed seventy years of lies and blanket denials by Soviet officialdom that censorship was not a feature of the Soviet system, and of course, many words of evasive apologetics from Western fellow-travellers.

The question of censorship, though quite distinct from anything Soviet, also arises in the 1990 Press Law's position with regard to the relationships binding a media outlet's founder, editor, editorial management and publisher of a media outlet. Article 15 ('The Founder, Editor, Editorial Management and Publisher of a Media Outlet') states that the founder establishes the 'basic principles' of a media outlet, but that the editorial management carries out the programme on the 'basis of professional independence'. In the economic circumstances of post-Soviet Russia the relationship between founder and editor has become an important issue for the independence of journalists.

For example, the notion of 'founder of the mass media' was alien to Soviet media legislation[13], so while the concept of a founder might be applicable to new media outlets created after the 1990 Press Law had come into effect, it made no allowance for the absence of a 'founder', as a legal requirement for Soviet mass media. One gets the impression that the concept of 'founder' was introduced so that party interests could retain some control. We might see it, in fact, as a pre-emptive strike against looming media privatization. Another important historical consequence of the Soviet period is that the relationship between editorial staff and the party was ideological, not economic. Economic matters and the control of the plant and assets were the responsibility of the publishing houses. Given that the ideological basis for any claim is now non-existent, the party or party interests must be seen as one of a number of owners vying for ownership.[14] When the editorial board of *Znamya* submitted their registration on the basis that working collectives had the right to found a medium of mass information, others made counter-claims, among them the board of the Union of Writers, and the Pravda publishing house.

Registration, something, which appears to be a mere technical formality from the point of view of the legislator, proved to be one of the main sources of conflict arising from the 1990 Press Law and its successor. In essence, this was a struggle to possess parts of, or all of, the vast publishing and media complex of the Soviet state. The problem, though more severe in the Soviet Union and the cause of many legal disputes in the Russian Federation, is in some ways analogous to the many arguments over the merits of public ownership and privatization that raged in Britain during the 1980s. The bitterness with which the party resisted the transfer of various media outlets into private hands suggests that it regarded them as its own property. It confirmed that all the party's talk of being the custodian of the common good was a façade behind which the party could use and dispose of assets and services as it thought fit; not so much a round table of equal access and use but a ladder of increasing privilege. Not only was public ownership of the means of production a practical failure, it was also riddled with legal inconsistencies that have emerged as privatization has progressed.

Perhaps the real key to understanding these disputes lies in the dominion exercised by envy over human affairs. Most governments, whatever their political persuasion, encounter fewer difficulties when nationalizing privately-held assets, reallocating privately-run services and assuming tight control over the disposal of privately-held products than they do when transferring assets and services, previously owned in common, to private ownership. In a society where, until recently, the ethos of collectivism was so widely and deeply inculcated, then the political, economic and legal problems associated with such a transfer are likely to be especially acute. Media privatization in Russia has been one of the most hotly disputed areas of the changes affecting ownership of state assets. On reflection this is not too much of a surprise. The relationship between the broadcast media and political power grows ever closer, which does nothing to dispel the belief that whoever controls the mass media, directly or indirectly, controls the state. Hence the bitter legal battles, and frequently murderous struggles, to control television, for example.

The language of the 1990 Press Law does not completely clarify where rights and responsibilities begin and end. Take for example the provisions of Article 35 ('Grounds of Liability for the Violation of Legislation on the Press and Other Media'). According to Article 35, 'Abuse of freedom of speech, the dissemination of information that does not correspond to reality' incurs liability. The inclusion of the term 'to correspond to reality' (*sootvetstvovat' deystvitel'nosti*) obfuscates rather than clarifies the impact of the law. Questions as to the inclusiveness of Article 35 can also be identified. According to Article 35 'attempts by journalists to influence courts entail criminal, administrative or other liability in accordance with USSR and Union-republic legislation'. Any reference to state officials and state organizations is conspicuous by its absence.

The question of liability for the dissemination of information that fails 'to correspond to reality' is further complicated by Article 38 ('Cases of Exemption from Liability for the Dissemination of Information that Does Not Correspond to Reality'). The stated exemptions are:

(1) if this information was contained in official reports;
(2) if it was obtained from news agencies or press services of state or public agencies;
(3) if it is a verbatim reproduction of speeches by People's Deputies at Congresses or sessions of Soviets or by delegates to Congresses, conferences or plenary sessions of public associations, or of official statements by officials of state and public agencies;
(4) if it was contained in sources' speeches that were broadcast live or in texts that were not subject to editing in accordance with this law.

Overwhelmingly, the exemption affects information from official sources (paragraphs 1–3). The burden of verification outlined in Article 32 ('The Journalist's Duties') is removed from the *journalist* but nothing is stated about the responsibility of official sources and agencies to verify their facts or to impart information and materials that 'correspond to reality'. True, Article 39 ('Compensation for Moral Damages') makes it possible, at least theoretically, to achieve some redress from official sources. However, the idea of 'correspondence with reality' is so vague and open-ended that any attempt to demonstrate moral damage based on it would be difficult to prove. In such a struggle, to demonstrate that moral damage had been inflicted the citizen would find himself on a most unequal footing with the state.

If this interpretation is correct, then there exists, in effect, a loophole that could be exploited by the government or, still in 1990, the CPSU. This conclusion is hinted at in paragraph 4 of Article 38 which states that exemption from liability applies if the information 'was contained in sources' speeches that were broadcast live or in texts that were not subject to editing *in accordance with this law*' [emphasis added]. But since paragraphs 1–3 of Article 38 remove the burden of verification (from the journalist) at the outset and, moreover, make no provision for official sources to disseminate information 'corresponding to reality', then any information so disseminated automatically falls outside the provision of Article 38. Again, one is left with the impression that Article 38 was written not with the interests of journalists in mind, or indeed the reading, watching and listening public, but those of officials who might occasionally – let us be charitable – find it expedient to be somewhat economical with the truth. These conclusions, if accurate, have serious consequences for the 1990 Press Law as a whole, since they threaten to undermine certain key provisions. For example, Article 5 ('The Impermissibility of Abuse of the Freedom of Speech'), Article 24 ('The Right to Obtain Information Through the News Media'), Article 26 ('The Right to Retraction and Reply'), Article 27 ('The Consideration by a Court of a Request for the Publication of a Retraction or Reply') and Article 39 ('Compensation for Moral Damages').

Despite the limitations of the 1990 Press Law, the formal abolition of censorship – the Law's key provision – and the liberalization of media activity paved the way for further legislative acts without which the privatization of the post-Soviet media would not have been possible. Equally important was the fact that the legislative process had been firmly placed in the public domain where it was subject to scrutiny and amendment, however acrimonious and vituperative that has turned out to be.

1992 MASS MEDIA LAW (AMENDMENTS AND SUPPLEMENTS)

After the dissolution of the Soviet Union the 1990 Press Law was superseded by the Mass Media Law of the Russian Federation 'Zakon Rossiyskoy Federatsii o sredstvakh massovoy informatsii', which was signed into law on 27 December 1991 and came into f orce on 6 February 1992 (hereinafter referred to as the 1992 Mass Media Law).[15] The 1992 Mass Media Law consists of a total of 62 Articles organized in seven chapters. It is a much longer and more comprehensive document than its Soviet prototype and the drafters have attempted to address some of the earlier failings. It is, too, a recognizably more contemporary law in that the drafters have taken cognizance of some of the changes brought about by information technology.

The 1992 Mass Media Law bans censorship, but, unlike the 1990 Press Law, defines it. According to Article 3 ('The Inadmissibility of Censorship'), censorship is the:

> [...] demand made on the editorial board of a medium of mass information on the part of official persons, state organs, organisa-tions, institutions or social formations to submit reports and materials for advance approval (apart from cases when the official person is the author or interviewee), as well as the imposition of a ban on the dissemination of reports and materials, or on separate parts thereof ...

Of course, what is known as prior censorship is only one of a number of ways of controlling and censoring information. Furthermore, the banning of prior censorship clashes with the provisions for the protection of state secrets or 'other secrets specially protected by law' stated in Article 4 ('The Inadmissibility of the Abuse of the Freedom of Mass Information').

Overseeing the protection of state secrets and other specially protected secrets almost certainly requires some form of state body (in contravention of Article 3). Also, the circumspect editorial board, mindful of the penalties and Article 4, might wish to confer with a state body to ascertain whether information that is to be published falls foul of Article 4. Yet Article 3 forbids submitting material for prior approval of officials, and forbids the creation and financing of state bodies for that purpose. So one wonders how the editor protects himself and his publication from prosecution. Given that Article 3 forbids censorship (as defined in Article 3), but that Article 4 proscribes the dissemination of state secrets, then the consequence is that the state can decide to punish the media outlet by claiming that Article 4 has been violated. Legal advantages enjoyed by the state are enhanced by the absence of any definition of a state secret (a flaw noted in the 1990 Press Law), so that the editorial board can quite easily and inadvertently fall foul of the law.

Then, of course, there is the question as to what are these other secrets. Seeking an answer to this question is made all the more difficult by the peculiarities of secrecy itself: the full range of secrets which would fall within this category of special legislative protection cannot be stated since with really sensitive information, one of the most effective means of protecting it is to hide the fact that you have a secret in the first place. Stating that you have secrets in areas X and Y merely encourages journalists and others to ferret them out. The other variation of course is that the state can deliberately mislead by luring journalists away from sensitive areas by calculated and well-timed leaks.

Another difficult task for the journalist and the courts is trying to resolve, or to find, suitable definitions of the many activities that constitute abuse of freedom of information. For example, what is religious intolerance and the propaganda of war? The relationship between secrecy and legislation also poses problems for the journalist in pursuing activities which might be in the public interest. Investigating corruption and incompetence exposes the journalist to the risk of prosecution under the law, since investigative journalism will by its very nature involve the search for, and publication of, state secrets and sensitive information, particularly where they are being used to shield official malfeasance. Under the terms of Article 41 ('Confidential Information') for example the editorial board must not disseminate information given on the understanding that it be kept secret.[16] In cases involving official incompetence and malfeasance then surely the whole point of informing a media outlet is so that it uses the information.

Registration of mass media outlets is another area where state supervision and control are intrusive and excessive. Chapter II ('The Organization of the Activity of the Mass Media') of the mass media law lays down the procedure for registration, a requirement which is taken for granted. Registration for media products intended for dissemination in the Russian Federation and beyond its borders and several (unspecified) *oblasti* and *kraya* must be submitted by the founder to the Ministry of Press and Information of the Russian Federation. For dissemination inside the Federation and down to the smallest administrative units then the founder must submit an application to the above Ministry and to the relevant organs of the State Inspection for the Protection of the Freedom of the Press and Mass Information Attached to the Ministry of Press and Information of the Russian Federation.

Article 10 ('Application for Registration') requires the applicant to provide ten specific pieces of information: (i) details of the founder and co-founder. (ii) title. (iii) languages in which the outlet will be published. (iv) the address of the editorial board. (v) the form of periodical dissemination. (vi) the area of dissemination. (vii) the general themes and specialization of the product (*tematika*). (viii) frequency of publication. (ix) sources of finance. (x) whether the applicant has connections with other media outlets.[17] Any changes in this registration information obliges the applicant to re-register within one month with the registering body.

On its own, excessive red tape in the registration process is not an insuperable obstacle to publication. In conjunction, however, with other prescriptive clauses the cumulative effect can be to create a regulatory environment that places too many options at the disposal of state officials for limiting and controlling journalistic activity. One example that has already been highlighted in the 1990 Press Law poses a number of problems for both the journalist and the courts, specifically where an interpretation of those parts of the 1992 Mass Media Law relies on the term 'to correspond to reality' (*sootvetstvovat' deystvitel'nosti*).

According to the provisions of Article 13 ('Refusal of Registration'), registration of a media outlet can be refused if information required under Article 10 is false, that is 'it does not correspond to reality'. In other words, an objective right/wrong, truth/false differentiation is applicable when determining whether to register a media outlet. Yet in other parts of the 1992 Mass Media Law where the failure 'to correspond to reality' involves sanction, the same right/wrong and true/false differentiation cannot be said to apply with the same clarity. Indeed, it may be entirely inapplicable, in view of the fact that any legal outcome will be contingent on an interpretation of 'correspondence with reality' which is open to dispute in a way in which a true/false determination cannot be. The effects of this wording can be appreciated in the provisions of Article 43 ('The Right to Refutation'). Readers of a media outlet have the right to insist that the editorial board correct information that does not 'correspond to reality' and that tarnishes their 'honour' (*chest'*) and 'dignity' (*dostoinstvo*). Article 62 ('Compensation for Moral Damage') takes the matter even further. Moral damages arising from the publication of material 'not corresponding to reality' that damages the 'honour and dignity' or causes other 'non-property damage' (*neimushchestvenny vred*) will be reimbursed on a decision made by the court. A straight lie or inaccuracy is one thing, a statement that impugns the honour or dignity of a reader is another matter, and one that opens up the possibility of endless litigation.

FURTHER PRIMARY LEGISLATION AFFECTING THE MEDIA

The Arbitration Information Tribunal

The election campaign for deputies to the State Duma and Council of the Federal Assembly of the Russian Federation in December 1993 took place against a recent background of politically-inspired violence and economic instability. In such an atmosphere access to the media for the various competing factions and parties would be a major source of disputes and could jeopardize the legitimacy of the whole electoral process on which the Russian Federation's move towards political stability depended. There existed, therefore, considerable pressures for establishing procedures, that, firstly, would guarantee fair access and, secondly, mediate as and when disputes arose. President Yeltsin's decree, 'Ob informatsionnykh garantiyakh dlya uchastnikov izbiratel'noy kampanii 1993 goda' ('Concerning Information Guarantees for Participants of the 1993 Election Campaign' N 1792), which was signed on 29 October 1993, attempted to meet just these aims.

Yeltsin's decree – with memories of insurrection still fresh – confirmed 'guarantees of free democratic elections'. In a lengthy document accompanying the decree, the terms and conditions for information guarantees, the prices for access to the various broadcast media and the creation of an Arbitration Information Court for the duration of the election campaign ('Treteyskiy informatsionnyy sud', hereinafter AIC) were set out. Points 1–25 of the Statute deal with the questions of access and points 26–41 specified the composition and tasks of the AIC. Since so much of the work of the AIC stems from the detailed definitions and prescriptions of the access arrangements, it is worth considering them first.

A striking leftover from the Soviet period is the word 'agitation'. It does not seem to have occurred to the Statute's authors that the use of such a thoroughly discredited notion as 'agitation' might be inappropriate in a post-Soviet legislative document. For example, 'reports, materials (mass information) which are intended to cause the voters to vote for or against one or another candidate or electoral association' (Point 2, para a) are defined as 'pre-election agitation'. Political advertisements, speeches, press-conferences, interviews, pre-election debates and round-table discussions are all considered (by the Statute) to be forms of pre-election agitation.

Point 5 specifies norms of broadcast time for the various broadcast media: two minutes in any twenty-four period for political advertisements; seventy minutes a week for speeches, press-conferences and interviews and 350 minutes for pre-election debates and round-table discussions. Point 8 of the Statute establishes the right of the Council of Ministers and the Government of the Russian Federation to set a limit for the amounts of time that can be purchased.

The problems of media access and the solutions put forward tend to obscure the criteria and basis on which the time limits have been arrived, why they in preference to any other limits were chosen and openness of the discussion itself. Such criteria are themselves a legitimate matter of public debate, but one in the climate which the government felt able to eschew. Point 26 of the Statute defines the task of the AIC:

> The Arbitration Information Court (henceforth – the Court) is to be formed with the aim of resolving the most complicated disputes brought about by the failure to observe the requirements of the legislation on the part of editorial staffs of the mass media, journalists, producers, candidates, electoral associations and electoral commissions declared for informing the electoral campaign in the mass media.

The AIC consisted of nine members appointed by the President of the Russian Federation.[18] Members of the Court have the right to request information in accordance with the rules laid down in Articles 39 and 40 of the 1992 Mass Media Law and to demand written explanations for violations of the Statute. As a collective legal body the Court could make: recommendations concerning the implementation of the Statute and on the content of the pre-election agitation;

consider complaints made against journalists and others; offer interpretations on the applications of statutes concerning the elections;
and of great importance 'within the limits of its competence and on its
own initiative or on the decision of a court to put before a court
expert conclusions on questions arising from the consideration of
complaints connected with the conduct of pre-election agitation with
the use of the mass media'. (point 30, paragraph 4).

One of the main problems caused by the detailed regulations for
the conduct of pre-election agitation is that it makes the need for
regulatory bodies ever greater. The regulatory body itself – in this
case the AIC – is called on to make judgements and recommendations in a complex labyrinth of rules.[19] The laudable principle that the
law should cater for and protect citizens' rights seems to have come
second best to a bureaucratic zeal for interference.

The Judicial Chamber for Information Disputes

The experimental use of an Arbitration Information Court in the
1993 election campaign paved the way for the setting up of a permanent government body to oversee the ongoing problems and
resolution of disputes associated with access to the mass media
arising from the Mass Media Law and other legislation. A presidential decree dated 31 December 1993 (N 2335) established the
'Sudebnaya palata po informatsionnym sporam' ('The Judicial
Chamber for Information Disputes', henceforth the Judicial
Chamber). One month later a further presidential decree confirmed
and published the Statute governing the scope and role of the Judicial
Chamber.[20]

The Judicial Chamber is an unusual body and one faced with a
daunting and complex array of tasks in the turbulent infosphere of the
Russian Federation. The role of the Judicial Chamber is defined as
follows:

The fundamental task of the Judicial Chamber is to assist the
President of the Russian Federation in the effective realisation of
his constitutional powers as the guarantor of the rights, freedoms
and lawful interests in the sphere of mass information which are
fixed by the Constitution of the Russian Federation (Chapter 1,
point 2).

In addition to any assistance to be rendered to the President there are
other tasks: (i) to assist in the provision of objective and reliable

reports in the mass media; (ii) to provide for the principle of equality of rights in the sphere of mass information; (iii) to protect the moral interests of children and youth in the mass media; (iv) to further the principle of political pluralism in information and political-social television and radio programmes; (v) to resolve disputes concerning the allocation of broadcast time of factions created in the Federal Assembly; (vi) to issue instructions on the correction of mistakes in reports of the mass media which touch on social interests (Point 4).

One of the more important long-term implications of the Judicial Chamber's work is that it must be bound by both Russian Federation and International Legislation as well as 'the requirements of the norms of journalistic ethics' (Chapter II, Point 8). The most important function of the Judicial Chamber is perhaps that it provides additional guarantees against censorship. Of the six functions specified as being within the competence of the Judicial Chamber, at least four have a direct bearing on the provision of information in the public domain.[21]

As a watchdog, the powers of the Judicial Chamber are limited. Within two weeks of having received a Judicial Chamber ruling state organs and official persons are to notify the Judicial Chamber concerning its implementation. The Judicial Chamber has no law enforcement capacity. Yet, the Judicial Chamber does have the power to insist that official persons and editorial staffs provide written explanations for 'unethical actions' (Chapter III, Point 19). However, the Judicial Chamber is able to activate Article 16 of the Mass Media Law, and within the provisions of Article 16, Article 4, as a means of bringing persistent violators to book. Additionally, the Judicial Chamber is acknowledged to be an expert body and is free to make recommendations to the government and to offer expert conclusions on matters connected with the mass media.[22]

The most obvious thing that can be said about this range of tasks is its enormous diversity and equally the huge responsibility shouldered by the members of the Judicial Chamber for its decisions. The least contentious roles would appear to be those concerned with the resolution of disputes over broadcast time and the corrective function exercised over reports.[23] Real problems start to emerge when the tasks move from the mechanistic into the realm of ethics and morals. For example, objective and reliable reporting is a highly desirable attribute of all the mass media but one doubts whether it can be enforced by a government body. The nature of a great deal of what is reported and interpreted as news lends itself to dispute. That a government body will be called on to make decisions, which in the word of the decree, are to be 'final' (Point 10), will strike many Russian journalists as intolerable. Such a style of reporting can only really become part and parcel of the media's ethos when sufficient numbers of journalists and politicians believe in, and support, the intrinsic value of objectivity and reliability. However laudable the aims of the Judicial Chamber are, one detects the legacy of the Soviet past in its approach and the execution of its judgments. As Frances Foster has observed: 'It uses a specific case or controversy as a springboard for a general discussion of legal and moral principles, rights, and responsibilities. It makes a conscious effort to guide and educate as well as decide and discipline.'[24]

Can a body of media specialists however wise and experienced really be expected to change the moral universe in which Russian journalists operate? Indeed, should they be expected to discharge what many would regard as an onerous and impossible task? Others take an altogether more negative view, arguing that the Judicial Chamber is a successor to the revolutionary tribunals of the communist past. Writing in *Rossiyskaya gazeta*, Vladimir Klimov has attacked what he regards as the too cosy relationship that exists between the Judicial Chamber and its government sponsors and what he perceives to be a lust for power on the part of the members of the Judicial Chamber. This drive for greater power and influence, according to Klimov, can be seen in some of the recommendations made in the Judicial Chamber's annual report to the President of the Russian Federation, 'O sostoyanii del s soblyudeniem svobody massovoy informatsii v 1994 godu' ('Concerning the State of Affairs with the Observance of the Freedom of Mass Information in 1994').[25] The report's recommendation that regional branches of the Judicial Chamber be set up to parallel regional branches charged with the protection of the press is seen as a grab for more power and influence.[26] Such criticism appears quite mild with what comes later. The main part of the title of Klimov's article – 'The Final Decision/Solution' – has sinister resonances in the twentieth century, and the subtitle expressly compares the actions of the Judicial Chamber with those of the *troikas* and the legal norms (or lack of) of 1937. For good polemical measure Klimov throws in a reference to the nineteenth century: 'In Tsarist Russia they denounced dissidents to the Tsar. In today's Russia the Judicial Chamber scribbles one to the President'.[27] Klimov also notes some contradictions arising from the Judicial Chamber's Statute and the Constitution of the Russian

Federation. According to Article 46 of the Constitution actions and decisions of state bodies can be the subject of an appeal.[28] Yet Point 10 of the Judicial Chamber's Statute (see above) states that decisions are 'final' (*okonchatel'nyy*), which presumably means that they cannot be the subject of an appeal. Equally, Point 8 of the Judicial Chamber's Statute states that the Judicial Chamber is to consider 'disputes and other matters stemming from the requirements of generally recognised principles and norms of international law and the international treaties of the Russian Federation'. Yet Article 118 of the Constitution (Chapter 7 'Judicial Authority') states: 'The administration of law can be carried out only by a court.' The Judicial Chamber does not have the authority of a court as defined by this article of the Constitution, yet has all the appearance of being one. 'The Judicial Chamber', as Frances Foster observes, 'ranges well beyond any traditional definition of a court.'[29]

Legal reform can only go so far. The biggest and most serious problem is the moral, ethical climate in which the journalists operate, and which they create for themselves, or to which they adapt. In the present circumstances calls for self-regulation will not be heeded because in the very recent aftermath of the Soviet experiment they will be associated with self-censorship. In part these problems are the problems associated with freedom, or to paraphrase Sir Karl Popper, the strain of civilization. Can we say, therefore, that perhaps the excesses of the Russian media are in some ways to be expected? That cases on which the Judicial Chamber has ruled are the natural, perhaps, logical outcome of so many years of totalitarian control? In the present circumstances one of the most effective policies of the Judicial Chamber may turn out to be the manner in which, in the words of Frances Foster, 'it uses each dispute as a point of departure to interpret and explain overall constitutional and legal guarantees of freedom of speech, press, and information and their legal and moral limits'.[30] Responsibility and self-control have to be learned, often painfully, as the rulings and judgements of the Judicial Chamber show. The best that can be hoped for is that slow incremental change – guided only in part by the Judicial Chamber – will affect the conduct of the mass media for the better. In the meantime the Judicial Chamber will find itself waging a war of attrition against the most destructive and anarchistic forces in the mass media, as well as some deeply hostile to the new press freedoms.

Secrecy Legislation and the Mass Media

The 1992 Mass Media Law includes no definition of a secret. Nor, as a consequence, is the range of any legislative application discussed. This legislative lacuna was remedied in 1993 with the promulgation of 'The Law of the Russian Federation Concerning State Secrecy' (21 July 1993, hereinafter the Secrecy Law). The Secrecy Law has a direct bearing on the work of the mass media and other publicity agencies and has been a major source of friction between Russian Federation journalists and the Russian military and other security services during the Chechen war. Article 2 of the Secrecy Law defines a state secret thus:

> A state secret is information protected by the state in the area of defence, foreign policy, the economy, intelligence, counter-intelligence and the activity of operational-criminal investigations, the dissemination of which can damage the security of the Russian Federation.[31]

Article 5 ('Information Which Can be Considered to be a State Secret') specifies in great detail those areas covered by the legislation. The main categories are: (i) military and defence matters including the contents of strategic and operational plans, documents of the military administration and command, the technical operational features of weapons systems, the dispositions of troops and the tactical-technical characteristics of military formations; (ii) information in the sphere of economics, science and technology. This includes any information in the above fields that might have a direct bearing on the state's military capacity and operational mobilization. Any information that reveals the volume and reserves of strategic raw materials (specific materials are undefined). Details of scientific research, trials or experiments that have any bearing on defence or have an economic significance are also affected by this paragraph; (iii) information in the sphere of foreign policy and the economy, specifically information 'about the foreign-policy and foreign-economic (trade, credit and currency) activity of the Russian Federation the prior dissemination of which could damage its interests'; (iv) information in the sphere of intelligence, counter-intelligence and the activity of criminal-investigations. Information in this category is subject to a wholesale ban. Given the still enormous capacity and influence of the former Soviet military-industrial complex and its influence on the economy of the Russian Federation generally (especially, for example, as it affects arms sales), then the reach and range of this particular article is enormous. The article also imposes, whether by design or accident, fairly severe limits on the themes that journalists can discuss in the press. Journalists who specialize, in say military and defence-related matters, and who are well-informed by virtue of access to sources of unclassified information available in the West, run the risk through intelligent deduction and speculation of falling foul of this article. It should be noted that meteorological data are not listed as being a state secret. This is an interesting omission since in certain military conflicts weather data can provide very useful intelligence about the enemy. Likewise, journalists who specialize in economics, particularly those whose tasks are to collect, collate and analyze economic and business data, are vulnerable by virtue of thorough professional analysis to prosecution.

The Secrecy Law classifies information according to three criteria (Article 6 'Principles of the Classification of Information'). They are lawfulness (*zakonnost'*); justification or foundation (*obosnovannost'*); and timeliness (*svoevremennost'*). The lawfulness of classification derives its force from Articles 5 and 7. As noted, the powers provided for by these articles are very wide-ranging and pose problems for assiduous and effective journalists and other private analysts. The power of the criterion of *zakonnost'* is strengthened by the manner determining the foundation of classification. The defining paragraph states:

> Justification for the classification of information consists in deter-
> mining by means of an expert assessment the expediency of the
> classification of specific information of its probable economic and
> other consequences of the act, proceeding from a balance of the
> vitally important interests of the state, society and the citizen.
> (Article 6, paragraph 3).

The manner in which the experts are appointed is of course crucial. Unless their independence is guaranteed and the process whereby they are appointed is subject to public scrutiny and discussion, then there exists a real danger that state agencies will select experts known to be favourable to the state, or in some way vulnerable to pressure. As a result, the credibility of independent experts and public confidence in them, so important in a civil society, would be seriously undermined. Again, similar problems can arise in the interpretation and application of the third criterion: 'The timeliness of the classification of information consists in the determining of restrictions for the dissemination of this information from the moment of its receipt (processing) or well in advance.' (Article 6, paragraph 4). If anything, questions of public scrutiny and the manner of the appointment of any experts become more important, given that this paragraph does not state how and by whom the determination is to be made. Since this process is not explicitly discussed and the procedure for a determination is not stated, then the timing of any determination will itself not be in the public domain. Only if such information is available is it possible for those acting and observing independently of the state to establish whether the requirement to decide any restrictions 'from the moment of its receipt (processing) or well in advance', has been carried out according to the terms laid down by the law. These omissions from the statute will encourage abuses and make effective monitoring very difficult, if not impossible. In the long term this will weaken the law's effectiveness, since the perception that officials are hiding behind either weak legislation, or legislation intended to protect them rather than the public interest, will encourage journalists and others to flout the law.

A typical feature of the Soviet media landscape was the absence of detailed and timely reporting of natural disasters and accidents, often, as in the notorious case of Chernobyl, with horrendous consequences for the public. Article 7 ('Information not Subject to Classification') specifies just such events which in the Soviet period would have been banned. Article 7 also provides for the punishment of state officials who attempt to classify such information. By and large one welcomes the provisions of Article 7 – they are in case long overdue and during the Soviet period were a constant source of embarrassment internationally – yet one detects some obvious potential clashes with the definition and scope of the state secret.[32] Again, a Chernobyl-type accident comes to mind. A very close relationship exists between the civil nuclear industry and the military establishment in Russia (as in the Western nuclear states) and a conflict of interests, between a public need-to-know (nationally and internationally) and the desire of the nuclear industry to maintain silence, if for no other reason than to hide its own incompetence, is not difficult to imagine. Given the potentially catastrophic consequences of nuclear accidents, and moreover of the Soviet record, then there needs to be an explicit presumption in favour of maximum publicity and openness during and after any emergency. Certainly, any Russian journalist who exposed the failings of nuclear plants should not be subject to the penalties of the law.

Questions of accountability and the transparency of decision-making arise from many of the Secrecy Law's provisions. The procedure for placing information within the present law is entirely within the authority of official persons and a special list (*Perechen'*) of persons invested with the authority to make such decisions. A government body then compiles a list of information regarded as state secrets, confirmation of which falls to the President. The government body responsible for this highly sensitive task is the *Mezhvedomstvennaya Komissiya po zashchite gosudarstvennoy tayny* (The Inter-Departmental Commission for the Protection of State Secrets).[33] From the point of view of defenders of the public right-to-know (and, it must be said, insatiably curious individuals) then publication of this list is a useful step since it draws attention to government omissions, highlighting potential areas for investigation. Within this overall main list further lists relating to selected areas will be drawn up. These detailed lists are subject to classification according to the criteria discussed above.

Article 13 ('The Procedure for the Declassification of Information') specifies four conditions in which information can be declassified. They are: (i) when international treaties signed by the Russian Federation require the open exchange of information; (ii) a change in the objective circumstances rendering the need to keep certain information secret superfluous; (iii) decisions made by the classifying authority after a periodical review of the original justification; (iv) the period of classification of a state secret may not exceed 30 years. However in exceptional circumstances, and on the decision of the Inter-Departmental Commission for the Protection of State Secrets, the period may be extended. The period of any extension of the classification is not specified. This fourth factor has an important bearing on historical research and access to various state and party archives. Paragraph 4, Article 14 ('The Procedure for the Declassification of the Holders of Information Comprising a State Secret') confers authority on state archivists to declassify material kept in their archive. The potential obstacle to access arises if the archive is 'liquidated' or if there is no legal successor. In such cases questions of declassification pass automatically to the Inter-Departmental Commission for the Protection of State Secrets, which then has the prerogative of whether to declassify the contents before or at the expiry of the 30-year period, or to extend it indefinitely. It should also not be forgotten here that the Commission has the power to classify as well as to declassify. So a situation in which an archive containing unclassified information and accessible to the public, but which for one reason or another had become a problem to the government, could be closed down ('liquidated') with the express intention of then classifying its hitherto unclassified material (for 30 years or indefinitely).

Law for Reporting the Activities of State Agencies in the State Media 1994

State media, that is those, whose founders are state agencies, occupy a huge position in the Russian mass media market. Their size, budget and reach raise serious questions of monopolistic abuse. For example, accusations from political opponents that such media are little more than propaganda outlets for the government, appear to have some substance when one considers the requirement that the state media broadcast what are called 'informational-enlightenment programmes' (Article 7). In states with a well-established liberal-democratic tradition no discordant note would be heard. In Russia, despite the efforts of the law's drafters, the ghost of the Soviet past continues to cast its shadow. Nevertheless, the government rightly believes that accurate and objective reporting of its activities has an important role to play in fostering trust between rulers and ruled, and thus furthering the growth of a civil society. Subject to close supervision, there is no absolute or objective reason why government programmes should automatically be dismissed as propaganda (as understood in the Soviet context).

The Federal Law 'Concerning the Procedure for the Reporting of the Activity of the Organs of State Power in the State Mass Media' (hereinafter the Reporting Law[34]) is, given the special nature of the state as founder, an important piece of legislation. This is readily appreciated if one bears in mind the reach and application of the Reporting Law. Written publications, newspapers, documents, decisions and informational-educational programmes relating to the Presidential office, the Constitutional Court of the Russian Federation, the government, the Federal Assembly, the Supreme Court and the Supreme Arbitration Court are all covered by the provisions of the Reporting Law. The law also affects the activities of state agencies and bodies in the regions and districts, areas where relations between journalists (state and private) and the officials are frequently acrimonious.

Articles 5 ('Obligatory Television and Radio Programmes') and 6

('Informational Programmes') specify a number of state functions that the relevant state agencies must broadcast. They are: statements made by the President of the Russian Federation, the Council of the Federation, the State Duma and the government, as well as the opening of certain official sessions, and the inauguration of the President.

The general provisions of the Reporting Law have a direct relevance to the Chechen war, since the government's position has been bitterly attacked by parts of the central press. Article 11 ('Other Televisual and Radio Programmes about the Activity of the Federal Organs of State Power') is of particular importance here, since it allows official persons the opportunity to initiate programmes about, among other themes, the state's domestic and foreign policy. The danger of official abuse is clear.

The 1995 Information Law

Even in the volatile and fluid conditions of an emerging market economy such as Russia, access to private and business information will require some form of regulatory control, or ground rules, if violations of personal privacy are to be avoided and protection is to be afforded to legitimate business interests. The rapid growth and proliferation of government and privately-maintained data bases, data banks and other information resources throughout the early 1990s have made the need for some form of primary legislation pressing. Greater contact with foreign firms and companies, and the threat posed by organized crime both in and outside the Russian Federation, have added to the pressure for legislation. 'The Federal Law Concerning Information, Informatization and the Protection of Information' which came into force on 20 February 1995 (hereinafter the Information Law), is a long and detailed document in which the drafters have attempted to strike a balance between the need to protect sensitive information while at the same time providing for the protection of individual rights and access to information.[35]

One of the law's strengths is that it defines many important categories and tasks connected with information. Paragraph 1 of Article 2 of the Information Law defines information as: 'details about persons, subjects, facts, events, phenomena and processes irrespective of the form of their presentation'. Informatization is defined as: 'the organizational societal-economic and scientific-technical process of the creation of the optimal conditions for meeting information requirements and realizing the rights of citizens, organs of state power, the organs of local government, of organizations, social associations on the basis of the formation and use of information resources.' Article 3 ('The Obligations of the State in the Sphere of Forming Information Resources and Informatization') demonstrates a firm grasp of the economic, social, educational and defence implications of information and its application.[36]

An important distinction is made by the Information Law between state-owned and privately-owned information. This is more than another repudiation of the Soviet past: it is an essential distinction for the development of the potentially enormous market of services and products based on information technology.[37] Without such a provision foreign and private investment on the necessary scale is not going to be forthcoming.

Article 11 ('Information about Citizens (Personal Data)') sets important limits with regard to the use and access of personal data, which are regarded as 'confidential information' and thus subject to restrictions on access. Two paragraphs are likely to pose problems for the burgeoning market in information services. Paragraph 1 states that:

> the collection, storage, use and dissemination of information about an individual's private life, and equally of information, violating personal, familial secrets and those of personal correspondence, telephone negotiations, postal, telegraph and other communications of a physical person without his agreement, apart from on the basis of a court decision, are not permitted.

Market research is heavily dependent on personal data, legally collected from sales and credit cards and population census data. Value is added by computer analysis which according to this article would be forbidden. Data have to be collected, collated, analyzed, disseminated and stored if the added value is to be of use to the market researcher and his customers. The details of paragraph 1 also have some bearing on the work of the Federal Security Services, the successor to the KGB. Telephone tapping (though the word 'negotiations' suggests business rather than personal matters) and the interception and reading of correspondence are, unless expressly ordered by a court, forbidden. Paragraph 4 obliges private organizations and private persons involved with the collection and processing of personal data – market researchers for example – to be licensed, which then brings the market researcher's data within reach of various government agencies.

Of great importance for the individual citizen are the Information Law's provisions for access to data and information. Article 14 ('Access of Citizens and Organisations to Information about Them') states that individuals and organizations have a right to 'confidential information' held on them. Access to secret information lies outside the provision of this law. Equally, Article 24 ('The Protection of the Right to Access to Information') must be seen as a key element in the guarantee of access to information and holding officials liable for failing to meet their obligations. Articles 20 ('The Aims of Protection'), 21 ('The Protection of Information') and 23 ('The Protection of Subjects' Rights in the Sphere of Information Processes and Informatization') provide legal guarantees for the protection of personal information and in the event of disputes, for the setting up of Arbitration Courts.

OTHER GOVERNMENT AGENCIES AND THE MEDIA

The Committee of the Russian Federation of the Press (Komitet Rossiyskoy Federatsii po pechati, *Roskompechat'*) inherited the legal and executive status of the Ministry of Press and Information of the Russian Federation and the Federal Information Centre. As the successor body of the Ministry of Press and Information, *Roskompechat'* assumes significant responsibilities and powers under the 1992 Mass Media Law, among which is to ensure that the mass media legislation of the Russian Federation is being observed. As its official title suggests, however, the *Roskompechat'* is concerned with the press. Its primary tasks, as defined by Chapter II 'Basic Tasks of *Roskompechat"* are wide-ranging. Some of the more important are: (i) the protection of free speech and the independence of the press; (ii) formulating and implementing measures aimed at the realizing of state policy in the field of book publication; (iii) ensuring that the Russian Federation's treaty obligations with regard to book publishing and the dissemination of books are implemented; (iv) ensuring that the mass media legislation is being observed; and (v) 'the formation of a culture of mass information, the strengthening of the legal, professional and moral foundations of the activity of the mass media' (paragraph 8). Whether the drafters of this Statute were making a point when they compiled these tasks is open to speculation, but it strikes one as odd that a criterion such as the protection of the freedom of speech should come in sixth place. All other tasks and aims must surely be predicated on this basic and inviolable freedom, without which the rest count for very little.

One of the basic functions of *Roskompechat'* is to prevent abuses of freedom of the press by the press. At the same time the body is charged with the responsibility of preventing censorship being carried out, among others, by state and government agencies. Quite clearly, *Roskompechat'* has an overlapping function with the work of the Judicial Chamber. Given that both bodies owe their existence and status to government decrees, and that *Roskompechat'* is part of the executive machinery, then worries about impartiality are not entirely unjustified.[38] Another potential flaw of *Roskompechat'* is its size and the intrusive reach of its legislative and executive status.[39] Its governing statute and powers suggest that its main aim is to maintain a suspicious eye on the press, negative control rather than encouragement.

PRESIDENTIAL PRESS SERVICE

Although established to meet the specific publicity needs of the President of the Russian Federation, the Presidential Press Service, by virtue of the individual it serves, access to him, and the resources it enjoys, may be regarded as a major player in Russia's media scene. Indeed, the Statute defines the press-service as 'an independent sub-unit of the President's administration' [...] 'with the status of a directorate within the main directorate of the President of the Russian Federation' (Chapter 1, 'General Conditions'). The current Statute was confirmed by President Yeltsin as late as 2 May 1996 replacing the earlier Statute, promulgated on 18 May 1995.

The two main tasks of the Presidential Press Service can be summarized as (i) promotional-informational and (ii) analytical. The first of these aims at securing the maximum dissemination of the President's position on given issues and ensuring that the representatives of the national and international media are, in the words of the Statute, given a 'full and objective' account of the President's activities (Chapter III 'Tasks of the Press-Service, paragraph 3).

In Western states the idea that a leader's press service should seek to influence public opinion would raise few eyebrows. That the Russian Presidential press service should be specifically charged with 'the forming, through the mass media, of public opinion about the activity of the President' (Chapter III, paragraph 4) is cause for concern in view of Russia's recent past.[40] The second main function is to analyze the press to determine the way in which the President's policies and statements are reported, and, one assumes, to prepare material for rebuttal. It is here perhaps that the danger of abuses – real or imagined – on the part of the executive arises. For both the Judicial Chamber and *Roskompechat'* are government agencies with their chairmen appointed by the President. A President disposing of a sizeable press service,[41] part of which was dedicated to analysis and monitoring tasks, and whose office exercised considerable control over the budgets and appointments of two key supervisory agencies, such as the Judicial Chamber and *Roskompechat'*, is in a powerful position to apply pressure directly or indirectly.

Subsequent to the promulgation of the Secrecy Law, a Statute defining the scope and detailed tasks and functions of the Inter-Departmental Commission was confirmed by presidential decree dated 20 January 1996.[42] The Inter-Departmental Commission is designed to function on the legal basis provided for by the Constitution, the Russian Federation Secrecy and Security Laws, and the Federal Information Law. The Statute's powers are thus formidable.[43] At the time of writing the legal position with regard to the proscription of agencies involved in censorship, as stated in Article 3 ('The Inadmissibility of Censorship') of the 1992 Mass Media Law is not clear.

Among the Inter-Departmental Commission's main administrative duties and powers are: the right to form lists of material to be classified; to make decisions pertaining to the declassification of information where this is not provided for by the Secrecy Law; to put forward proposals on the legal regulation of the protection of state secrets; to consider those requests for information on the part of government agencies that may be outside the provisions of the Secrecy Law; to determine the procedure for the declassification in the event that no organization exists to implement that task or in the event that it has been abolished; to assess the likely damage done to the security of the Russian Federation in the event 'of the unsanctioned dissemination of information' (paragraph 4, part 9) and equally the damage done to non-governmental bodies and private citizens of classifying information. Additionally, the Commission is required to examine, at the behest of the government, the joint use of information in international treaties. The likely task here is to assess the impact of such agreements on the degree of openness, which, by virtue of treaty obligations, would be imposed on the Russian Federation. The Commission also assumes responsibility for the 'coordination of the work of organising the certification of the means of protecting information' (paragraph 4, part 14). This task is poorly defined, as a result of which the full remit is not clear, and thus the potential for institutional abuse exists in a very sensitive area. Censorship is, after all, the protection of information, or the strict control over its dissemination.

SUMMARY

1 August 1990 is a watershed in the history of the Russian media and of the Soviet state: censorship was publicly recognized for what it was and outlawed. There is every reason to believe that the banning of censorship, and the expectations of greater accountability engendered by its banning, were crucial factors in mobilizing opposition to the coup a year later. If so, that nurturing of public-spirited intolerance of party lawlessness, and the resistance it encouraged at a crucial juncture, may prove to be one of the greatest and most far-reaching consequences of any piece of Russian legislation this century.

For all its imperfections the 1990 Press Law provided a solid foundation for post-Soviet legislators to build on. One of the first major legislative acts of the new federal government was the enactment of a new mass media law in February 1992, that owes a great deal to the 1990 Press Law, and that, in turn, paved the way for other legislation. Despite these legislative successes a number of general weaknesses can be identified.

One obvious problem, and one, given the birth pains of the new state, that is unavoidable, concerns the sheer volume of new legislation. There is now a bewildering array of decrees, statutes and laws affecting the public, both as consumer (viewer, reader and listener) and as a legal subject with rights and responsibilities, and of course journalists themselves. Much of this growing complexity is the consequence of legal refinement, but it also suggests a certain tightening and control on the part of the state. Too much legislation, particularly that trying to legislate for the unforeseen, can be destructive of the very thing it exists to support. This zeal for legislation can, in part, be attributed to the absence of a strong tradition of independent legal scholarship (and an independent judiciary). In their absence all responsibility for drafting and enacting legislation belonged to the state.

The state's presence is powerfully reflected in bodies such as the Judicial Chamber and the Russian Federation Press Committee, to name two important state agencies, and in the many other agencies, affiliated to, or controlled by, the Presidential office. The Judicial Chamber's terms of reference are unusual, even quixotic, and whether one believes that there is a role for such a body or not (in my opinion there is), a substantial element of Russia's journalists resent its judgements, seeing it not as the watchdog of press freedom, but as the bodyguard of state prerogative and privilege. Another significant cause of legislative overload is that, once again, in the absence of private traditions and organizations, the state is being called on to fill the gap. This does nothing to facilitate a light regulatory touch.

That journalists be free to print what they wish is in itself an insufficient precondition for the growth of a civil society. Freedom imposes responsibility. The habits and culture of responsible journalism will not be acquired where the state, through excessive and intrusive legislation, unintended or not, bears down too heavily on the journalist. Government agencies will be resented and resisted. Confrontation between government and press has its uses, but a condition of near permanent, media war between the state and important sections of the media is no more desirable than the incestuous relationships obtaining in the Soviet period between the party and media. The experience of the Western liberal democracies, reinforced by the contemporary Russian experience, shows that there are definite limits to what can be achieved by media legislation.

3 Russian Journalism's Time of Troubles

Political control over mass media in Russia occurs in the forms of prior restraint, pre- and post-publication pressure and censorship; government and corporate secrecy; state and corporate advertising and lying.   Mikhail Gulyaev

If newspapers are useful in overthrowing tyrants, it is only to establish a tyranny of their own.   James Fenimore Cooper

INTRODUCTION

The battering endured by Russian journalism in the last eight years goes way beyond anything experienced by their Western colleagues. True, the introduction of new technologies in Britain was bitterly resisted, with ugly scenes of public disorder, but such opposition did not take place in conditions of political and constitutional collapse. Russian journalism's problems go much further than the need to grapple with new technologies. Journalists have been caught up in sweeping and often violent change, as well as being beset by powerful corporate and criminal interests, the two frequently being indistinguishable from one another. Four main challenges can be noted. The first has been the need to find a new set of political principles to replace the coerced certainties of Marxist-Leninist ideology; a thoroughly discredited and bankrupt ideology, to be sure, but one whose replacement with the principles of liberal democracy has turned out to be fraught with difficulties, as Soviet journalists themselves have discovered in their metamorphoses to Russian journalists. The notion of a *tabula rasa* is beguiling but illusory. The past does not easily relinquish its grip, as the Bolsheviks discovered after 1917. The second challenge is to be found in the nature of the new vested interests, corporate and criminal that are fighting to control, among other things, the huge advertising revenues of the electronic media. Third, there is the web of legislation that now envelops the journalist. Finally, there has been the Chechen conflict that has pushed the

95

newly-established democratic conventions to the limit, and that, in too many well-recorded incidents have failed badly.

A VIABLE FOURTH ESTATE (?)

The fourth estate evolved from fundamental changes in the relationships between ruler and ruled in the aftermath (in England) of the Civil war and the impact of the scientific revolutions occasioned by Newton's discoveries.[1] At its heart lies what can be best described as an idea and assumption of reasonableness; that is the belief that with sufficient evidence and the application of scientific principles of argument, men of good faith can resolve problems. Unwritten rules determined that both parties to the discussion would be bound by any outcome. This was, therefore, a moral and ethical contract, as much as an intellectual one. The belief that the press could and should influence the rulers of the day was generally accepted, and the association of the freedom of the press and the liberties of the people, was widely recognized, *inter alios*, by David Hume. Naturally, in those societies where no serious challenge had been made to the idea of autocracy (as in Russia for example), this intellectual contract could not exist, and thus the political and economic benefits could not ensue.

Despite the unpromising historical parallels the concept of the fourth estate is an attractive solution to Russia's journalists as they try to define their role in the post-Soviet reconstruction. But the idea of the fourth estate makes certain assumptions about a society, and presupposes that certain conditions are extant. The most obvious omission is a tradition of reasonableness and compromise – in both senses of the word – that are most certainly not the dominant feature of the post-Soviet media.

As profound and unique as the legacies of the Soviet period undoubtedly are for the growth and development of Russian journalism, the history of other states points to some recognizable problems, and possible solutions. The legislative foundation is one example. Press freedoms enjoyed in Western states did not spring up ready made: they were asserted in conflict, wrested from reluctant governments, and moulded by social custom and the challenge of new technologies. Legislation accompanied these changes. The established liberal democracies, whose model of a fourth estate is something to which many Russian journalists aspire, can offer some guidance. In other ways they are ignorant and helpless onlookers, conscious that Russian journalists must grapple with problems that the West (specifically the Anglo-Saxon West) has not had to face.

Two questions are crucially interwoven with the discussion of the fourth estate. To quote Frances Foster: 'Is conventional wisdom correct that press freedom is a precondition for the democratic, law-based state? Or is the democratic, law-based state a precondition for press freedom?'[2]

Both questions tend to ignore the manner in which the law-based state and the growth of press freedom have evolved. Press freedom and the civil society have grown together symbiotically over a long historical period. Once again the English model of parliamentary democracy, as it exists today, is a useful guide. It is the outcome of a civil war and many bitter struggles between ruler and ruled over many centuries. The wholesale import of a Western model to Russia in the hope that Russia would somehow become a liberal-democratic society in a fraction of the time taken by the established liberal democracies was always, of course, somewhat utopian.

Monroe Price has used the expression 'inventing independence',[3] which perhaps hints at the more fundamental question of whether independence can be invented, or imported from outside. The aftermath of colonial withdrawal is instructive. It teaches us that liberal democracy cannot be imposed if the conditions are not right, and very frequently, the conditions will not be right. The overriding assumption here is that liberal democracy is by far the best form of civil governance, an attitude that has triumphally swept the world in the aftermath of communism's collapse. The twentieth century suggests, however, that totalitarianism is more likely to emerge from a weak democracy than from an authoritarian state. Is it, then, too outrageous to suppose that the path to democracy from totalitarianism is better achieved, and more likely to endure, after a period of authoritarian government? If true, then this is not a comforting thought for those who believe in instant liberal democracy. No state, not even a liberal democracy, can function without authority. The role of the fourth estate, as traditionally understood, can be seen to be part of the authority structures of the state, yet at the same time it is separate and distinct from them. Its independence is contingent on the interdependence of these structures, that is the interacting relationships between people, government, legislative and executive bodies. Without these interacting relationships the mediatory, analytical, critical role of the fourth estate, from which the liberal democracy derives so much benefit, cannot exist. Or to put it another way: it is the stability and endurance of the constitution – written or unwritten – that creates and fosters the fourth estate, and is in turn acted upon by the fourth estate.

The demise of official ideology, formally recognized in 1990, with the removal of 'the leading role of the Party' from Article 6 of the USSR constitution, poses, so argues the American legal scholar, Peter Krug, a special problem with regard to the public interest. He notes:

> The effect of these changes was to remove Marxist ideology and the regime's version of communal values from their place as the primary determinants of the 'public value' of mass information and commentary, thereby curtailing any legal support for the press's duty to criticise. Without these ideological moorings, the role of the press was cut adrift from any 'public interest' foundation. As a result, information as a 'public value' in the 1990s no longer functions as legal rationale and therefore has been rendered inapplicable to cases of personality rights protection.[4]

One might argue that removing the ideologically-imposed duty of the press to attack the enemies of the regime marked the beginning of public interest not its end. Also, the notion of 'public interest' and a public right to know certain things were major factors and demands in the dissident movement which started after 1956. They grew up independently of the state. Indeed, we can see Gorbachev's *glasnost'* campaign as an attempt to mobilize public interest against the enemies of reform. *Glasnost'* backfired on Gorbachev because he believed – mistakenly – that the party could remain the sole determinant of what constituted public interest while at the same time permitting and actively encouraging endless exposure of the party's failings and the historical legacy of Stalin. *Glasnost'* inadvertently facilitated the removal of the 'Party's leading role'. While there may not be a current legal foundation for 'public interest', which, had there been, would have been very useful for Gaidar and *Izvestiya* in their legal battle with Zhirinovsky, that public interest does exist. What is now of great urgency is that it be recognized in law.

Some Russian journalists, it must be noted, are markedly sceptical towards any idea of a fourth estate, and its chances of success in contemporary Russia:

> In the real conditions of contemporary Russia with its democracy still unsettled, with its extremely complicated conflict of power between the centre and the regions, the mass media – frequently

against their will – are taking upon themselves the role not only of moral judge or compass of authority (a custom inherited from the Soviet past), but also the role of a direct partner or counterbalance to power, compensating in so doing for the backwardness of both the institutions of power and of civil society. In such a trend journalism is being urged on by both the mentality of the journalists themselves and by the mentality of the mass recipient (the reader, listener and viewer), who, without having learned to perceive the mass media as instruments of power, became accustomed in the first years of *glasnost'*, in the rosy, romantic period of *perestroyka*, to perceive these media as the main instrument in the struggle against authority.[5]

Note the concluding remarks, the observation that the media are perceived as the 'main instrument in the struggle against authority'. Opposition to authority is, in certain areas and at certain times, an important role of a free (and responsible) press. All-out and unceasing attacks in which the government is attacked merely because it is the government is another matter entirely. Some journalists see their task as being confined to that of a 'carrier/bearer of information',[6] in which no interpretation or analysis is offered to the consumer, simply data, news and information. If we bear in mind that one of the main tasks of the fourth estate is to add value to the raw material of news and information, then the role of a mere provider, though undeniably valuable, is in itself insufficient. It represents a move away from a politically influential and accountable institution.

Another group welcomes government participation and is wary of the excesses that, it argues, are a direct result of too much journalistic independence and financial insecurity. Then there are those, who, uncertain of the future, look back at the Soviet period with a sense of nostalgia.[7] Two clear camps emerge concerning the question of ethical codes and the inculcation of any corporate spirit or professional ethos: those who are against, or at the very least sceptical (the majority); and those who favour some form of ethically-binding code (the minority).

Such an ethical code was approved in June 1994 by the Congress of Journalists of Russia. According to the journalist O. G. Lobyzova (*Krasnyy sever*), the code is an important step forward for Russia's journalists, a definite move away from the Soviet past. She notes:

The appearance of the Code bears witness to the fact that after the collapse of Soviet journalism, its fragmentation and going its own way, the mass media have created a fundamental system of references, have laid the foundations of journalist traditions and a code of professional conduct.[8]

There is a great deal of optimism here and a strong hint of question-begging. The physical and ideological structures that supported Soviet journalism have undoubtedly collapsed, or in the case of the latter are so despised and discredited among the majority, that they do not represent a problem (among journalists). But not all the practices and habits of the Soviet period have been jettisoned. As she notes, the practice of journalism 'in conditions of dictatorships differs completely from journalism in conditions of democracy'[9], yet by no stretch of the imagination can transition from totalitarian to democratic state be said to be complete. The reach of the ethical code is, she asserts, quite clear: 'It is not the code of the *Cosa Nostra*, but rather a Hippocratic oath, where the fundamental commandment is thou shalt not harm.'[10]

Of course, much depends on the position we adopt when assessing the meaning of what is understood by 'harm'. Corrupt politicians will undoubtedly resent being exposed and pilloried in the open press, and the notion of harm was repeatedly used by the Russian government and the military to defend the selective news blackout in the Chechen war. In contemporary Russian conditions an honest journalist is going to 'harm' some individual or some organization.

V. L. Bogdanov (Union of Russian Journalists), has also defended the ethical code, in part, one suspects, to recapture what he laments as Russian journalism's loss of *dukhovnost'*, a curious notion for the modern journalist, and one which seems to be conspicuously out of place in the modern world. The real danger from Bogdanov's proposals stems not so much from any utopian recreation of the past, but from the huge number of privileges that he wishes to see made available to members of the Union of Russian journalists. D. A. Yur'ev (*Utro Rossii*) has likened these privileges to a fantastic bribe, a way of controlling journalists by offering them access to creature comforts in return for docility. This danger is far from exaggerated when the journalist's identity card or papers 'can almost acquire the significance of a pass into a painstakingly protected zone of professional rights, advantages and privileges'.[11] Gaining access to this pass, becomes, or can become, in other words, an effective way of deciding who becomes and who does not become a journalist, in the final analysis the right to practise one's profession. For example, the Congress of

Journalists in June 1994 approved a code of ethics 'the acceptance, approval and observation of which is an indispensable condition for his membership of the Union of Journalists of Russia'.[12]

Fear is one of the driving forces among those opposing the creation of ethical codes and the corporate spirit, the fear that *korporativnost'* is merely a more marketable version of *partiynost'*. As E. V. Yakovlev (*Obshchaya gazeta*) notes: '[...] today I see practically no possibility of an association of the press on an independent basis, because, as I said above, the corporate spirit is being formed through *partiynost'*.[13] From this sense of the past stems the author's fears concerning the fourth estate in Russia:

> The press has never been the 'fourth estate' and certainly must not become one. It must not, since, if the legislative power even to the slightest degree is dependent on the electorate, and if the executive power is dependent on the legislative power, which itself assumes power through the choice of the voter, and from the president, who once again is chosen by the citizens, then the 'fourth estate' is absolutely arbitrary.[14]

True, the notion of the fourth estate was utterly alien to the Soviet press (and the reasons for that are obvious). That said, the possibility of the press's assuming a responsible role akin to the fourth estate is not automatically precluded. In a totalitarian state such as Soviet Russia, the idea that the legislative or executive institutions should be influenced by the people had no standing whatsoever. In a society, however, where the public is conceded a voice, and has powers to make their voice heard, then the legislative and executive will be influenced by the public. The problem is not one of totally isolating or insulating the legislative or executive from the public it serves – an impractical and hardly desirable situation – but one of creating suitable institutions both official and unofficial which act as filters of ideas, which retard the real dangers inherent in the arbitrariness of public opinion. Any danger does, however, inhere as much in the immaturity of democratic leadership in Russia, as in the fickle nature of public opinion.

According to D. A. Yur'ev (*Utro Rossii*), the new corporate spirit, or the search for it, is a 'form of the old nomenklatura'.[15] There is, he argues, a definite reason for this situation:

> This specific problem has been created first and foremost by the transitional condition of the Russian state, the absence – even in a

rudimentary form – of the skills of a functioning information establishment under conditions of democracy, and of the bankruptcy of
those structures, which pretend to the role of being the constituent
parts of a Russian civil society.[16]

More worrying still is the frank admission that Russian journalists are
not entirely blameless:

> One can also not accept the rules of the game and the utterances
> which have been imposed by the authorities. Unfortunately,
> Russian journalism has proved itself to be boundlessly receptive
> and has easily sought out cooperation with the 'Ministry of Truth'
> in all its manifestations. This comes as no surprise. The former
> Newspeak violated the creative personality. When the fundamen-
> tal mass of a newspaper text contained neither information nor
> any emotional meaning and when one could serve a prison
> sentence for divulging information, then creative personalities
> which had been suppressed, sought means for giving an outlet to
> their unclaimed emotions. As a result of this various ways of
> imitating meaning were opened up.[17]

If I have understood Yur'ev correctly, he argues that Russian journalists have still to free themselves of the attitudes and ways of the
Soviet period; even that the Russian government and the journalist
are in some way both locked into the old ways and deceits. Debate in
such circumstances is cosmetic, a way of justifying what has already
been decided. These various habits, both of the government advisers,
lobbyists and the journalists themselves are conspiring to bring about
the very reverse of what is expected (by some): 'All these give rise in
one form or another to a completely specific – extra-governmental,
extra-state, supra-ideological structure – a monopolistic monster
exercising total control of all the mass media.'[18]

Yur'ev's views find some support from I. M. Dzyaloshinskiy
(Russian Association of an Independent Press), the author of a
detailed study of Russian journalism.[19] Lenin's view of the journalist
as an organizer, propagandist and agitator is, Dzyaloshinskiy suggests,
still influential since one of the contemporary approaches towards
journalism places it above society, seeing the reader (viewer, listener)
as an object to be controlled and manipulated. The final aim of this,
'control-technocratic approach' is, according to the author, to achieve
a specific response from the audience. One of the defining characteristics of this paradigm, and one manifest in the Russian Federation, is:

[...] the striving towards a harsh programming, a normativisation of all sides of professional activity, including the moral sphere. Once again it should be pointed out that the authoritarian approach is in no way an appendage of the sad past. And today there are quite a lot of journalists, who, while sincerely considering themselves to be democrats, in the professional sphere adhere to an authoritarian-technocratic professional ideology.[20]

The pull of the past and the urgent need for journalists themselves to find their place is a central theme reflected in the many arguments concerning the need for a 'spirit of corporatism' or a 'corporative foundation' for Russian journalism. Opinion among journalists as to what is meant by *korporatsiya* and thus what it entails for their profession is clear cut: some welcome it as a suitable and pragmatic institutional framework to replace the Soviet one; others, for precisely those reasons, are concerned that it is yet another attempt to control journalists. Or, ask others, is *korporativnost'* a natural process allowing journalists to be more concerned with information and its provision, and less concerned with ideological or political commitment, the promotion of a greater detachment integrated within the emerging market relations? Whereas others, it has been noted, associate this word with ... 'the threat of monopolisation of the mass media by a political power or discrete financial-industrial groups'.[21]

The problem of ethical codes in general is exacerbated by two conflicting tendencies. The first is the perception among some journalists that such ethical codes are an intrinsically desirable thing to have; that they enhance the professional status of the journalist, placing him on a par with the legal and medical professions. In such a way, it is argued, the profession of journalism will be taken more seriously both in and outside Russia. (One of the more outspoken advocates of this first tendency is Bogdanov, head of the Union of Journalists). The second problem is the perception that these ethical or professional codes of conduct are a means of controlling journalists by government officials and bureaucrats; that the call for a corporate spirit is in fact the rebirth of the nomenklatura in another form.

Whatever a journalist's attitudes are, it is fair to say that the question of journalistic ethics is a major consideration. Many initiatives have already been implemented, for example the Declaration signed by a number of Moscow-based journalists in February 1994. Similar such ethical codes are under consideration. None of the choices that stand before Russia's journalists with regard to ethics is easy. There is professional disagreement about the nature of ethical codes and whether they are necessary, and, externally, pressure is being applied by various power structures, particularly those who are calling for press freedoms to be protected from what they regard as irresponsible journalists. Media legislation, the setting of norms and rules by officials and the establishing of what constitutes the proper procedures, all affect the arguments.

The question of ethical codes, whether enforced from outside, or adopted from a growing sense of professional independence and need, will of course be largely shaped by the pressures and requirements of those working in the mass media. Journalists' assessment of the state of their own profession is gloomy indeed. It is a profession under siege from government and powerful business interests, threatened by organized crime, financially insecure and overwhelmed by legislation.

The power of the media – in their capacity as an emerging fourth estate, or some other independent, still-to-be-defined identity – inheres in their ability to offer informed and coherent challenges to the government policies of the day. If violent and premature death are indicators of effectiveness, then Russian journalists are, despite the burdens under which they must operate, managing to be effective: they are exposing official corruption and malfeasance and maintaining credible attacks on the government. Perhaps the greatest threat to their freedom, apart from the obvious one of death, is that much information which should be in the public domain, is not. True, all journalists cultivate official and unofficial contacts – and thus run the risk of being used as the witting or unwitting tool of politicians, the degree of such vulnerability being much greater in Russia's present situation. Circumstantial evidence for this assertion can be seen in a significant difference between the media in the West and that in Russia. 'The primary function of mass media in Russia', argues Mikhail Gulyaev, 'is not to attract and hold large audiences for advertisers' [...] 'but to attract and hold large audiences for individual politicians who either already control or strive to control the mass media'.[22] Then there is the degree to which journalists themselves actively compromise their own independence or regard it as a disposable commodity in the struggle for power, or to move closer to the centres of political power.

Manipulation of journalists is also facilitated by their huge stake in the print and broadcast media. The Moscow-based press enjoys greater independence than the regional press which is still answerable to local administrations. These differences can also be observed between central and regional television. The same problems apply to local television stations.

Yet another threat to journalistic independence (or the desire for it) emerges with the increase in corporate investment.[23] There are risks for a heavy-handed investor, not the least of which is the destruction of the media outlet's independence. Private monopolies, unlike state ones, must reckon with the possibility that their monopoly can be attacked by other investors. The biggest threat to independence remains, however, the state. Figures from the Russian Media Institute show that almost 90 per cent of the Russian media are the recipients of state subsidies.[24] It is the process of allocation of state subsidy that makes it possible for the state to effect control. For example, not all media outlets are entitled to receive government subsidies.

The growth of independent media is stifled in other ways. The press is largely dependent on state-owned publishing houses. Newsprint is also a state-controlled material, as is the distribution system. At every stage in the production process from licensing, suitability for state subsidy, access to vital information, through printing to distribution and a range of penalties, the journalist feels the heavy hand of the state. Television is no better off. Both state-controlled and independent television and radio stations have to allocate up to two-thirds of their budget to pay for transmission and energy costs.[25] Transmission facilities are totally controlled by the Russian Ministry of Communications and electricity is controlled by the United Energy Systems company (both state monopolies). Privatization of energy companies would be a useful step, and deregulation of the Russian telecommunications industry also requires urgent consideration.

Another aspect in the struggle for information can be seen in the fact that some media enterprises – such as ITAR-TASS, *Komersant-daily*, *Izvestiya*, Interfax News Agency and *Argumenty i fakty* – seem to enjoy privileged access to government information. The Russian–American Freedom of Information Commission noted in its report, 'Workshops Focus on Freedom of Information', that the above groups opposed the introduction of freedom of information legislation. If a small group enjoys privileged access, in effect a monopoly, then it is not too difficult to see why they would wish to preserve it. Freedom of information legislation would undermine this monopoly. Whether this is a conscious policy of divide-and-rule being used by the Russian state against journalists is not clear but the outcome is not dissimilar to such a policy.

The situation in Russia is one in which journalists owe allegiance to one particular group. Those who would be genuinely independent do not have the capital. The problem is that in post-*glasnost'* Russia the public has come to rely on the media to a much greater extent than in the past. This trust would sometimes seem to be misplaced. Consider, for example, Gulyaev's views with regard to the media professional. He argues that the media professional has three tasks: to serve as an effective channel of information transmission for the authorities; to extend his own power base; and to seek personal or corporate profit. To this Gulyaev adds the problem of bribes and what he calls 'ordered stories'. The advertisement, for all the effectiveness and élan of its creator, is still an advertisement and recognized as such. An advertisement that hides itself behind the mask of pseudo-objectivity or impartiality of reporting or in-depth interview is likely to appear more convincing. Clearly, if a business 'orders' a story, it is also buying the right to set the tone, almost the right to insert its own prepared stories. Such behaviour is unlikely to go undetected and will do nothing to assist the growth of a truly independent media. A serious reputation for objectivity and fairness is not something that can be created overnight. Nor should it be squandered for short-term gain. It is the product of a long-term commitment which becomes recognized both domestically and internationally. Allowing stories to be bought can destroy the paper. To quote R. S. Gol'dberg (*Tyumenskiy kur'er*):

> A newspaper which sells itself, however strange this sounds is completely disadvantageous for the person who buys it. As soon as the reader understands that the paper has been bought, he reacts in a definite way. The publication loses its reader and following after him the advertiser and ceases to bring in any income to him who purchased it precisely with the idea of profit in mind.[26]

A proven reputation for objectivity and impartiality has considerable market value in itself where the provision of news services and data are crucial for business success. The greater the reputation for objectivity and impartiality, the more attractive a media product is to the corporate or other vested interests wishing to exploit the brand name's reputation as a vehicle for its own views, and in turn the greater is the need for media outlets with an established reputation to resist the blandishments of vested interests, private or state. A reputation for objectivity and impartiality is a fragile commodity and easily undermined or destroyed. Once damaged, moreover, it cannot easily be restored. In consequence Gol'dberg is probably correct to conclude: 'As soon as a period of stabilisation ensues then the hour of independent newspapers will have arrived. Not only because this will be required by society but because independence will turn out to be economically advantageous.'[27]

Yet this argument poses an interesting question. In a relationship between consumer and supplier, one that is market-dominated, the brand name of a particular product assumes great importance, particularly for advertisers. Many papers of the Russian Federation retain names that were part and parcel of the Soviet terror and propaganda machine and opposed to any form of free speech. It is one of the many curious features of the end of the Soviet Union that the post-Soviet founders of newspapers such as *Pravda* or *Izvestiya* felt able to retain these communist trademarks (a similar phenomenon can be observed with ITAR-TASS) without any apparent sense of historical embarrassment, or raised eyebrows in the West. One wonders what the reaction worldwide would be, were a German entrepreneur to publish a paper under the title of *Der Völkische Beobachter*, or *Der Stürmer*.

A balanced relationship between state and corporate interests on the one hand, and the media professional on the other, has yet to be consolidated in Russia (it may never emerge). In this respect, the Soviet past still casts a very long shadow. 'All media transitions', as Monroe Price reminds us, 'build not only on the innovators, but on those who were previously in control, the existing pool of journalists and the existing journalistic tradition.'[28] This legacy has, of course, implications for the drive for independence. Western media outlets, which to the beleaguered Russian journalist must seem to be enviably free, do not enjoy total independence, if indeed such a thing is possible. They are, after all, dependent on their readers to buy their services. Then there are certain limitations set by government some of which are intrinsically desirable, and in certain circumstances government intervention can make a crucial difference. Consider an example from Britain. Until the mid-1980s the single biggest threat to the press did not come from government. It came from within the industry itself, from the disruptive and intimidatory behaviour of the big print unions. Employment legislation, introduced in 1980, 1982 and 1984, helped the newspaper proprietors to break free from the trade-union stranglehold. If we doubt the total independence of the media – in the widest sense of the word – then we can also question that of the universities which are directly reliant on government funding. If 'absolute' independence is a myth, then this suggests that there is no such thing as an 'absolute' monopoly, whether of an ideological kind such as was the norm in the Soviet Union, or, so some would claim, in the media empires emerging in the West (cf. Ted Turner and Rupert Murdoch).

Analyzing the Marxist-Leninist criteria of *partiynost'* and so on, Price has noted:

> The idealized early understanding of these principles must be discerned to interpret developments in the current transition. They establish the vocabulary of the past, a use of words that must be kept in mind when dealing with the present. Without such a grounding, the contemporary usage of words like 'independence' or 'objectivity' can be a snare.[29]

It should be borne in mind that 'independence' was a dirty word in the collectivist Soviet Union and that the notion of objectivity was dismissed as a bourgeois fallacy. The drive for independence and the recognition that objectivity is essential for the journalist is rich in irony for the symmetrical interpretation of Soviet and Western media practices, that until very recently, was common. Irrespective of the merits of this argument, one can agree with Price's assertion that: 'These different perceptions of objectivity are an important factor in understanding the transition.'[30] As a result:

> For those schooled in the Soviet period, for those with a memory, the new objectivity could mean simply that a new theory – the theory of capitalism – would be the scientific worldview, and objectivity would consist of demonstrating its wisdom. Objectivity might become that picture of the world that corroborates the then-government's scientific approach to a particular problem.[31]

This assessment ignores, I suggest, the ability of Russian journalists to understand the nature of objectivity. The supposition that this could happen arises from the seductive view that there is no such thing as objectivity. With regard to scientific objectivity, capitalism has demonstrated certain advantages when compared to Marxism-Leninism. But this misses the point: there is after all no such thing as capitalist or Marxist-Leninist objectivity. Advocates for capitalism make no claim that it has a monopoly of objectivity. What they are entitled to claim, however, is that the political ethos that supports capitalism has also proved to be extremely conducive to great scientific and technological achievement. So closely related are they indeed that one might be tempted to conclude that one is not possible without the other.

One must also ask whether any serious Russian journalist today is going to be influenced by Marxist-Leninist criteria. Those trained under the Soviet system are finding it difficult to jettison the hold, but for the newer, younger journalists, these criteria are to be treated with contempt. For these reasons the following assessment is somewhat doubtful: 'A free-market solution to demand and supply of information is inconsistent with principles of *narodnost* if it means that large sections of the community would be without access to information.'[32]

There exists some confusion here about the nature of *narodnost* and what it means, if it means anything at all, in the post-Soviet period. The accessibility which is implicit in *narodnost*, was, as is noted, intended for reasons of ideology. Saturating the masses via the media with Marxist-Leninist ideology and outlawing anything different was deemed the best way to indoctrinate and school the masses for their place in the new world. Financial considerations, that is the need for these media products to be self-supporting, were not important when private business was also outlawed. State subsidy was all that was necessary. *Narodnost* implies accessibility but has nothing to do with the cost of accessibility. The sole concern for the party was that the media disseminated the current ideologically-correct views.

Now if we transfer the criterion of *narodnost* to the post-Soviet media, then things look slightly different. We find a market-place for ideas and views. In a market-place of competing ideas, there can be no place for a party-subsidized, ideologically-driven criterion such as *narodnost*. The fact that the business of printing and publishing has become more expensive is a consequence of the breaking of the state monopoly, and the not unimportant realization that Marxist-Leninist economics failed to deliver. It is by no means certain, as Price claims that: 'Continuing subsidies for newspapers, [...], bespeaks a societal determination that information ought to be linked to the largest possible audience.'[33] Subsidies are highly addictive and once a paper becomes dependent on one then the removal is likely to be very painful. People no more have a right to receive subsidized information and media services than they have a right to receive subsidized food or clothing. If every would-be publisher of a newspaper claimed and received the right to have access to printing facilities at reduced prices, then the function of the market-place would be subverted, for the sanction of failure would no longer exist. The lingering influence of *narodnost* – if it is that at all – owes more to a failure to understand the function of a free-market, on both sides of the former Iron Curtain, rather than to any legacy of access based on the old ideologically-prescriptive model.

Price's observations on the difficulties of the old journalists trying to adapt to the new ways are important in the extent to which they reveal the intellectual confusion among the journalists. We note the persistent belief that the only difference for a Soviet journalist and the post-Soviet journalist lies in the fact that the former worked under ideological pressures, the latter under commercial ones; that both are as bad as one another, an insidious view, particularly when it leads to the belief that: 'Censorship could be said merely to be the decision of the founder – a state-related entity – as to what should be in a journal, a decision taken by publishers world-wide.'[34]

Indeed, censorship could be said to be this, but it would be wrong as these Soviet journalists would have known. If a journalist lost his post at *Pravda* because of a lack of ideological reliability or vigilance, then it was not a simple matter of getting another post at, say, *Izvestiya*. Since the party owns everything and determines the ideological line to be taken on *all* papers – in this context all news is undoubtedly ideological – then the hapless journalist who falls foul of his editor has nowhere to go. Thus it is disingenuous to compare the lot of the Soviet journalist with that of his Western counterpart in such a way. We can also see that the state monopoly is many times worse than the private variety. If the Western journalist falls foul of his editor, he can find work elsewhere, since there is a market for different views and different writing.

CRIME AND THE CHECHEN WAR

The severe pressures on Russian journalists are compounded by organized crime with the threat and use of violence against selected journalists undermining progress towards a more open society.

The Glasnost Defence Foundation (GDF) maintains records concerning the persecution of journalists both in the major urban centres of Russia and the former Soviet republics. The GDF also collected and disseminated information on the plight of journalists in the Chechen war zone.[35] Persecution covers a wide range of violations, from bureaucratic obstructionism, intimidation, and beatings by unidentified assailants, to murder. For example, in 1994 18 journalists were killed on the former territories of the Soviet Union.

There were seven murders in the Russian Federation, two in Belarus, one in Armenia, five in Tadzhikistan and two in Georgia. One American journalist was killed in an air attack launched by the Russian air force in Grozny.[36] Even without the murders the overall picture is one of an undeclared war against journalists in all the former republics, including Russia. Government officials not only appear utterly inert in the face of this onslaught, they are in many cases almost certainly implicated.

The murders of Dmitriy Kholodov and Vladislav Listiev on 17 October 1994 and 1 March 1995 respectively are two of the better known cases. Kholodov was the military correspondent of *Moskovskiy komsomolets* who was investigating corruption in the Russian army, specifically that senior officers in Russia's Army Group West were involved in illegal arms sales. In one article he came close to accusing the former Army Group West commander, Colonel-General Burlakov, of being responsible. Kholodov was also investigating claims that Russian special forces were training – one assumes for large sums of money – members of Russia's mafia gangs. Kholodov died when he opened an attaché case that, he believed, contained documentary evidence, confirming these suspicions. Russian military intelligence (GRU), the mafia and the Federal Counter-Intelligence, (formerly the KGB), have all been blamed. In the atmosphere of rumour, counter-rumour and disinformation it is impossible to say who did kill Kholodov, and one doubts whether the murderers will ever be brought to justice.

Aside from the obvious reason of silencing an investigative journalist who was possibly starting to discover too much, Kholodov's murder was yet another warning to journalists of what was in store if they probed too far or were not amenable to persuasion, part of an on-going campaign to terrorize journalists whose reports, despite apparent public displays of apathy on the part of officials, were hitting home. Kholodov's murder, wrote Grigoriy Baklanov, the well-known prose writer and former editor of *Znamya*, was a shot at 'democratic Russia',[37] a view supported by most journalists. *Novoe Vremya*'s Kronid Lyubarskiy went even further, arguing that terror was being used as censorship, and that the more brazenly the murder was carried out, the greater the intimidation effect. Paraphrasing Osip Mandelshtam's famous remark, Lyubarskiy concluded that: 'in Russia [...] it is not only poets that are respected, but also journalists'.[38] *Nezavisimaya gazeta*'s Andrey Bayduzhiy saw Kholodov's murder as a symptom of Russian society generally: 'the death of

Dmitriy Kholodov shows not only the depth of the chasm of criminal terror into which Russia is sliding and continues to slide'.[39]

Listiev, a 38 year-old television journalist, was shot dead outside his Moscow home. Speculation as to the reason for Listiev's murder centred on his executive directorship of a newly-created share company at Ostankino. Prior to its creation, revenue from advertising amounted to 5 billion rubles. Thereafter, it climbed dramatically to 35 billion rubles. It has been suggested that the decision to stop advertising on the first channel was the most likely reason for the murder. Listiev's murder was the fourth such case involving the head of an advertising consortium in the year leading up to his death.[40] Immediately after the murder *Izvestiya* put forward three explanations.[41] The first supported the view that advertising revenue had been the main cause. It was the intention of Ostankino to restrict advertising on the first channel to a number of companies under its direct control. Up until then advertising time had been controlled by others who in the new arrangement would be the losers. The second version of the murder posited that certain persons wanted to exploit the murder of the undeniably popular Listiev and the outrage that would ensue for political reasons: to call for the removal of the President and or certain ministers. The third version suggests that the murder was a pretext for a thorough examination of all Ostankino's affairs, especially financial, with the aim of bringing it under complete official control. This in turn would be used to justify the introduction of tough new legislation to help with the struggle against crime, which would include the introduction of censorship and the cancellation of elections.[42]

The Chechen war has proved to be another severe challenge to Russian journalists. They have had to contend with the murder and beatings of their professional colleagues, overlapping and conflicting emergency legislation in the war zone itself, and all kinds of minor obstructions ranging from denial of visas, limited accommodation and poor communication links to their papers in Moscow. The war attracted large numbers of foreign journalists and they, and the various international organizations that they represent, reported enormous difficulties in accreditation and access.

Journalists who work in war zones must, naturally, accept the risk of being caught in cross-fire, shelling and air attacks. The risks go with the job. But there are other dangers in the Chechen war one of which was deliberate attacks on journalists by the combatants themselves. 1995 saw a sharp escalation in the number of journalists being killed simply because they were journalists. Moreover, such apparently indiscriminate killing is far easier to conceal in a war zone when it is either difficult or impossible to collect forensic evidence and the perpetrators have the anonymous protection of an unofficial or official uniform.

Two murders in 1996 were particularly shocking even by the standards of the Chechen war.[43] Both victims were women and both had been subject to 'execution-style murders', in the words of the Committee for the Protection of Journalists (CPJ).[44]

Nadezhda Chaikova, the correspondent of *Obshchaya gazeta*, was murdered some time in March 1996. A follow-up investigation carried out by colleagues from her paper discovered that her body had been dumped in the village of Gekhi, some 20 kilometres from Grozny. Photographs taken by the local prosecutor's office after the body had been discovered show that Chaikova had been beaten, blindfolded and shot in the back of the neck. On 9 May 1996 Nina Yefimova, a Russian reporter, resident in Chechnya was found dead. She too had been shot in the back of the neck. Her 73-year-old mother had also been murdered. ITAR-TASS reported that Yefimova and her mother had been abducted from their apartment on the night of 8 May 1996. It has been suggested that Yefimova was murdered because of the stories she had written on crime in Chechnya.

Despite overwhelming military advantages in terms of equipment and sheer fire power, the war went very badly for the Russian army. Whatever the strictly military reasons for its generally poor performance, the Russian army failed to come to terms with its having to conduct military operations in the presence, albeit controlled, of a large contingent from the domestic and international print and broadcast media. This is the first time that the Russian army in either its Soviet or Russian-federal variant has had to face hostile criticism from journalists in and out of a war zone, and the Russian army has, to put it mildly, found it extremely difficult to adapt to their presence. During the early 1980s Soviet difficulties in Afghanistan seemed to provide a ready-made parallel with America's involvement in Vietnam. Yet the openly sceptical and hostile tone adopted by the Russian media suggests that the Chechen war is a closer analogue.

The disagreement over whether Russia was prepared for this conflict is revealing, in part, for the light it casts on why this war has proved to be so divisive. For example, Peter Khlebnikov, the co-director of The Russian–American Information Press-Centre has argued that Russia – the government, the military and the press – were not prepared for the war in Chechnya. Aleksandr Il'in, the editor-in-chief of *Pravda* rejected this, citing the experience of Soviet papers in covering wars such as the Great Fatherland War (1941–45), the Korean war and Mao's campaigns in China.[45] The point that has to be made here is that coverage of the wars mentioned took place in an atmosphere of total ideological conviction and in conditions of total censorship. All three wars took place when Stalin was in charge so there was absolutely no chance of any deviation from the party line whatsoever (it is worth noting that he does not cite the war in Afghanistan as an example, since there were voices raised against it and criticism inside the Soviet Union was widespread. Some of the most influential articles were written by Mikhail Kozhukov, correspondent of *Komsomol'skaya pravda*). The conditions and opportunities for reporters in the Chechen war bear no resemblance to the coverage of these earlier conflicts. The Great Fatherland War was a life-and-death struggle against the Nazis. This was certainly not the case in Chechnya. Again, the Korean war posed no threat to the Soviet Union, nor did the war between the nationalists and communists in China.

The army's opposition to journalists and the reporting of the war in the press of the Russian Federation followed a number of distinctive lines. Senior Russian officials publicly accused Russian journalists of either accepting bribes from emissaries of the separatist leader, Dzhokhar Dudaev, or openly supporting his forces. For example, on 21 December 1994 Vyacheslav Volkov, Deputy Leader of the Presidential Administration let it be known that: 'Several special centres for supplying Russian journalists with disinformation about events in Chechnya have been set up in Moscow.'[46] Nikolay Egorov (10 January 1995) then stated that 'these days the mass media are in the hands of those whose interests lie in Groznyy [...] The mass media have declared war on the state, the government and the President.'[47] A month later, and worryingly for the credibility of the Russian press, Sergey Gryzunov, the head of *Roskompechat'*, admitted that he did 'not exclude the possibility of attempts to bribe'.[48] In fact, the barrage of such accusations was set in motion by none other than President Yeltsin, who on 27 December 1994 put forward the view that: 'Without Chechen money a number of mass media outlets in Russia would not function.'[49]

One of the more interesting responses to the coverage of the war in the Russian press was made in an anonymous letter, published in

Rossiyskaya gazeta (31 January 1995), purporting to have been written by Russian troops serving in Chechnya. The author(s) noted:

> A cruel uncompromising war is being fought on the territory of the Chechen republic the consequences of which will determine the future not only of the Northern-Caucasus region but of Russia as a whole. [...] We wish to draw your attention to the fact that the Russian Army is, in essence, operating in conditions of encirclement. From the front, it is opposed by bands of professional murderers and mercenaries which have been gathered from all over the world, and from the rear blows are struck by those who are enemies of strengthening Russian statehood, who are ensconced in a number of mass media outlets, and those who are part of separate pseudo-patriotic movements and social organisations of the country. Systematically insulting the Russian Army, its soldiers and officers, these people risk nothing at all. They do not spill their blood, nor are they prosecuted according to the law for their criminally disdainful attitude towards servicemen and towards the army as a whole. [...], many Russian mass media are disinforming the population, deliberately exacerbating the political situation in the country, and undermining Russia's authority in the international arena.
>
> It is not difficult to note that the constant attacks on the Minister of Defence and the leadership of the Armed Forces are part of a well-planned and organized information-psychological war against Russia.
>
> The open subversive propaganda has an influence on the morale of the rank and file and assists criminal activities not only in Chechnya but also in many regions of Russia.
>
> [...] We are ready to endure and overcome anything provided that people stop spitting in our face and shooting us in the back.[50]

Whether this letter was indeed penned by soldiers serving in Chechnya is an open question. The outrage and anger felt towards journalists are, however, all too genuine. An alarming feature of this response is the tenacious belief that criticism of the Russian army and other national institutions is propaganda and, therefore, to be dismissed and its authors vilified. The claim that such attacks are 'criminally disdainful' is surely an unwelcome leftover from the communist period when criticism of the army – apart from the *glasnost'* period – was not permitted. We are left with the impression that any criticism is regarded as simply criminal and therefore to be punished. The letter also hints at dark conspiracies organized by foreigners. What is not clear is why the Russian army has proved conspicuously unable to deal with these 'professional murderers and mercenaries'. Journalists, Russian and foreign, are, one suspects, being used as scapegoats for a number of operational and planning failures on the part of the Russian military leadership.

This overwhelmingly negative and hostile appraisal of Russia's media received a further boost in a report written by a Commission of the State Duma charged with examining the causes of the Chechen conflict. Stanislav Govorukhin, repeated the substance of army assertions and then singled out various journalists and their papers:

> The Commission cannot but help analysing as well the position of the mass media in the Chechen conflict. Russia's Armed Forces, the interior troops and special sub-units carrying out their orders, are subject to condemnation.
>
> The overwhelming majority of the mass media, including the electronic media, have initiated a wide-ranging, and in terms of world practice, unprecedented, campaign of persecution of their own Armed Forces, charged with the task of restoring constitutional order in the Chechen Republic. In essence this is a situation, seldom seen in world history, when the majority of the press are on the opposing side.
>
> [...] And, in the opinion of the Commission, it is precisely those representatives of the fourth estate who must bare some responsibility for the troubles and suffering connected with Chechnya. Events in the villages of Assinovskaya and Samashki are examples illustrating such active disinformation. It is quite clear that deliberately false descriptions of 'bestial acts' of Russian soldiers not only stiffened the resistance, but also made it possible for Western countries yet again to apply financial pressure to Russia.
>
> The extent of this total counter-propaganda initiated by the mass media confirms the planned nature of this unprecedented information action.
>
> A definite aura of moral superiority, purity and nobility has been created around the criminal regime of Dudaev. No little effort has been spared on the creation of this aura by Andrey Fadin of *Obshchaya gazeta*, Kronid Lyubarskiy of *Novoe vremya*, Valeriy Simonov, Igor' Rotar', Andrey Pavlov and Evtushenko of *Komsomol'skaya pravda*, Yulia Khaytina of *Moskovskiy komsomolets*, Elena Afanas'eva of *Novaya ezhednev-*

naya gazeta, Elena Grigor'eva of *Moskovskie novosti*, Dmitriy Muratov of *Novaya ezhednevnaya gazeta* and many others. The newspaper *Argumenty i fakty* printed a manual for soldiers on desertion from the army.[51]

Unfortunately for Russian journalists, accusations of bribe-taking or being bought by Dudaev are all too plausible. Many Russian newspapers face severe financial difficulties and are known to be hostile to the government's position in the Chechen war. Even in the absence of proof such accusations are difficult to disprove. Moreover, the idea of buying or exploiting sympathetic journalists either as individuals or in front organizations to further a specific cause was standard Soviet practice.[52] There is no automatic reason why such techniques should be discontinued merely because the Soviet Union no longer exists.

Alongside the military conflict the Russian government has also found itself embroiled in a protracted legal battle with journalists. The most obvious question is one of legal control over the activity of journalists in armed conflicts. There are two aspects to this particular question. First, there are a number of laws that overlap, and in some cases contradict one another, and second there is an absence of any detailed provision in law for conflicts such as that in Chechnya. This means that legislation existing at the time Russian troops were deployed has been adapted to the situation and that new legal measures have been introduced *ad hoc* as the conflict progressed. Under the pressure of the war the process of legal consultation has been hurried, as one might expect, and this has led to still greater confusion and inconsistencies. To complicate things still further, neither martial law nor a state of emergency was declared in Chechnya.

A consequence of this has been that journalists and government have relied heavily on the provisions of the Russian Constitution and the 1992 Mass Media Law. With, however, the promulgation of the resolution 'Ob obespechenii gosudarstvennoy bezopasnosti i territorial'noy tselostnosti Rossiyskoy Federatsii, zakonnosti, prav i svobod grazhdan, razoruzheniya nezakonnykh vooruzhennykh formirovaniy na territorii Chechenskoy respubliki i prilegayushchikh k ney regionakh Severnogo Kavkaza' ('Concerning the Provision of State Security and the Territorial Integrity of the Russian Federation, Legality, Rights and Freedoms of Citizens, the Disarming of Unlawful Armed Formations on the Territory of the Chechen Republic and

Contiguous Regions of the Northern Caucasus'), the government created a legal situation which had more in common with the undeclared state of emergency in which human rights and freedoms could be subject to some limitation.

A consequence of this resolution was that certain powers, normally only available in a state of emergency, were now at the disposal of the security forces within the operational area. It should be noted that in a decision of 31 July 1995 the Constitutional Court of the Russian Federation ruled that a number of statutes in this resolution were unconstitutional.[53]

Another legal consideration is how the provisions and norms of the 1992 Mass Media Law fit in with, or are at odds with, legislation regulating the behaviour of the military and MVD troops, most particularly 'Zakon o vnutrennikh voysk' ('The Law Concerning the Interior Troops'). The 1992 Mass Media Law works in conjunction with constitutional guarantees. Weighing up the 1992 Mass Media Law and the Law Concerning the Interior Troops, Aleksey Voinov concludes:

> [...] irrespective of the fact that the [1992] Mass Media Law and the Law Concerning the Interior Troops of the Ministry of Internal Affairs formally enjoy equal judicial force, the statutes of the Law Concerning the Interior Troops (in particular Article 29 of the said Law) and the norms of other special legislation and official normative acts must be interpreted in connection with the statutes of the Russian Constitution, international acts concerning human rights of which Russia is a signatory, and the statutes of the Mass Media Law.[54]

Then there is the precise legal status of the Provisional Information Centre and the requirement to receive accreditation from it. The author argues that the accreditation requirements introduced with the creation of the Provisional Information Centre are at odds with the accreditation laid down in Article 48 of the 1992 Mass Media Law since they introduce a new form of accreditation, that of accreditation in a zone of armed conflict.

The accreditation requirements of the Provisional Information Centre also contradict Articles 29 (parts 4 and 5), 55 (part 3) of the Constitution of the Russian Federation, Article 19 (parts 2 and 3) of the International Covenant on Civil and Political Rights (1966), as well as Articles 1 and 47 of the 1992 Mass Media Law: '[...] since it introduces preliminary conditions not provided for by federal law the

execution of which is necessary for the implementation of the constitutional right to information'.[55]

The exercise of journalists' rights in a conflict zone, particularly
those guarantees covering photography and recordings, is not quite as
clear-cut as the author suggests:

> Interfering with the taking of photos of servicemen, military instal-
> lations and the movement of troops and equipment cannot be
> justified by the necessity to observe state or military secrets, since
> in themselves servicemen, military installations and the movement
> of troops do not constitute state or military secrets a category
> which is only applicable to specific persons, installations or move-
> ments, and in the event of a decision being taken to classify these
> data as a state secret, then it must be taken by a competent official
> person. Moreover, the 'Law on State Secrecy' does not include
> information about the movements of troops in the list of informa-
> tion which is to be considered a state secret.[56]

The assertion of the journalist's right to take whatever photos he
pleases is naive and dangerous. It is completely unrealistic to expect
the army to allow journalists to take photos, unsupervised in a
conflict situation since such information can have deadly consequences.[57] Soldiers, whose lives may depend on secrecy being
maintained, are not, no matter what the law says about journalists'
rights, going to assist journalists. On the contrary, they will see journalists as another enemy and act accordingly. This state of mind can
be seen in all major conflicts where the press and the media have
asserted a right to be in the conflict zone: Vietnam; Northern Ireland;
the Falklands War; the Gulf War; and Chechnya. The author's assertion that such photography is within the reach of the law is far from
clear. The Secrecy Law confers a large amount of operational discretion on the authorities, which in some ways it must do.

In a similar vein, the author asserts that journalists who are not
taking part in any military operations must not be fired on either by
the army or by 'armed formations' (the Chechen forces). These
'armed formations' are by their very nature outside the law and thus
are not going to be bound by it, even more so, when, as far as they are
concerned, the law cited is a law of the Russian Federation, the very
state against which they are waging armed conflict.[58]

The problems outlined so far are not just confined to the Russian
press trying to operate in Chechnya. There is plenty of evidence to
show that parts of the Chechen press faced similar problems. Well

before the deployment of Russian troops and the outbreak of hostilities journalists whose stance towards Dudaev could be described as sceptical found themselves on the defensive. There was, for example, a great deal of hate propaganda aimed at Russia and at those in Chechnya who preached moderation.

Appearances of moderation on the part of Dudaev prior to 1994 were deceptive. The comments of Ruslan Karaev, editor-in-chief of *Vozrozhdenie*, are worth noting:

> We concerned ourselves with an analysis of what was going on, analysis of the regime, of the political and economic condition of society. For a long time this paper was cited as confirmation of the fact that there was democracy in the republic. When people came to the republic from abroad Dudaev would show them our paper and say: look, you see our press is not suppressed. But this was a short interval between 91 and 93, then they started to interfere with such papers.[59]

Nor did the Chechen Constitution offer much help to beleaguered journalists. The paper *Spravedlivost'* was closed down and the staff fled to Moscow. The Chechen-language paper *Daymokhk* was more or less left to print critical remarks in Chechen, but when material in Russian was printed the paper's staff received threatening phone calls.

In some ways the situation mirrors that which obtained in the former Yugoslavia prior to its disintegration: media wars both in and among the republics came before the shooting war and made a shooting war much more likely.[60] Moreover, as in the case of Chechnya, when the shooting war replaced the media wars, acts of brutality by both sides became commonplace, and even acceptable.

CONCLUSION

Grave financial difficulties, the search for new political allegiances, a campaign of intimidation and murder waged by organized crime (often it seems with the tacit approval of the government), a complex legal situation and, of course, the enormous challenges and dangers of covering the Chechen war, suggest that Russian journalism can only ever be at best an anaemic version of what has long been taken for granted in the West.

As bleak as things are, there has been progress and there are successes. To date, Russian journalism's finest hour has been the coverage of the Chechen war. The government, despite its massive resources, has lost the moral and intellectual arguments, having violated its legal obligations. Frequently and uncomfortably for the government this has been done in the full glare of publicity. Non-governmental organizations such as the Glasnost Defence Foundation have played a crucial role in keeping these violations in the public eye both at home and abroad. This has undoubtedly kept the government on the defensive. Some remarks by Sergey Yushenkov, chairman of the Defence Committee of the Russian State Duma, should be noted: 'Everything which is happening in Russia is, in my opinion, a terrible test, a check of the democratic press. The press has passed this trial. The authorities, unfortunately have not ...'[61]

350 years on from John Milton's eloquent and powerful defence of press freedom in *Areopagitica* (1644) the relationship between governments and the press, and what in the twentieth century has become the mass media, is as strained as ever. Technology, especially the new electronic media, is creating new tensions in the final years of the twentieth century, but there is another, perhaps more fundamental reason identified by Erskine, in his defence of Thomas Paine in 1792, which is as cogent as ever, and one, it seems to me, which helps to explain the Russian situation, and from which Russian journalists can draw some succour: 'Other liberties are held *under* governments, but the liberty of opinion keeps *governments themselves* in due subjection to their duties. This has produced the martyrdom of truth in every age, and the world has been only purged from ignorance with the innocent blood of those who have enlightened it.[62]

Part III Shaping the New Infosphere

4 A Survey of Russia's Culture and Media Wars

What Huxley teaches is that in the age of advanced technology, spiritual devastation is more likely to come from an enemy with a smiling face than from one whose countenance exudes suspicion and hate.

Neil Postman

The writer's special role in Russian society is well documented and needs no further explanation. As a vehicle of political and intellectual protest, literature has shaped Russian society, or been intimately involved with its fate, in a way that is quite unusual, even unique, when compared to Western societies. Russian writers took it upon themselves to champion various social and intellectual causes, which after 1917, and especially 1934, though receiving the ideological sanction of the party, had the range of themes severely circumscribed.

This distinctive calling survived more or less unchanged right up to the fall of communism. In the final phase of communism's demise, however, this traditional role was itself vulnerable to the forces and shifts attacking communism. When communism fell, Russian literature was orphaned, the long-standing relationship between radical revolutionary and literature, initiated when the typographical age reached Russia, and which was co-opted by Lenin, came to an end.

The *glasnost'* period was the breaking of the backlog of banned and censored works, something that had to happen before any new directions could be pursued. Packed with revelations, the *glasnost'* journals offered the reader the chance to catch up with the past, to discover new authors and ones hitherto banned, to read informed and open criticism of the Soviet state's icons. The release of documentary evidence and the opening up of historical and literary archives were unprecedented in a society accustomed to paranoid secrecy. But this media frenzy should not distract us from more fundamental shifts. *Glasnost'* was Russian literature's swan song, at least as it had existed and been read and venerated since the nineteenth century. The abolition of censorship, the liberalization of the mass media in general and the proliferation of information technology have all conspired to bring about these changes and then to consolidate them.

For most of the communist period the writer had to cope with the all-powerful, explanatory mechanism of Marxist-Leninist ideology and the violence of the state. In the post-Soviet period the relationship between great art and censorship, and even, outrageous as it may sound, the degree to which censorship may be considered to be a positive factor for literary activity, raises awkward questions for the radical left and libertarians.

The abolition of censorship has greatly increased the prestige and influence of the electronic media, creating a huge demand for the sort of programming that, during the communist period would have been considered at best 'bourgeois', or at worst 'ideological diversion'. The cult of the television personality, videos, soap operas such as *The Rich Also Cry* (*Bogatye tozhe plachut*), represent a further weakening of the traditional relationship between reader and writer. Of importance here, of course, is the reaction of writers themselves to these profound cultural shifts. How do they react to a culture which, more and more prefers to watch videos of the *Terminator* ilk to reading the Russian classics.

During the *glasnost'* period when print and broadcast journalists were discovering the intoxicating experience of making life unpleasant for party politicians, trial-by-media became associated with Western ideas, another example of Western excess, it was claimed. The same resentment is still to be found among Russian Federation politicians but they and their aides are learning to deal with a critical and pervasive media. Writers, particularly those who prospered under the Soviet system, and other bearers of Russian culture, still regard the media, television especially, with a mixture of contempt and visceral loathing. Their hostility cannot, however, be dismissed out of hand. Prominent and respected writers such as Rasputin, Mozhaev, Belov and Bondarev have accused both late-Soviet and contemporary Russian television of polluting the minds of the people, in particular youth. Rasputin objects to what he regards as 'the moral permissiveness and lustfulness, the unscrupulousness and sensationalism of the mass media', 'the liberation from all norms' and 'the cacophony of frenzied music'.[1] Equally censorious is Sergey Vikulov, a former editor of *Nash sovremennik*: 'Now everyone sits in front of the TV and stares at it. They watch what they are shown, and even when they can't sit any longer, they still watch TV.'[2]

Rasputin and his colleagues firmly identify this state of affairs with the influence of the Western media, particularly television-programming, radio formats and game shows. A frequently voiced criticism is that the Western media promote a materialistic outlook that is inimical to the cultural traditions and growth of Russia. These writers fear that a nation targeted by sophisticated advertising campaigns – the Cola war is one example – will lose its way in a miasma of irrelevant consumerism and will be bogged down by trivia. These are familiar utterances to Western culture-watchers and indirect support for the fears expressed by Rasputin and others can be found in the writings of Western scholars. 'Television', concluded Neil Postman, in an informed and speculative study of the effects of television, 'does not extend or amplify literate culture. It attacks it.'[3] Reading Postman's comments, Russian opponents of the spread of Western television programming and viewing habits, would emphatically agree. Embedded in Postman's remarks, and much else of what he writes on this subject, is a belief that literate culture is superior to that offered through the television screen, and that television's seemingly unstoppable influence and pervasiveness trivializes what it touches; that the medium of television is unsuitable for the discussion of serious questions; indeed that it is intrinsically unable to deal with such issues. But Postman goes even further. Of the commercial he notes: 'By bringing together in compact form all the arts of show business – music, drama, imagery, humor, celebrity – the television commercial has mounted the most serious assault on capitalist ideology since the publication of *Das Kapital*.'[4]

Yet, on the other side of the former Iron Curtain Western-style commercials are seen as being the very essence of aggressive, brash, persuasive and conspicuously successful capitalism, the very antithesis of what was offered on Soviet television and therefore something to be embraced and enjoyed with gusto. So on the one hand television is considered to be the destroyer of literate culture, or at the very least as undermining it, and on the other hand as an essential element in a prosperous capitalist society. How are we to understand these two distinct views?

One of the most significant features of television, and this especially applies to the interactive applications of the computer, is its volatility. It encourages a change-for-change's-sake approach, a restless search for novelty to keep the attention of viewers. A potentially more serious consequence of such electronic volatility is the opportunity for electronic censorship, arising from the speed and ease with which electronic text can be edited.

The merits of television (and the computer) and books are closely linked to the bitter arguments that have raged in America over recent years between supporters and opponents of political correctness. Until very recently Russian literature and culture were largely free of the American-style obsession with race, sex (read gender) and culture and the canon of great literature. The irony that seems to have been missed by all observers is that what appears to Russians to be the unwelcome intrusion of yet another, insidious Western fad, is in fact the return of the original product, wrapped in the rainbow-packaging of American West-Coast, left-wing radicals, with a hefty dose of Maoism, to the culture whence it came. For political correctness was a Marxist-Leninist construct designed, as the name suggests, to lay down standards of orthodoxy – the correct approach – to questions of class and ideology, culture, and even psychiatry where holding incorrect views was equated with insanity.[5] In the words of Chairman Mao: 'Not to have a correct political orientation is like not having a soul.'[6]

The attack on the great canon of literature, a cornerstone of the American political-correct programme, is entirely coherent if you believe that the canon plays a vital role in transmitting cultural and moral values from one generation to another; that it imparts confidence and resilience. If your intention is to destroy this cultural transmission, then again, it is perfectly logical to seek to reduce the status of the canon by the inclusion of lesser known, supposedly neglected writers, to the extent that it is no longer a canon, let alone a great canon. 'Great', as in great canon, is an affront to the levelling instincts of the tenured radicals.

Television and the electronic interactive medium can be very useful allies in achieving this aim. For both technologies are universal and enjoy the prestige of having played a big part in the downfall of communism. They are, unquestionably, seen as the wave of the future. But, an exclusively television-based education is no help in recognizing and disarming the sophistries of political correctness, nor indeed the promises of instant Huxleyian happiness contained in advertisements. More demanding intellectual training is required. This vulnerability is something of which Russia's new cultural guardians are instinctively aware. Russia's great canon of literature – Pushkin, Lermontov, Gogol, Turgenev, Dostoevsky, Tolstoy, Pasternak, Bulgakov, Grossman, Solzhenitsyn, Tsvetaeva and Akhmatova – was, possibly still is, Russia's moral and intellectual centre. The screen leads away from that centre, not to it.

In a world that is ever more swamped with television images, the literary, reading-based education – the Great Books if you will – as a vital tool in analysing the electronic media should not be under-estimated. An individual who has benefited from a study of literature acquires intellectual skills that cannot be claimed for an education that relies too heavily on television and electronic images. The Great Books and print-based literacy are a form of immunization against the absurdities of the electronic image, be it disseminated via the television or the computer screen. Witness the manner in which the Nazis and Soviets exploited the image, blending play and ideology (*Kraft durch Freude* and GOTOVO respectively). A culture in which education is biased too heavily in favour of the image will produce citizens without the intellectual apparatus and, therefore, protection, given by studying literature, or by simply reading a great deal. Such adults are vulnerable to the various half-truths, distortions and lies, that are such staple fare of the media in their many forms. The concept of literacy, the baggage of cultural assumptions encoded in the idea of the Great Books, with all its undoubted flaws and arbi-trariness, is to be preferred to the chaotic 'educational' supermarket offered by the screen. Multi-media and the whole range of opportu-nities afforded by the information superhighway are here to stay, but they cannot replace print-based literacy.

Objections to Western influences are nothing new in Russian thought. The Slavophile/Westerner dichotomy was a characteristic feature of the nineteenth-century intellectual landscape. It raised questions of abiding concern to Russian artists and thinkers: should Russia move closer towards the West? (the Westerners' position); or should she turn her back on the West, relying instead upon her own traditions and intrinsic strengths and virtues? (the Slavophile posi-tion).

With varying degrees of success communism suppressed these arguments. But it is clear from the utterances of Rasputin and many of his fellow writers that the issue is still very much alive. It is no coin-cidence that some of the most outspoken criticism of the media originates from writers whose work venerates the traditions of *Rus'* and who attribute a key role to the media for the decay of rural life. In one respect, therefore, hostility towards the Western media may be seen as a continuation of the search for answers to the apparently insoluble questions of Russia's destiny posed by the Slavophiles and Westerners.

The objections of Rasputin and his colleagues cannot be dismissed out of hand as the ravings of nationalist extremists. On the other hand, given that an essential part of overcoming the 70-year legacy of totalitarian rule necessarily involves removing the formidable barriers erected by the commissars of culture, then, inevitably, there are going to be cultural casualties, as isolation comes to an end and West meets East. Agreed: *Dallas* and *The Rich Also Cry* are poor substitutes for the poetry of Pushkin and Pasternak, but the god-like status of these poets was a reflection of the social, and intellectual dysfunctions caused by the Soviet state, a misdirection of intellectual and moral resources that were denied other outlets.

The choice is between a move towards an open and free society, in which the writer loses his status as cultural oracle (or must compete with other cultural oracles), and one in which cultural and economic change are retarded for the benefit of a small group of writers. Somewhat overstated perhaps, but not too much. The poetry of Pushkin makes fine food for the spirit in the concentration camp, but better surely that there be no 'enemies of the people' and no concentration camps. The extent to which the Soviet infosphere was breached suggests that complete cultural isolation is in any case not only not possible (not even it seems in North Korea), but hardly desirable. Russia's great literary tradition, has nothing to fear from the West or contact with it. Familiarity with the West did nothing to impede or to destroy the growth of literary greatness in nineteenth-century Russia. Pushkin, Lermontov, Turgenev, Tolstoy and Dostoevsky are in no way reduced in stature by virtue of any contact with the West. The reverse is surely true. Moreover, with the relentless proliferation of substandard courses in Western universities and the insidious influence of feminism and other excrescences of political correctness, the Russian classics are a powerful reminder of what we in the West stand to lose.

Other objections to the current media climate, especially some of those emanating from the regular contributors to *Nash sovremennik*, need to be taken with more than a smidgen of salt. The threat to Russian culture allegedly posed by the electronic hysteria of Western heavy-metal bands and their Russian imitators bears not the slightest comparison with the calculated and systematic destruction visited on Russian culture by communism.[7] Are Russian tractor drivers really running such a risk by listening to the inanities of pop music on their Japanese personal stereos as they plough the steppe? Communism, not the programming of Western media, was the implacable enemy of Russian culture. Nor was this desecration ever openly discussed. The freedom that permits Russian television to open a window onto the

West, also permits Rasputin (and others) to speak out about what is perceived to be cultural pollution.

Censorship, and specifically the sense of identity that this imparted to the writer, is inextricably linked to power, especially those writers and cultural activists who supported the system. Soviet-style socialism placed incomparably greater emphasis on the role of intellectuals than did German-style National socialism. The CPSU grew out of intellectual and political struggles and the Marxist – eventually – Marxist-Leninist body politic reflects this past in the heightened prestige accorded to the intellectual. One of the great attractions of Soviet communism for writers and intellectuals was precisely the promise of wielding power and being taken seriously by rulers who portrayed themselves as philosopher-kings. It was an intoxicating promise. Many were seduced, little realizing that in the process they colluded in their own moral and intellectual destruction. One of the consequences of this incestuous relationship was the loss of intellectual independence. For it is inconceivable that the party intellectual would break with the latest party line. Self-censorship was essential. So the intellectual who despises the *hoi-polloi* for their ignorance, their lack of class consciousness and who is sworn to liberate them from their serfdom, is himself a slave to lies and party propaganda. Even if he knows or believes them to be false, he must remain silent. One of the reasons why so many Western writers, intellectuals and scientists admired the Soviet Union was because they believed that the special privileges and status accorded such people in the Soviet Union should be reciprocated in the West. Naturally, they preferred not to know too much about the fate of persecuted writers. As George Orwell famously noted in 1946 when writing about the Russophile infatuations of British intellectuals: 'The direct, conscious attack on intellectual decency comes from the [Western] intellectuals themselves.'[8]

Perversely, the absence of censorship and persecution in the West is something that the left-leaning intellectual feels most keenly. Unable to free himself from the notion of class struggle, he is convinced that the failure on the part of the Western state to terrorize him, to arrest him and to censor his work – that is, to do the sorts of things that were routinely done throughout Central and Eastern Europe – is in no way indicative that he is not being persecuted. To his conspiratorial mindset it means that the persecution is so subtle, so diabolical, and so well hidden, that only his acutely honed intellectual faculties that the bourgeoisie, dulled by crass materialism, do not possess, are able to discern the 'hidden agenda' or the 'repressive tolerance', intended to silence him. The Soviet writer, even the moderately successful hack, could harbour absolutely no illusions about what resistance to the state entailed. For him, unlike his comfortable and free Western colleagues, persecution was vicious and prolonged long after 1953.

Censorship of the kind practised throughout the Soviet period (omnicensorship[9]) undermines social life, prevents economic prosperity and attacks intellectual endeavour. Progressive impoverishment follows, and by the time the problem is realized systemic collapse is unavoidable. On the other hand, for all its destructive and insidious effects, especially as exemplified by socialist realism, censorship left the creator and mediator of culture – the writer, artist, painter and dramatist – in no doubt about the value of art and literature. 'Censorship', as Neil Postman observes, 'after all, is the tribute tyrants pay to the assumption that a public knows the difference between serious discourse and entertainment – and cares.'[10] Art was not a commercial activity pursued for profit, but one devoted to high moral and ethical (supposedly) purposes. Writers mattered and the fact that they were so comprehensively persecuted can be seen as a manifestation of the profound importance attached to them by the party.

By and large the writer was a privileged functionary. There were privileges of two kinds: access to scarce material goods and services denied to the population; and a definite position and status in the Soviet scheme of things, which claimed the legacy of the nineteenth century. It is the loss of this unique intellectual and moral role after 1991 that marks the profound change. If the abolition of censorship can thus be said to be the beginning of cultural renewal, and Russia's rejoining the intellectual community of nations, it also signifies a major change in the position of literature – serious or otherwise – in Russian society.

Censorship – based on, and justified by, Marxist-Leninist ideology – offered certainties to the writer. The writer defined himself by his reaction to these certainties. Soviet ideologists argued that History was moving towards a definite end: the end of capitalism and the triumph of socialism; that is History had a meaning. It was not a maelstrom of inexplicable events but a process from which, with the aid of Marxism-Leninism, certain laws of social and economic change could be deduced and manipulated. These laws would facilitate the transmutation of morally autonomous, rebellious, freedom-loving, self-improving individuals pursuing their own ends into docile and malleable insect-humans working away in one giant, socialist ant-hill.

A writer living and working in such a culture must contend with a view of History that itself has a strictly defined structure: a beginning (the growth of class war in the ancient cities of Greece and Rome), a middle (the battle between capitalism and socialism that gathers momentum from the Industrial Revolution onwards) and a glorious resolution (the classless society in which everybody is compelled to be equal and party decrees have replaced the Decalogue). Day-in, day-out, the party's message is hammered home: we know the meaning of History; History is with us; those who do not march with History will be crushed by its wheels.

For a writer to create a structure which did not reflect the party's interpretation of History required enormous intellectual and moral resources. In effect the story-telling technique – the beginning, middle, the end – had already been kidnapped by the party: there was only one story to tell and that was the story of class war and its inevitable victory. The writer either endorses the party's view – he becomes the party's mouthpiece – or he retreats into his own world, the private world of emotion and nature. Finally, he can rebel. So, again we see the importance of socialist realism for the party; a doctrine designed to ensure that writers wrote in a manner that was consistent with the party's world view. Socialist realism, then, was not just another literary technique or school of thought. As Czesław Miłosz, notes in *The Captive Mind*:

> 'Socialist realism' is much more than a matter of taste, of preference for one style of painting or music rather than another. It is concerned with beliefs which lie at the foundation of human existence. In the field of literature it forbids what has in every age been the writer's essential task – to look at the world from his own independent viewpoint, to tell the truth as he sees it ...[11]

Socialist realism was intended, therefore, to be a fundamental and irreversible break with all preceding literature and art. Henceforth, there was only the Method, and that is socialist realism. These profound and obvious differences have not stopped Michael Schudson from coining the term 'capitalist realism' as a counterpart to 'socialist realism'.[12] By inference, we are given to understand that American advertising supports a totalitarian system as bad as anything that existed in Soviet Russia. Advertising executives may well indeed portray an idealized life via the advert, but the viewer is free to reject it. Acceptance of the advertiser's vision was not compelled, and criticism did/does not lead to the concentration camp.[13]

For its part, socialist realism was an ideologically-driven doctrine imposed with the aim of bringing about the complete and final Sovietization of Russia in the realm of intellectual and artistic endeavour. There is nothing remotely analogous or comparable to these aims in the practice or theory of liberal, free-market economics. In fact, the relationship between great art and capitalism has been enduring and beneficial. It should also be obvious that advertising in the capitalist West is predicated on the existence of a market for goods and services, something that was absent in the Soviet Union. Socialist realism, which began by undermining literature, offered its readers a wholly mythical interpretation of the birth of the Soviet state and a vision of contemporary society and its bounties, which, to use the Russian expression 'did not correspond to reality'. Socialist realism formalized the end of history and as a result it remained locked in its Leninist-Stalinist time-capsule, even as it was clear that Soviet society was changing. Western advertising is not really bothered by the end of history (it's bad for business). As the social and economic needs of the target audience change so the advertising strategies designed to reach that audience must also change. Adaptability is crucial to success, something conspicuously missing in socialist-realist hermeneutics. 1990s advertising is altogether more subtle, technically proficient and entertaining than the advertising of even ten years ago. So, should we be tempted to admit even the loosest of comparisons between socialist realism and its alleged capitalist counterpart, then the time-frame must also be specified.

Curiously, however, there is a Soviet influence on Western film-makers and advertisers. The feminist and race industries' obsession with role models reminds us of the socialist-realist, *polozhitel'nyy geroy*. The basic premise owes much to the Soviet past, as Bertolt Brecht, one of its loyal supporters put it, the aim is to show the world: 'nicht wie sie ist, aber wie sie sein soll.' If advertising or soaps show enough women or members of various ethnic groups in traditionally white-male roles, so the argument runs, then reality will conform to the social blueprint of the script. The fact that some of these adverts, films and series are also highly entertaining only serves to make the message easier to get across. To what extent it is consistent with social and economic reality is of course another matter.

The Soviet censorship machine did not achieve its aim. In spite of all the repressions, the violence and ideological incantation and the support of many influential Western intellectuals, Russian literature did not become the totally compliant servant of the party.

Perhaps, first of all, we can say that socialist realism undermined itself. Socialist realism encouraged the growth of a large bureaucracy of literary functionaries whose job was to oversee their fellow writers. Status in this bureaucracy depended on qualities that had very little to do with creativity. As is usually the case in such bureaucracies, a form of negative selection takes place. The less talent or less interest a functionary has in writing, the more he devotes himself to scheming and securing privileges within the organization. Having reached a certain position, he finds that his interests will diverge sharply from those interested in writing. His prime task now will be to ensure that his political masters – the guarantors of his status and privilege – are not offended by mere writers. He might deny it furiously, but such a writer-functionary is an important part of the censorship apparatus. Simonov, Tvardovskiy and Fadeev were notable exemplars of the writer-bureaucrat.

A second consideration must be the links with the classics of the nineteenth century that continued throughout even the darkest days and moments of the Soviet period. It is possible, I suggest, that had writers such as Pushkin, Tolstoy, Dostoevsky and Chekhov not been read during the Soviet period words such as 'democracy', 'spirit', 'freedom' and 'individual' would have been irreversibly corrupted. These and other writers were the standard against which Soviet claims of social and intellectual progress could be measured. Nineteenth-century literature was a refuge from party lies and trickery, a safe harbour for the intellect and spirit. The party grossly underestimated the danger posed by the classics for its control of artistic activity. The classics did not assist the building of the brave new world. On the contrary, they were weakening its foundations from the very beginning.

A third consideration is that the party theorists and pedagogues failed to realize that if the medium, by means of which information and ideas are received, is changed, the manner in which people perceive and evaluate information can also change. Propaganda and political messages, in other words, tend to be medium-contingent. The scope of these changes can be appreciated in the transition from a purely oral culture to one in which the printed word is dominant, and currently, one in which the transition to multi-media and IT is under way.

Where so much was left unsaid, what was said assumed great importance. In such a society the writer is of course much more than just a writer: he is a forum for all kinds of ideas that, in say, Britain or America would be discussed in specialist journals. While it was undoubtedly the case that much useful information about the state of Soviet society could be gleaned from a careful reading of literature, and it frequently proved to be more insightful than the standard social science areas such as history, economics and sociology, it is hardly a desirable state of affairs for the discussion and analysis of serious social and economic problems.[14]

The flood of revelations about Stalin and the many admissions of failure concerning contemporary Soviet society that were the staple fare of *glasnost'* needed no writer to act as mediator or interpreter. Statistics of horror, mass murder and gruesome incompetence spoke for themselves. The breaking of censorship also broke the party-sponsored bond between 'the people' and the writer. It also led to the outbreak of a media war. Released from the chains of Soviet censorship, television came into its own. It is surely no coincidence that some of the most ferocious criticisms of television have come from writers who are only too aware that their monopoly of attention has been broken.[15] Liberation of television has also been accompanied by the publication of Western authors, hitherto banned or mutilated by censorship, such as George Orwell, Aldous Huxley, John Steinbeck and Graham Greene. To these illustrious foreign rivals can be added the spread of video-cassette recorders and the legal and pirated copies of Western films. Competition for attention is fierce. Anticipating the current situation, Vladimir Voinovich has argued that: 'The overwhelming majority of Soviet writers simply could not exist without censorship because they could not withstand the competition.'[16]

Competition for the scarce resource of attention is only part of the problem. The breaking of the party's information monopoly is first and foremost a question of personal freedom, the freedom of individuals to decide for themselves what to read without being supervised. One of the most assiduously maintained cultural divisions of the period of Soviet–West confrontation was that the average Soviet citizen moved on a higher cultural and intellectual level than his counterpart in the West; that Soviet citizens were not interested in pulp fiction, soap operas, detective stories, thrillers and the sensationalism and scandalous fare of the tabloids, preferring instead to read poetry, play chess and visit the opera. The eagerness with which the Russian reading and viewing public has abandoned Tolstoy and turned to Western videos and Mexican low-budget soaps is a brutal rejection of party-approved culture-behaviour in favour of fun. Not surprisingly, those writers who resisted the party – in the case of Solzhenitsyn magnificently so – feel cheated, almost let down. They might argue that their contribution to bringing about the end of the Soviet system has been shamefully ignored. They undoubtedly feel a strong sense of personal rejection that manifests itself in stinging criticism of Western cultural influences, rock music, and in Solzhenitsyn's case, the obsessions of the younger writers with self-expression. Boris Paramonov's response to Solzhenitsyn on this point is worth noting since it identifies what is most likely to be happening in Russia:

> What Solzhenitsyn fails to realise is that this shift is not just an aesthetic but a cultural historical change phenomenon heralding the emergence of a new mentality in Russia – individualistic bourgeois consciousness. The shift marks a genuine historical change and presages the final demise of communism. That the new Russian tends to be purely commercial or aesthetically elitist should be greeted as a sign that this historical transformation is becoming irreversible.[17]

It is not unreasonable to assume, therefore, that the continued growth in importance of the electronic media and their continued striving towards intellectual autonomy will continue to hasten the demise of the writer's traditional role in Russia; that the cult of the media personality, supported by an increasingly confident telocracy, will supplant the writer as the cultural oracle. There are a number of reasons for this silent revolution, some obvious, some less so.

Firstly, and most obviously, the writer's monopoly has been broken. The genuinely liberal and humanistic ethos of the nineteenth-century writer was one of a commitment to social change. The special position of the writer was predicated on the belief that the people needed the literary intelligentsia to speak for them. Under Stalin, the writer was intended to be a social engineer. But does a society that has found its voice need writers as its mouthpiece? Put another way: why read a Solzhenitsyn when you can watch a Donahue? Secondly, it would be consistent with a pattern already observed in the West. Thirdly, the technology associated with the propagation of the electronic image enjoys tremendous prestige. Finally, economic cooperation with the West can only serve to accelerate the integration of this technology at all levels of Russian society.

If we accept these likely changes and the assumptions on which they are predicated as given, then it goes some way to elucidating the single-minded hostility of so many writers towards television. Writers are culture watchers. They are well aware that television threatens their unique position. In fact, rigid censorship of television in Eastern Europe actually favoured the writer. Now, with the abolition of literary censorship writers fear that the word will be no match for the image.

Writers will fight back in the traditional manner. It will not be too long before we will see the publication of a novel whose major theme is television. There are some precedents. Both Zamyatin and Platonov exploited themes of media in works that were published in the late 1980s.[18] East European writers anxious to warn the reader of the perils of the electronic media will find food for thought in the work of Aldous Huxley, George Orwell, Ray Bradbury and Philip K. Dick. Their as-yet-unwritten works will stimulate the growth of a new criticism. They will mark the *incunabula* of a significant and lively dialogue between the various media. Again, there will be valuable insight for Western scholars. Literature's place in Russian culture has indeed changed, but it has not been written off, rather it has been rewritten.

5 The Internet in Russia

> How will a society founded on [paternal] guidance cope with the
> wilds of x-rated cyberspace? [...] They expect that whole highways
> of data will flow through their city. Yet they also seem to expect
> that this won't affect them.
>
> William Gibson

INTRODUCTION

Socialist autarky and participation in the global exchange of products
and services based on IT are mutually incompatible. So Russia's
embracing the Internet is a welcome sign of speedy remove from the
Soviet past, and the possibility of any reversal. Compared with the
arrival of the Internet in Russia, the changes affecting television
programming and the fears expressed about them are far less important than they seem. True, Russian television has experienced major
developments, but IT has, as in the West, forced journalists, government agencies, universities, business, wider economic activity and, of
course, the private citizen to make huge conceptual leaps from the
recent past, in a way in which television has not.

Information technology – a broad term at best – makes the information society a possibility, or rather it enhances the importance of
raw data and information in the process of wealth creation and in
political decision-making. Russia, for reasons that were examined in
Part I, was not a major innovator in the computer industry. As a
result, the theoretical and practical aspects of the information society
developed in the West have established the *de facto* standard of
comparison. That is not to say that specifically Russian aspects
cannot be identified, but that for the foreseeable future the Western-
inspired paradigm will be the one to be emulated. I would argue that
the following four areas need to be considered: (i) the nature and
promise of the information society itself; (ii) Russian Federation and
international legislation that has a direct bearing on the use of IT;
(iii) the global consequences of American dominance in the provision of IT; and (iv) commercial and non-commercial networks in the
Russian Federation.

BANGEMANN AND GATES: POTHOLES ON THE ROAD AHEAD

Since the early 1990s two distinct approaches to the information society have emerged in the West. For purposes of argument and simplification I call the two approaches individual and corporatist. The first approach (individual) is fiercely entrepreneurial and resists state intervention and is exemplified by the success of individuals such as Bill Gates, as outlined in his book, *The Road Ahead* (1995); the second approach (corporatist) is embodied in *The Martin Bangemann Report, Europe and the Global Information Society: Recommendations to the European Council* (1994). Bangemann and Gates recognize many of the key problems with which the architects of the information society, in any of its manifestations, must grapple. Yet, as one might expect, the degree of emphasis varies from one problem area to another, particularly when it comes to state intervention and regulation, and it is here that some significant differences in approach are apparent.

Gates, unlike his European antagonists, is an expert salesman. For all his undoubted insight and expert knowledge of the industry and of the possible directions it might take, he has a powerful vested interest in the development of the technology. The vision offered by Gates in *The Road Ahead* is, for better or for worse, a direct appeal to electronic self-fulfilment and self-gratification:

> There will be a day, not far distant, when you will be able to conduct business, study, explore the world and its cultures, call up any great entertainment, make friends, attend neighbourhood markets, and show pictures to distant relatives – without leaving your desk or armchair. You won't leave your network connection behind at the office or in the classroom. It will be more than an object you carry or an appliance you purchase. It will be your passport into a new, mediated way of life.[1]

If Gates can be said to be pushing any one theme of IT hard then it is education. IT is accelerating the spread of distance-learning and other forms of non-traditional education. As a result the market for all kinds of IT products and services continues to grow worldwide.

The *Bangemann Report* is altogether far less straightforward. The authors acknowledge the enormity and scope of the changes that are taking place as a result of the penetration of information technology. An immediate concern is that Europe's approach is 'still too fragmentary'.[2] There is some clarification of this with the observation that: 'An information society is a means to achieve so many of the [European] Union's objectives.'[3] Given that one of the European Union's prime objectives is ever closer political and monetary union, one may ask whether the information society as understood in this report will facilitate, or is intended to facilitate, these specifically political goals rather than enhance Europe's competitiveness. Central to the *Bangemann Report* is the belief that IT can bring Europe's nations together. In this scenario IT is seen as a form of societal and economic cement whereas practice suggests that IT can fragment societies, highlighting differences among various groups. It may indeed be possible to impose non-economic requirements on the main users of IT but only at the cost of negating the intrinsic advantages accruing from the use of IT itself. The authors note: 'Europe's ability to participate, to adapt and to exploit the new technologies and the opportunities they create, will require partnership between individuals, employers, unions and governments dedicated to managing change.'[4]

Precedents inside the European Union for managing change in some sort of partnership are far from encouraging (witness the horrendous waste and distortions brought about by the Common Agricultural Policy). The greater the number of partners, the greater the likelihood that irreconcilable conflicts will arise, or will exist in the first place. This is especially the case when there exist serious differences in the area of social and economic goals and interests. IT has been one of the most powerful and effective means for allowing companies and corporations to lay off large numbers of workers at all levels. This is an area in which it is difficult to see any form of effective partnership emerging. Companies that retain superfluous employees burden themselves with extra costs. If they are forced to retain workers then they will relocate to low-cost areas, or areas free from intrusive and costly legislation.

The notion of partnership that the *Bangemann Report* fosters assiduously rests on the authors' assumption that the creation of a 'European information society'[5] is possible. Again, one cannot but conclude that the authors have missed the point about the impact of IT. One might well talk of an 'information society', though its definition might not be as inclusive as the authors would wish, but there is nothing specifically 'European' about the opportunities and risks posed by the information society. It is a global phenomenon. So, if the notion of the 'European information society' is indeed intended to be a protective barrier against harsh economic changes, then the costs will be greater than the supposed benefits, and will be likely to exacerbate the social and economic tensions it is meant to ameliorate. The global nature of the information society is conceded later in the same report when the authors correctly note: 'Since information infrastructures are borderless in an open market environment, the information society has an essentially global dimension.'[6]

Other inconsistencies emerge as well. While acknowledging that market mechanisms are the best way forward and rejecting subsidies, *dirigisme* and protectionism, the authors worry that the information society in Europe will not be 'a strategic creation for the whole Union', but 'a more fragmented and much less effective amalgam of individual initiatives by Member States, with repercussions on every policy area, from the single market to cohesion'.[7] A strategic creation is only possible if you have a strategy. Who are the strategists? Businessmen or the bureaucrats of the European Union? If the long-term goal is to retain control via some form of bureaucratically enforced standardization, then the perceived lack of strategy is justified. If, however, non-market solutions are imposed then this will lead to the very problems of subsidy, *dirigisme* and protectionism.

The authors' expectations of the sort of changes that can be delivered by this technology provide some useful indicators as to the Europe they wish to see created, or possibly preserved. One can identify potential losers, who also happen to be among the biggest, and in many cases the most profligate spenders of public money. 'A more caring society with a significantly higher quality of life …'[8] may well be a laudable goal. Unfortunately, the authors do not share their thoughts with the reader as to what they mean by a 'more caring society'. So it is difficult to take issue with them on specific areas. There is, however, one area that poses an enormous threat to the attempt to control public welfare spending to which too many Europeans have become accustomed.

Caring for Europe's greying population is already proving to be a major drain on public finances across Europe and expenditure is likely to increase as we move into the next century. Some very hard choices will have to be taken about the source of funding for this growing area of social welfare provision. If one takes the view that those who exploit IT to create wealth are likely to be few in number, much fewer when compared to the mass employers of the recent past, then it is difficult to see where the tax revenues will come from to support the vision of a more caring European society. The outcome can only mean more government intervention and increased expenditure, or expectations will have to be reduced.

One can also question the expected consequences for bureaucracy. The authors hope for: 'More efficient, transparent and responsible public services, closer to the citizen and at lower cost'.[9] Implicit in this hope are large reductions in the numbers of bureaucrats at all levels of government, thus adding to the burden of unemployment, or if governments refuse to implement painful decisions, adding to the costs of overmanned bureaucracies. Overmanning is costly to maintain, and overmanned bureaucracies are inimical to efficiency.

If we look at business organizations of comparable scale and budget then we can get some idea of what is in store for Europe's bloated bureaucracies if Europe's politicians are indeed determined to reduce the cost of government. Consider the effects of IT on banking and the financial sector: greater productivity, efficiency gains and profit, but drastic reductions in the number of employees. Given this horrendous blood-letting, it is not clear how Europe's politicians will be able to reconcile more efficient public administration with current manning levels and at a lower cost. Something will have to give. The nature of the social challenge is glossed over in superficial terms. The authors observe: 'The widespread availability of new information tools and services will present fresh opportunities to build a more equal and balanced society and to foster individual accomplishment.'[10] The opportunities created by IT are unlikely to be equally disseminated in and among societies. This is inherent in the creative process itself. Creating a new product, developing a new idea or adding value to an existing product is something that is highly individualistic. It cannot be driven by a committee. Many of the wealth creators and entrepreneurs of the past had to rely on the procurement of large amounts of natural resources, and a manufacturing process that was at the mercy of trade union intimidation and disruption. The multiplicity of small, discrete, commercial, creative and intellectual enterprises that are able to exploit the opportunities of IT do not find themselves dependent on a single supplier and have access to a limitless amount of data and information. And they do not require expensive and space-consuming plant and infrastructure. The levels of employment and wealth creation that will be needed to reduce unemployment and social costs in Europe will not be delivered by IT. IT can be used to exploit an idea, to market a new product or service, but overwhelmingly it raises the rewards for individual achievement and recognition. In other words, it is socially and economically divisive. Regarding the social challenge, the authors are quite right to conclude:

> The main risk lies in the creation of a two-tier society of have and have-nots, in which only a part of the population has access to the new technology, is comfortable using it and can fully enjoy its benefits. There is a danger that individuals will reject the new information culture and its instruments.[11]

for which they advocate the solution:

> By pooling resources that have traditionally been separate, and indeed distant, the information infrastructure unleashes unlimited potential for acquiring knowledge, innovation and creativity.[12]

Much depends on how these resources are pooled. Are they to be pooled by a free and voluntary assembly of commercial and academic interests, or does the call for the pooling of resources, mask further bureaucratic and coercive intervention and legislation, both of which are hostile to a market that is still developing? Again, despite perhaps the authors' best efforts to avoid such an impression, the bureaucratic itch to intervene, to regulate, is detectable:

> Thus, we have to find ways to master the risks and maximise the benefits. This places responsibilities on public authorities to establish safeguards and to ensure the cohesion of the new society. Fair access to the infrastructure will have to be guaranteed to all, as will provision of universal service, the definition of which must evolve in line with the technology.[13]

The management of risk and benefit is not something that can be solved by bureaucratic diktat. Vague talk of safeguards remains just that since it is not clear what is to be safeguarded (bureaucrats' jobs or European markets from tough competition?).[14] Nor can we have much faith in the ability of bureaucrats to ensure the cohesion of society. There is no such thing as a 'single European society'. Attempts to regulate for cohesion in one country will not necessarily work, or will have unintended consequences, invariably negative, in another. This merely inflames the appetite for still more intervention to correct the original error.

One can also question whether officials are competent to determine what constitutes 'fair access' and thus whether universal provision should be guaranteed. These are decisions which should be made by individuals using the service and willing to pay for it. Nor can entrepreneurs and other innovators draw much comfort from the call that the definition of universal access '*must* [emphasis added] evolve in line with the technology'.[15] This amounts to a tax on innovation. Universal access which is achieved by the commercial success of a product's market penetration is of quite a different order from universal provision of an IT product (such as, say electronic mail) deemed to be desirable by officials. The former is a market success story, which has had to overcome the sanction of failure, and one whose continued success cannot be taken for granted; the latter is the fruit of bureaucratic intervention unimpeded by the fear of commercial failure and carrying quite disproportionate political costs for those who might wish to remove it at a later date. That is not to say that some stimulus to disseminate a product, other than the commercial imperative, will always be automatically ruled out. It does, however, mean that we need to be quite clear about the costs and benefits. Government bureaucracies do not provide us with an unimpeded view. Universal access to electronic mail (for example) may well be a societally desirable goal. On the other hand, the cost of provision may well outweigh the supposed benefits. The history of other communication products and services suggests that the market is a far better regulator than the bureaucratic committee.

The authors note the dangers posed by 'monopolistic, anticompetitive environments'.[16] Yet they fail to distinguish between a private and state monopoly. This failure obscures the demonstrable fact that deregulation of telecommunications industries has had a marked effect on the growth and use of IT, specifically in Britain and the US. The issue of regulation is tackled in a somewhat roundabout way. The authors state: 'The key issue for the emergence of new markets is the need for a new regulatory environment allowing full competition.'[17] The issue is not regulation but deregulation. (In fact, it is worth noting that the word deregulation does not occur once in the entire report). Rules made by bureaucrats constitute an obstacle to the penetration of IT. Also, given that the contours of the market are poorly defined in many key areas, then any attempt to regulate in the absence of knowledge will stifle the market, not assist it. Projects with promise will be stillborn. Regulation is necessary, but it needs to be a very light touch, establishing general operational principles rather than trying to regulate the minutiae of day-to-day business activity. Regulation is not, to paraphrase a well-known Russian proverb, the mother of invention.[18] The authors of the *Bangemann Report* try very hard to minimize the level of state control necessary to bring about their aims. They do not succeed. The failure to resolve the problem stems from the very nature of the European Union itself. Deregulation and privatization of telecommunications markets are by no means uniform throughout the European Union, which of course gives advantages to those states who have deregulated, such as Britain. European-wide regulation to reverse or to limit the advantages of deregulation acquired by individual states is a perverse use of bureaucracy. Also, the use of English in the global information market is undoubtedly a matter of standards. The dominance of English on, for example the World Wide Web, is a direct result of the dominance of the North American computer and software industries, not a calculated insult to the sensibilities of the French.

The concerns and aspirations of Gates and Bangemann suggest that there are wide-ranging opinions and differences between the United States and continental Europe as to what constitutes the information society. The following features – by no means exhaustive – can be noted: (i) the penetration of IT puts a premium on life-long education; (ii) IT opens up virtually limitless opportunities for leisure and entertainment; (iii) according to Gates, IT makes 'friction-free capitalism' a possibility;[19] (iv) the information society is a global development; (v) no nation, if it wishes to prosper, can remain outside this global information exchange; (vi) 'The information highway is a mass phenomenon, or it is nothing';[20] (vii) There are opportunities for social engineering.

There is no obvious reason why the information society or information highway cannot be a mass phenomenon, but we need to be clear what this would entail. Gates quite rightly stresses the need for life-long education, particularly that type of education that emphasizes problem-solving skills.[21] The trouble is that these skills are not equally distributed among populations. Consequently, access will not in itself be enough: what you do with access will be more important. If, as Gates observes, 'Informational tools are symbolic mediators that amplify the intellect rather than the muscles of their users',[22] then IT will tend to accentuate the innate intellectual differences between people, not remove them. There is for example a qualitative intellectual difference between a scientific researcher using the Internet to help him solve a problem connected with, say, some aspect of global warming, and those sending a love letter via electronic mail. Equal access, even if it proved to be a desirable policy, would not necessarily guarantee equal outcome. An outcome such as this will have implications for education and employment (and the rewards of education and employment).

The Case against the Universal Provision of Electronic Mail

At the time of writing, the specific question of the universal provision of electronic mail has not arisen in the Russian Federation. So far it is a question for the more prosperous North America and the European Union. As, however, the infrastructure of the information society is created and spreads throughout the Russian Federation, and the advantages of such a basic service become more widely perceived, it is likely that the question of, if not universal provision, then some form of state-sponsored provision of e-mail and other information services will start to concern Russian policy-makers.

The Rand Organization sponsored a study of just this question and the study will be taken as the focal point of the case against such universal provision.[23] While it is recognized that conditions in North America (the area on which the Rand study was based) are of course not identical to those in the Russian Federation or Europe, the Rand study, nevertheless, raises the same basic questions for all societies.

The case for the universal provision of e-mail (estimated at $1 billion per year[24]) or any limited provision for that matter, must demonstrate that unlike other media of communication – such as radio, television, press, telephone and fax – e-mail confers unique advantages without which societal and economic well-being will suffer. This has not been demonstrated. The press, the television, radio, cinema, telephone all assist in the promotion of democracy (or rather they have that potential) but individuals using such products and services have to pay for them.

Quality of use and quality of material on the network are important considerations. Are we really to believe that the average inner-city or rural recipient of welfare (and their counterparts in Europe and the Russian Federation) are going to discover the joys of participatory democracy by virtue of their being given a computer or e-mail card when hitherto they have not had the slightest interest whatsoever? The presumption is utopian. There is nothing wrong with people sending, say, love letters via e-mail, but should the costs of this be carried by the taxpayer? Given that there will not be, and indeed never can be any kind of quality control (censorship in other words) of personal communications, or the material they access electronically (a point upheld by the American courts in the challenge to the Communications Decency Act), then the assumption that universal access to e-mail funded from the public purse will have societal benefits, must remain speculative. For in all situations, apart from those judicially-sanctioned exceptions, we will simply not know what is being sent. Given that there are considerable variations in individual abilities to evaluate information, then the claim that 'equalizing information benefits' is possible, is highly questionable.[25] All are not equal here by any means.

Projections of statistical data indicate that the diffusion of PCs into US homes will be considerably slower than is the case for TV.[26] Moreover, even if the diffusion rate were higher we would still not be able to know anything about the uses to which PCs were being put, that is once again: all PC users are not equal. The study makes certain assumptions about benefits of 'targeted services'[27] for low-income groups, namely that electronic mail will increase general literacy as well as computer literacy. Once again we are back to quality use not just any use. How is an individual who is barely literate in a conventional sense, going to become literate by starting to send electronic mail messages? Grammar, style and knowledge of English are still required. Electronic mail use will not correct individual inadequacies, it will merely amplify them, and in some cases bring them to a much wider audience.

Information cited in the study leads to the conclusion that the question of access to electronic mail, or any other such media product, can only be a matter for the individual. For example, the authors note that 'many low SES [Socioeconomic Status] households own television sets and TV-based game machines', yet 'most low SES groups have had minimal exposure to computers and may therefore be intimidated by them.'[28] Also, 'many low SES households own television sets and receive cable'.[29]

The facts are not disputed, but it is not at all clear why the taxpayer should subsidize the provision of electronic mail to a low SES household, which, in spite of its low SES, can, nevertheless, still find the money for a television set(s) and TV-based games (by no means cheap). If the members of such a household wanted to acquire a PC, they could, if they so wished, dispense with the TV and video games. That they do not do so indicates that they have made decisions as to where their spending and consumer priorities lie. The low SES household whose staple intellectual nourishment is American TV and a diet of violent videos is, one suggests, highly unlikely to forgo these transient pleasures for the altogether less exciting, and more demanding civic obligations of participatory democracy via the electronic medium. We come back once again to the question of self-selection. The determining factor here is not money, but interest, which in turn is fuelled by one's possession of a lively intelligence. Would the same low SES household also have a reasonable claim on the public purse for books and newspapers? And what sort of papers and books? *Playboy*? *The National Enquirer*? Or *The Brothers Karamazov*? A low SES household that was interested in the benefits of a PC and had to make a choice between the purchase of a TV or a PC could decide to buy the PC. Granted, it is possible, though by no means demonstrated, that it might be desirable were all families, irrespective of their SES able to afford colour TV sets, TV-based game shows and the advantages of a PC. That they cannot is not the fault of those who can. If the low-income SES households have limited funds at their disposal then they must make choices as to what items will receive priority. They are not entitled to make any claim on the public purse. Nor should they be encouraged to believe that they have some claim on the public purse. Such personal decision-making is a vital process which all who aspire to economic responsibility and maturity must undergo. It is an intrinsic part of responsible citizenship, and anything that attacks or undermines the acquisition of such responsibility, helps to create financially irresponsible citizens.

LEGISLATION AND THE NETWORKS

For many reasons – size, potential GDP, military and economic capabilities, historical and cultural – the development of computing and computer networks in the Russian Federation is of great importance. The survey of Russia has identified enormous difficulties, expected problems and some unexpected progress and surprises. Using the baseline approaches summarized above (Gates/ Bangemann) it is possible to come to some preliminary conclusions. Consideration of these conclusions can be deferred until after an examination of the main Russian laws and statutes pertaining to IT, and a description of the commercial and non-commercial main computer networks and projects.[30]

Computing in the Russian Federation is currently affected by five pieces of primary legislation that are additional to the provisions of the 1992 Mass Media Law and its amendments. In chronological order of adoption they are as follows:

(i) 'Zakon Rossiyskoy Federatsii o pravovoy okhrane programm dlya elektronnykh vychislitel'nykh mashin i baz dannykh' ('Law of the Russian Federation Concerning the Legal Storage of Computer Programmes and Data Bases', adopted 23 September 1992, hereinafter The Data Base Law).

(ii) 'Polozhenie o Komitete pri Prezidente Rossiyskoy Federatsii po politike informatizatsii' ('Statute Concerning the Committee Attached to the Presidential Office on the Policy of Informatization', confirmed 17 February 1994, hereinafter the Roskominform Statute).

(iii) 'Federal'nyy zakon o svyazi' ('Federal Law Concerning Communications', adopted 20 January 1995, hereinafter The Communications Law).

(iv) 'Federal'nyy zakon ob informatsii, informatizatsii i zashchite informatsii' ('The Federal Law Concerning Information, Information and the Protection of Information', adopted 25 January 1995, hereinafter The Information Law).

(v) 'Federal'nyy zakon ob uchastii v mezhdunarodnom informatsion-nom obmene' ('The Federal Law Concerning Participation in the International Information Exchange', adopted 5 June 1996, hereinafter The Law of Information Exchange).

THE DATABASE LAW

Given the dramatic increase in the importance of computers and software products for the Russian Federation, a law of this kind was urgently needed. The law provides some legal protection for the software designers, and goes some way to allay the genuine concerns of foreign software companies about the dangers of piracy (though Bill Gates might think otherwise). As with so much Russian Federation legislation, however, enforcement has often been woefully inadequate. The law consists of 4 chapters and a total of 20 articles: chapter 1 ('General Conditions'); chapter 2 ('Exceptional Authorial Rights'); chapter 3 ('The Use of Computer Programmes and Databases'); chapter 4 ('Protection of the Author's Right'). Foreign companies will note the contents of paragraph 5 of Article 3 ('The Object of Legal Storage'): [...] 'the legal storage does not apply to the ideas and principles forming the basis of a computer programme or a database or any other element thereof, including the ideas and principles of organising the interface and algorithm, and in addition the programming language'. It should also be noted that Article 13 ('The Right of Registration') confers the option of registering (for a fee) the property rights to a computer programme or database with the Russian Agency for the Legal Storage of Computer Programmes, Databases and Topologies of Integral Microsystems. The law provides no indication of the precise institutional affiliation of this agency, its wider powers and system of appointing its members.

ROSKOMINFORM STATUTE

Roskominform consists of a total of 12 persons, with its head, as in the case of the Judicial Chamber and *Roskompechat'*, directly appointed by the President of the Russian Federation. The budget for 1994 was just under 512 million rubles. Paragraph 1 of the Statute describes *Roskominform* as a state body that 'ensures the co-ordination of work on the implementing of state policy in the sphere of information in the system of state organs, including those bodies attached to the Presidential office of the Russian Federation, the federal organs of executive power, and the organs of the executive power of the subjects of the Russian Federation'. While advisory functions are ascribed to *Roskominform* its remit is far more significant, since it exercises direct and indirect control over an emerging market, and one that is vital to Russia's prosperity in the next century.

Roskominform's tasks are set out in paragraph 3 of the Statute. Some of the most important for the development of IT and its applications in Russia are: (i) participation in the working out and implementation of state policy in the sphere of informatization; (ii) establishing national priorities in the sphere of informatization; (iii) the working out of draft legislation and other normative acts of the Russian Federation on questions of informatization; (iv) the responsibility for procurement of federal information systems; (v) co-operating with foreign countries and international organizations on questions of informatization.

The range of these tasks confers considerable power on *Roskominform*, and, for better or worse, gives this body an enormous say in the development of IT. For example, *Roskominform* is specifically charged with 'the creation and development of federal and regional information systems and networks, with ensuring their compatibility and mutual operation in a single information space of the Russian Federation' (point 6, paragraph 4). Such a role for a government body seems to suggest that the Russian Federation is not prepared to leave the development of the strategic information network to entrepreneurs and the market generally, a view reinforced by point 16 of the same paragraph. Point 16 deals with the crucial question of standards, which in this case, is to be monitored by *Roskominform* in conjunction with the Russian Federation Committee on Standardization, Metrology and Certification. Such authority to set and to regulate for standards can be destructive of the personal initiative and willingness to take risks on the part of non-government organizations that have largely led the IT revolutions in the West. One can only conclude that the Russian Federation's willingness to insist upon these intrusive powers is born of fear, the fear of losing control. The precedents suggest that excessive legislation can impede the development of strategic information networks, but not push it forward with the necessary speed and flexibility required to adapt to the pace and magnitude of change.[31]

THE COMMUNICATIONS LAW

The Communications Law 'establishes the legal basis for the activity conducted in the area of communications implemented under the jurisdiction of the Russian Federation, determines the authority of the organs of state power concerning the regulation of the indicated activity, and in addition determines the rights and obligations of physical and juridical persons, participating in the indicated activity or of those availing themselves of the services of communication'. (preamble). The law embraces all current communications services, such as postal, television, satellite, radio, cable, telephone, telegraphy and computer.

Great emphasis is placed on working with international bodies, particularly the International Postal Union, in the matter of establishing common-carrier standards. There is a stated commitment to incorporate best practice in communications and the management of networks developed internationally (paragraph 6, Article 5, 'Principles of Activity in the Field of Communications'). The provisions of the following articles should be noted:

Article 8 ('Official Communication Networks, Dedicated Communication Networks of Physical and Juridical Persons') establishes that: 'dedicated communication networks may be created on the territory of the Russian Federation by any physical or juridical persons, including foreign investors possessing the recognised legal status'. (paragraph 2).

Article 13 ('Control of Communication Networks in Emergency Conditions and in a State of Emergency') provides for representatives of the state 'to have priority use, and in addition to stop the activity of any networks and means of communication irrespective of government affiliation or form of ownership'. It should be noted that paragraphs 1 and 3 of Article 5 are subject to limitation in accordance with Article 13.

Article 32 ('The Secrecy of Communications') states that personal communications are protected by the Constitution of the Russian Federation and that the approval of a court is necessary for any interference with this right.

Article 35 ('The Use of Languages and Alphabets in the Activity of Communications Enterprises') states that Russian must be used within the borders of the Russian Federation.

Article 42 ('International Cooperation') states that: 'The Russian Federation assists in the development of international cooperation in the field of communications, and as well as in the solution of problems of legal regulation in the field of communications' (paragraph 1).

THE INFORMATION LAW

The Information Law affects all forms of communication throughout the Russian Federation. (Articles 2, 3, 11, 14, 20, 21, 23 and 24 have been discussed in Chapter 2).[32] Additional articles that will affect the area of IT and electronically transmitted information should be noted. In accordance with Article 7 ('State Information Resources') organizations [...] 'which specialise in the formation of federal information resources and (or) information resources jointly implemented on a contractual basis are obliged to acquire a licence for this type of activity in organs of state power' (point 4). Article 12 ('The Realisation of the Right of Access to Information from Information Resources') provides explicit recognition of the link between access to information and the effectiveness of government and non-government organizations: 'Access by physical and juridical persons to state information resources is the foundation of implementing social control over the activities of state organs and those of local government, of social, political and other organisations, as well as of the state of the economy, ecology and other spheres of societal life.' (point 1, paragraph 2).

Article 16 ('The Development and Production of Information Systems, Technologies and the Means of Provision Thereof') arrogates a powerful role to government. Point 1 notes that: 'All forms of the production of information systems and networks, technologies and the means of provision thereof comprise a special branch of economic activity *the development of which is determined by the state's scientific-technical and industrial policy of informatization'* (point 1, emphasis added). Granted, we do not find words such as 'solely' or 'exceptionally', but neither is there any explicit provision for non-state bodies to determine the policy. If we bear in mind that the aim of informatization is 'the creation of the optimal conditions for meeting information requirements and realizing the rights of citizens, organs of state power, the organs of local government, of organizations, social associations on the basis of the formation and use of information resources', then there is a clear conflict between the state and the private entrepreneur. IT and informatization are indeed special branches of economic activity, but then so are the management of pension funds and futures. The government has no special or unique expertise here. Nor can it claim any special privileges. Point 2, for example, notes that 'state and non-state organisations, as well as citizens have various rights to the development and production of information systems, technologies and the means of provision thereof'. The extent and definition of these 'various rights' are by no means clear.[33] Moreover, there seems to be a tacit presumption in favour of the government as the dominant player in the research and trials of information systems (point 3, paragraphs 1 and 2). The particular provisions of this law are wholly inconsonant with the dramatic successes achieved by private individuals in the West. Despite all the lessons of the last thirty years they represent the Russian government's determination to control an industry whose success has been due to freedom from government interference and intrusive regulation. That, additionally, these provisions are reinforced by the role of *Roskominform*, suggests that the Russian government puts its control of this area very high on its agenda, but that in order to achieve this control, some measure of success that might otherwise have been achieved without it, can be forgone.

THE LAW OF INFORMATION EXCHANGE

The Law of Information Exchange sets out the terms and conditions for the participation of the Russian Federation in what is called the 'international exchange of information', defined as 'the transfer and receipt of information products, as well as the rendering of information services across the state border of the Russian Federation' (Article 2 'Terms Used in the Present Federal Law and Their Definition, paragraph 11). The aim of the law is 'the creation of the conditions for Russia's effective participation in the international exchange of information within the framework of a single global information space' (Article 1 'The Aims and Sphere of Operation of the Present Federal Law', point 1).[34]

As with other similar legislation this law ascribes a powerful role to the government and its agencies in the provision of services and infrastructure. Again, one can note that while private investors are not excluded, their role is secondary when compared with that assumed by the state. A potentially controversial role for the state is defined in Article 4 ('The Obligations of the State in the Sphere of the Exchange of International Information'). The state, it is noted:

> [...] creates the conditions for the protection of the country's owners of documentary information, information resources, information products, of protecting the means of exchange of international information, of protecting the users from information of poor quality and that which is unreliable, as well as from unscrupulous competition on the part of physical or juridical persons of foreign states in the information sphere (paragraph 7).

While acknowledging the best intentions of the drafters, there is, it has to be said, a rather ominous echo in the state's intention to protect its entrepreneurs and citizens from the perils of accessing information in the international sphere. During the recent Soviet period the 'protection' of the supposed interests of the fraternal working class was the standard justification for sending in the tanks. In the post-Soviet period the presumption of such a right to police the intellectual life of Russian citizens is no less intrusive and no less disconcerting, even if presented in such an apparently benevolent form.[35] Apart from any objection to the presumption of the state to intrude in such a manner, there are likely to be grave difficulties of acceptable definition when dealing with terms such as 'poor quality' (*nekachestvennyy*), 'unreliable' (*nedostovernyy*) and 'unscrupulous' (*nedobrosovestnyy*), even more so when in international terms a consensual definition is likely to be remote. How, and by whom, are these definitions to be determined? They are far too vague and permit too wide a range of interpretation. As a result, these terms leave open the possibility of serious abuse by government officials. Protection from supposedly 'unscrupulous' competition has potentially serious economic consequences for the import of Western (overwhelmingly American) cultural products. Are they to be subject to import tariffs or other forms of discriminatory costs?

Article 8 ('Restrictions when Taking Part in the Exchange of International Information') imposes restrictions on certain categories of documentary information that can be exported, such as state secrets (as defined by the Secrecy Law), archive material and Russian national property. The merits of each separate case for export will be determined by the government (point 1, paragraph 3). That the owner of such information resources can appeal a government decision is small consolation for the violation of the basic right of the owner of private property to dispose of that property as he wishes. For example, one can envisage a situation in which valuable documentary information will be generated by a private Russian company, say in a collaborative venture with a foreign company or working alone, that then wished to sell the information to a foreign company, or that by virtue of contractual obligations had to share all information. The Russian government, having decided that it wishes to retain the benefits of this collaborative venture for the sole use of Russia, would, by invoking Article 8, be violating the law of contract and private-property rights. In collaborative research, the successful outcome of which could lead to significant technological gains, and would be very lucrative for the private partners, a potential foreign partner would need to consider the likelihood of Russian state intervention very carefully before embarking on any such project. One can say that the dangers of such projects not proceeding because of the justified fears on the part of foreign companies that intellectual property rights would be violated, which would lead to the loss of shared expertise and investment to Russia, would far outweigh the gains sought by the Russian state.

The provisions of the law designed to protect confidential information are only applicable to those physical and juridical persons, 'possessing a licence for work with confidential information and using certified means for the exchange of international information' (Article 9, 'The Use of the Means of International Information

Exchange', point 2). Given that 'protection' could easily be construed as 'control' some operators might decide to forgo the government's protection. The limited application suggests that the government will protect (however protection be defined and interpreted) only if it exercises total control.[36] The government seems to be using the licensing requirement, quite deliberately, as a means of limiting the independence of private operators. If accurate, then the limited application of Article 9 (point 2) violates the principle of equality before the law. For without the equal application of this principle to all physical and juridical persons, there can be no equality before the law. Equality before the law applies to all citizens, not some, and irrespective of their profession.

The dangers inherent in the vagueness of words, such as 'unreliable' are graphically illustrated in the provisions of Article 14 ('The Provision of Protection for Citizens, Juridical Persons in the Russian Federation and for the State from Unreliable, False, Foreign Documentary Information'). Article 14 represents a major threat to on-line free speech. The two points state:

1. The dissemination of unreliable, false [*lozhnyy*] foreign documentary information, received as a result of international exchange, on the territory of the Russian Federation is not permitted.
2. Responsibility for the dissemination of such information falls on the legal subject of the international information exchange, who has received such information and (or) disseminates it on the territory of the Russian Federation.

The dangers to free speech are two-fold. The first set arises from the failure to define 'false', or arguably, the impossibility to do so, in a way that takes into account the nature of the international electronic medium; the second set from the technical aspects of acquiring, storing and disseminating information when using the Internet.

By an unusual coincidence, six days after this law was adopted by the Russian State Duma, an American court in the Eastern District of Pennsylvania granted a preliminary injunction to the American Civil Liberties Union (ACLU) who had challenged the provisions of the American government's Communications Decency Act 1996 (CDA).[37] The nature of the challenge and the issues it raises are directly comparable to Article 14 of the Russian Law of Information Exchange.

The American government's aim was to limit the spread of material considered to be 'indecent' and 'patently offensive' (Section 502 of the CDA). Crucial to the success of the ACLU challenge were the lengthy evidentiary hearings. It was recognized in the introduction to the findings of fact that: '[the Internet] presents unique issues relating to the application of First Amendment jurisprudence and due process requirements to this new and evolving method of communication' (II, Findings of Fact).[38] Fundamental technical obstacles to the government's position emerged that convinced the judges that the benefits of the Internet far outweighed the negative sides.

The findings of fact made some important points about the nature of the medium that any government intending to limit or to control the medium cannot afford to ignore. First, the Internet does not exist as a concrete, physical structure. There is no vast empire of real estate scattered round the world controlling the network. Small networks of computers – local area networks (LANs) – are connected to other networks. The Internet is a network of networks. Multiple means of reaching the end destination for a message is one of the Internet's most important features. Messages can travel direct from sender to receiver or be re-routed through other computers. Packet switching makes it possible to send parts of a message via different routes. At the end of the transmission, whatever the routes involved, the packets are reassembled and the message is available to the receiver.

As was noted in the evidentiary hearings, the Internet challenges the statutory term 'content provider' which normally equates to 'speaker'. On the Internet, what in traditional terms will be one 'speaker', can be many. There are also obstacles to age verification on the Internet. Various procedures suggested for verification all have major cost implications for organizations or individuals on low budgets. Credit-card verification creates delays and thus bottlenecks. It undermines one of the virtues of the Internet: speed. Another suggestion would be to tag all material deemed offensive; that is it would be labelled according to its suitability. Tagging would however involve a huge burden, the larger the amount of information that had to be reviewed. Given that the Internet is a global phenomenon, a world-wide consensus would be required with regard to what is meant by the term 'indecent'. Caching also makes control of indecent material difficult if not impossible. By storing material that is frequently used caching reduces costs and saves time. Also, the provider has no control over the material that is cached and the provider has no control over secondary and multiple redistributions via access to caching.

In their ruling the judges noted the effects of the extra costs:

The CDA will, without doubt, undermine the substantive, speech-enhancing benefits that have flowed from the Internet. Barriers to entry of those speakers affected by the Act would skyrocket, especially for non-commercial and not-for-profit information providers.

The CDA would, it was argued, drive providers away fearful that they may be in breach of its rulings. Moreover, the provisions of the CDA would be overwhelmingly in favour of big corporations and commercial providers who could afford the costs of verification, tagging material and reviewing the material on line. Raising the costs of entry for small-scale information providers would necessarily limit the information available on the Internet and lead to a situation in which the big providers enjoyed a monopoly. Thus the CDA attacks free trade under the guise of protecting minors. As the court noted:

The CDA's wholesale disruption on the Internet will necessarily affect adult participation in the medium [...] Since much of the communication on the Internet is participatory, i.e., is a form of dialogue, a decrease in the number of speakers, speech fora, and permissible topics will diminish the worldwide dialogue that is the strength and signal achievement of the medium.

As for the crucial terms 'indecent' and 'patently offensive', it was noted in the Applicable Standard of Review:

The CDA is patently a government-imposed, content-based restriction on free speech, and the speech at issue, whether denominated 'indecent' or 'patently offensive', is entitled to constitutional protection.[39]

The dangers posed by the CDA to free speech in the American republic are not of academic interest to outsiders. They have a very real bearing on all global communications using the Internet. Given that the Internet is a truly global communications network, attempts undertaken in one country to limit the medium or to control the dissemination of information, data, ideas and just plain gossip are likely to have global repercussions.

One accepts that in framing this legislation the American government had set itself worthy aims, to wit, to prevent the spread of pornography and other offensive material via the Internet. It seems highly unlikely that this aim would have been achieved, and that a number of undesirable consequences for the protection of free speech in the US and its advance and consolidation abroad would have ensued. In many states, especially those emerging from long periods of communist rule, support for open and free speech is still not universal. In such countries freedom of speech faces challenges from resurgent communist/left-wing forces and extreme nationalists, not accustomed to the free exchange of opinion and ideas.[40] One suspects that these opponents of free speech would have welcomed the Act's becoming law in America, not out of any need to protect America's minors from pornography. Far from it. The CDA would have justified harsh domestic legislation to control the Internet and access to it. If America, the world's leading democracy can limit freedom of speech on the Internet in the interests of removing indecent or patently offensive speech (however defined), then, it could be argued, there would be nothing to stop far less tolerant political systems enacting similar laws under the pretext of protecting decency, cultural values and a whole raft of special information needs. As one of the judges noted: 'Any content-based regulation of the Internet, no matter how benign the purpose, could burn the global village to roast the pig.'

It can be seen then that Article 14 of the Russian Law of Information Exchange must create the very same problems identified in the challenge to the provisions of the CDA. The Russian Federation legal draughtsmen have demonstrated the same technical ignorance of the Internet that proved to be the undoing of the CDA. Equally, one can argue, the difficulties of definition and application of words such as 'false' (*lozhnyy*) and 'unreliable' (*nedostovernyy*) pose the same threat to domestic free speech as 'patently offensive' and 'indecent' do in the American context. Foreigners can be as 'unreliable' and 'false' as they wish. It is, however, the Russian Internet Service Providers who must run the risk of any criminal sanctions, which does nothing to develop the maximum possible Russian participation in the global information exchange.

A NEW CULTURAL IMPERIALISM?

During the Cold War cultural imperialism was a standard accusation made by the Soviet Union against the West in an attempt to limit the broadcasts of Western radio stations to the Soviet empire. As far as

Soviet propagandists were concerned, the 'free flow of information' was a mask for cultural imperialism. The free flow of information was dismissed as something being:

[...] not restricted by any judicial or political frameworks, of the dissemination of information-propaganda products of the leading capitalist press, radio and television concerns. Put forward by American ideologists and propagandists so as to justify the global expansion of the press monopolies of the USA in a spirit of open interference in the internal affairs of other states and the imposition of imperialist ideology and the 'Western way of life'.[41]

Had the Soviet Union succeeded in the 1970s (with the help of many African and Asian states) in limiting the broadcasts of the BBC, RFE/RL, VOA and Deutsche Welle, then the peoples of Central and Eastern Europe would have been even more isolated from the outside world than they were.[42] The 'voices', as they were known, were a highly successful and cost-effective way of breaching the communist monopoly of information.

With the influx of Western videos and the adoption of television-programming after 1991, accusations of cultural imperialism are once again being made. The target of the anti-cultural imperialists is invariably Hollywood, or indeed any of the conspicuously successful achievements of America in technology, sport or business. Accusations of 'cultural imperialism' are not really substantial intellectual arguments at all. They are manifestations of cultural envy, and even, a sense of cultural instability and inferiority.

There is no coercion to watch the latest offering from Hollywood. Presumably, adults intelligent enough to know that Hollywood is trying to enslave them with American low-brow films are also intelligent enough to decide to turn the television off. The fact that the offerings of Hollywood are universally available does not provide satisfactory empirical evidence in support of 'cultural imperialism'. What it does show – in the absence of any coercive mechanism – is that American cultural products are extremely popular: people watch them because they like them.

The amalgam of violence, intrigue and action – the staple diet of Hollywood's success – cannot be divorced from the wider economic and technological success of America generally. And here perhaps is a powerful reason for the national bodyguards of culture to insist that they must be protected from the likes of *Terminator* and *Robocop*. What these self-appointed guardians are trying to protect is a state-subsidized film industry that cannot compete with its American rival. Consequently, assessments such as the following, should be treated with caution: 'Wiring the consumer empire (or interconnecting it by satellite) increases the technology that can expand the allegiances of consumerism, akin to establishing the infrastructure for resource extraction in the colonies of old.'[43] Behind the supposedly neutral infrastructure that disseminates news and information we are really to understand that hideous new forms of slavery and exploitation are being prepared. Consumerism is about choice and choice involves making decisions. The makers of products and services can attempt to sell a product: they can also fail to sell a product. The decision is one to be made by the consumer. Those who believe that there is such a thing as cultural imperialism resent the choices that people make because these choices are inconsistent with their Utopian visions of how a society should be. The parallel with socialist realism is obvious. They persuade themselves that the consumer is 'exploited' by capitalists. 'Cultural imperialism' and 'electronic colonialism' are figments of an imagination obsessed with conspiracies. No electronic taskmaster drives the poor consumer-slave to the video-factory where he is compelled to watch the latest offering from Hollywood.

The success of the Internet has given accusations of cultural imperialism a new lease of life. Anatoly Voronov, the head of Glasnet, one of Russia's Internet Service Providers, has argued that the Internet/World Wide Web:

> [...] is the ultimate act of intellectual colonialism. The product comes from America so we must either adapt to English or stop using it. That is the right of any business. But if you are talking about a technology that is supposed to open the world to hundreds of millions of people you are joking. This just makes the world into new sorts of haves and have nots.[44]

The dominant use of English on the World Wide Web has nothing to do with any form of colonialism. Rather, it must be viewed as a user standard such as the Web itself or some of the more successful browsers and other user protocols. Successful cultures generate vast amounts of data, information and knowledge, some profound, some utterly trivial. This storehouse of knowledge and cultural exports can overwhelm the cultural space of other countries, but its status within the boundaries of another culture cannot be taken for granted. People take what they want, discarding the rest. The fact that they manifest a distinct liking for America's offerings, be they Watergate,

Hollywood or the Internet, suggests that domestic markets are failing to fulfil a need.

COMPUTER NETWORKS IN THE RUSSIAN FEDERATION

Russia's networks fall into two main categories: those that are primarily oriented towards scientific research and educational provision; and those that are commercial providers. A small group of networks, with overlapping tasks, do not fit neatly into either category. What follows is a brief summary of each network according to whether it is educational/scientific or commercial. An attempt will then be made to draw some general conclusions about their aims and status. It must be stressed that the survival rate of some of these networks in the economic conditions of the Russian Federation varies enormously. Thus any such survey is of an on-going process. All information concerning these networks is taken from their own W^3 sites.

EDUCATIONAL/SCIENTIFIC NETWORKS

FREENET (The Network for Research, Education and Engineering). Links Russian research institutes, universities and academies. FREENET was founded in July 1991 by the N. D. Zelinsky Institute of Organic Chemistry. FREENET provides basic Internet services and other information services to some 350 academic and educational institutions. It is funded by the Russian Foundation of Basic Research and the State Committee of Higher Education of the Russian Federation. FREENET's basic objectives are the following: (i) provision of open networking services; (ii) provision of reliable network connectivity to researchers; (iii) assistance to basic Russian-based research; (iv) assistance to the development of modern IT in education. FREENET and UNICOR (see below) represent Russia in the Central and East European Networking Association (CEENet). Based in Moscow, it has a branch based at the Technical University of Chelyabinsk.

GlasNet. The first non-profit, non-government telecommunications network in Russia. GlasNet aims to provide easy and inexpensive exchange of information between users in Russia. It has been operating in Moscow since March 1991 and is a Member of the Association of Progressive Communications (APC). See GreenNet in

England. Electronic version of *Nezavisimaya gazeta* available on GlasNet server. Based in Moscow.

IEMNETWORK (Institute of Experimental Mineralogy of Russian Academy of Sciences). Based in Chernogolovka.[45]

INFORIS Legal Database. Based in Nizhniy-Novgorod. By far the best legal database in the Russian Federation.

REDLINE (Russian Educational LINE/*Rossiyskaya obrazovatel'- naya liniya*. REDLINE was founded in June 1994 by the Russian Ministry of Education, The Central Committee of the Trade Union of Workers in Education and Science, *Uchitel'skaya gazeta* and the firm *Innotek*. Its main activity is the collection, analysis and processing of information relating to education, as well as the setting up of data bases. REDLINE lists other organizations similarly engaged, currently 72. It also provides e-mail service at low cost of entry. An important task is the setting up of the data base known as *Vse Obrazovanie* that will embrace all spheres of education in all the legal subjects of the Russian Federation. The project is funded by the American Agency for International Development and the Eurasian Foundation. Based in Moscow.

RELARN (Russian Electronic Academic & Research Network). Initiated by the Russian Ministry of Defence, Russian Academy of Sciences and the Kurchatov Institute. RELARN was founded by an agreement concluded on 20 March 1993. Registered as a juridical person 24 May 1993. An association of scientific and teaching organizations. RELARN was founded by the following organizations: the Russian Scientific Centre; the Steklov Mathematical Institute; Institute of Space Research; the Lebedev Institute of Physics; the Central Economic-Mathematical Institute; the Scientific-Research Institute of Nuclear Physics MSU; the Russian Scientific-Research for the Development of Societal Networks; and the Institute of Theoretical and Experimental Physics. The main aims of RELARN are: (i) to increase the effectiveness of scientific-research work; (ii) to inculcate new forms of education (iii) to carry out special-purpose programmes; (iv) to widen contacts with foreign scholars and scientific centres by provision of an optimal medium of information exchange.[46] RELARN is based in Moscow and St Petersburg.[47]

RELCOM. Created in 1990. Started out as a small communications network intended for scientists at the Kurchatov Institute of Atomic Energy. August 1990 linked up with Eunet (European Network). Four dedicated lines in Moscow. Internet Service Provider, e-mail and commercial information. Based in Moscow.

RIPN (Russian Institute for Public Networks). Founded in 1992 by the Russian Committee of Higher Education and Kurchatov Institute. Main aims are: (i) to develop computer communications in the interest of research; (ii) to coordinate networking in Russia; (iii) to promote research studies in the field of computer communications; (iv) to support organizations in gaining access to information resources via public networks.

RUNNet. Russian Federal University Networking Project RUNNet started in March 1994. Implemented under the programme 'Universities of Russia'. Aims to create information space for participation by Russian universities in domestic and international information exchange. Federal nodes located in the main university centres. Core federal nodes located in St Petersburg and Moscow.

UNICOR (University Networks of Knowledge). Established 1992 by the Russian State Committee on Higher Education. Main aims are: (i) the development of a university network infrastructure; (ii) development of data bases and information resources.

COMMERCIAL PROVIDERS

AOOT 'SVYAZINFORM' (*Aktsionernoe obshchestvo otkrytogo tipa*). Approximately 39 per cent state-owned (11.4 per cent foreign). Aims to provide high-quality domestic intercity and international telephone communications, radio and television broadcasting. Based in Chelyabinsk.

DEMOS (Dialogue Unified Mobile Operating System). Founded in February 1989 as software and network company. Initially based on mainframes. Founder of the RELCOM network. Close links with the Russian government and other state institutions intimated. Based in Moscow.

DUX Joint Stock Company. Founded May 1994. Internet provider with Internet-café. Development of software for networks. Commercial information for subscribers. Based in St Petersburg.

ELVIS+ (Electronic Computer and Information Systems/ *Elektronnye Vychislitel'nye i Informatsionnye Sistemy*) founded in November 1991, in Zelenograd. Company works with Sun Microsystems, Inc. Main research area is the design of key elements for wireless computing networks. Most of the staff recruited from the space industry and military-industrial complex. Internet Service Provider. Strong links with American-based companies such as Sun

Microsystems, SunSoft, FirstPerson, Cylink Inc, Federal Systems Group and Motorola. ELVIS+ seeks partnerships with foreign companies wishing to enter the Russian market. ELVIS+ used to advertise partners' products and services. Based in Moscow.

GARANT. Legal database resource for both foreign and domestic clients. No other information available. Based in Moscow.

INTERCOM. Founded in May 1994. Based in Saratov. Formerly known as The International Centre of Business Information (*Tsentr Mezhdunarodnoy Delovoy Informatsii*). In January 1995 the network was serving 55 subscribers. By mid-March 150 subscribers. Became an ISP in May 1995. November 1995 completion of dedicated line from Saratov to Ul'yanovsk. By January 1996 the number of subscribers had risen to 240. 1 February 1996 INTERCOM concluded deal with the Oreanda agency to provide financial information to subscribers. Real-time, world-wide access possible.

RosNet. Commercial telecommunications network. Founded October 1993. Based in Moscow.

SUMMARY OF NETWORKS AND PROBLEMS

The vast majority of the networks are based in the large urban centres. In descending order of concentration they are: Moscow; St Petersburg; Ekaterinburg; Novosibirsk; Nizhnyy-Novgorod; and Pereslavl-Zalessky. The academic networks show a great deal of overlap and many seem to be competing with one another. From the information provided it is not clear what advantages are gained from the existence of RUNNet, RELARN and say, UNICOR, especially when money and expertise are scarce. RELARN has by far the largest presence on the Internet. It provides the full text of its charter, details of various meetings, data of use and costs as well as bibliographies and the full texts of conferences. Commercial providers offer the full range of Internet services (electronic mail and access to the World Wide Web), as well as share-dealing services and on-line databases access to which is governed by subscription.

Despite the overwhelming urban concentration computer nodes are distributed throughout the Russian Federation and what one might call the index of interconnectivity continues to grow. The concentration, outside the commercial providers, of Internet resources in the universities is not just the recognition that universities and scientific institutions are natural participants in the global exchange of ideas and information, but also that in all major cities universities are major cultural and societal institutions in their own right.[48] As such they are the ideal base for developing local information infrastructure bases.

Many of these projects are designed to promote the growth of distance learning in the former Soviet Union (FSU), especially RELARN (Russian Electronic Academic and Research Network) and some observers see this as one way to convert Russia's huge military-industrial complex to non-military aims.[49] The World Bank's stance, for example, is that this conversion programme can succeed. The main thesis seems to be that 'in union there is strength'; that a collaborative venture is likely to be more successful and less expensive.[50] It is not clear whether this is a general business strategy or one that has been developed by the World Bank in response to specific conditions in Russia and Eastern Europe. For if Russia possesses 'ample technological resources' [...] 'to build a technologically advanced distance education system',[51] why does Russia need to cooperate with other states? If Russia can shoulder the burden of research and development alone, then it makes no sense to share the burden with the former, fraternal, socialist states, who are now competitors in a world market. The benefits of any breakthrough would then accrue to Russia which could use this infra-structure to gain a dominant position in the market place throughout Central and Eastern Europe. There are, moreover, considerable political benefits accruing from market dominance. Whether such Russian dominance will be realized is by no means a foregone conclusion. Nevertheless, the history of the region would suggest caution for the smaller states before entering into any binding financial and political commitments with Russia.

While it is the case that the network infrastructure does lend itself to 'be used first and foremost to produce educational services for domestic markets',[52] it is also the case that the infrastructure can be used for other purposes, especially if they confer advantages in the military sector. Let us hope that the massive, Russian military-industrial complex can be restructured towards more peaceful aims, but this is far from a foregone conclusion. One of the key lessons of the 1991 Gulf War was that heavy investment in IT can pay handsome dividends on the battlefield. The same infrastructure for distance learning can deliver a massive boost to the military-industrial complex. The present Internet was after all the product of the need to share information among scientists and contractors involved in defence-related research. Military products can be a major earner of hard currency. There would be no shortage of buyers for high-tech, STEALTH weaponry. Also, as advanced economies and post-industrialized societies come to rely ever more on their information infrastructure, so the utility to an opponent of attacking that infrastructure increases. Strategic information warfare (SIW) in which states seek to disrupt and to destroy the information resources of their opponents marks a new stage in warfare. Banking, financial services, telephone networks, policing and public administration – the vital infrastructure of capitalist Western societies in other words – all rely on the transfer of large amounts of raw data and information and are prime targets.[53] It would be an irony indeed, if Western support resulted in a strengthening of the Russian military-industrial complex when the declared aim is to diversify into other areas.

Much has been said about the growth of the knowledge-based economy, but what about the social consequences for a country such as Russia where grossly inefficient state industries have been protected and pampered for 70 years? The consequences of shifting from the heavy industries have been severe enough in the West. Given the lack of any private enterprise and the skills associated with such activity in the East, the problems of switching to a knowledge-based economy are much more widespread, more severe and prolonged in the former Soviet Union than in the West.

This does not automatically mean that Russia is liable to be relegated to permanent second-best as the West and America surge ahead. As in the countries of the European Union, there is a need to reconcile two different approaches towards IT (individual/corporatist). The legislative and administrative thrust of the Russian Federation supports the view that the favoured approach is one of control, even at the loss of some gains in productivity. Fears of deregulated chaos and supposed market anarchy are real, and there is a perception (rightly or wrongly) that Russia is vulnerable to electronic exploitation and that this must not be allowed to happen.

Of significance for the planned links of Russian universities, as envisaged in RUNnet, is the fact that: 'core federal nodes located in Saint Petersburg and Moscow are key parts of the backbone, and almost all backbone administration and channel control will take place at these nodes'.[54] Will all roads on the Information Super-Highway lead to Moscow? It raises serious questions of control which have yet to be resolved. Some are technical and financial: who will be responsible for the maintenance of the networks, especially those that are wire-based? And can private networks finance themselves?

Assuming that these non-political factors can be resolved and that the attempts of hostile politicians to exploit them can be blunted, then excessive regulation will fail on two counts. Firstly, it will not work. It is almost impossible to control an information environment such as the Internet and the many databases and online information services that are available without a massive and costly effort on the part of government agencies, and of course without running the risk that the advantages offered by the Internet will be negated. Private encryption facilities will only serve to increase the problems of government surveillance. A striking and little known feature of Soviet-style censorship was the cost. The equivalent of many millions of US dollars was spent on jamming the BBC and VOA. Worst of all, it did not work. The Russian government has neither the money nor the time to repeat such costly failures. Nor can it afford to incur the opprobrium attached to such activities. Moreover, there is something about electronic data that resists caging. It is exceptionally adept at seeping through apparently closed systems. To quote Gordon Cook: 'The network has a built in immune system that acts to destroy secrecy and thwart the plans of anyone who would develop policies of network operation and expansion in secret.'[55]

Secondly, the net gains of attempting to control flows of information that can be done in the short term are far outweighed by the losses. This is the one crucial lesson of Soviet-style censorship. Norbert Wiener's understanding of the problem expressed nearly fifty years ago proved entirely accurate: '[...] no amount of scientific research, [...] will be adequate to protect us for any length of time in a world where the effective level of information is perpetually advancing. There is no Maginot Line of the brain.'[56] Such an approach failed the Soviet system, and it is difficult to see how it might work in the information environment of the 1990s and early twenty-first century. State control would merely provide opportunities for a new type of hero, the Internet commando, to attack the government's electronic redoubt from the vastness of cyberia.

To date the picture of IT in Russia and elsewhere throughout Eastern Europe might suggest a comparison with David and Goliath. There seems little doubt that in the short term the advantages have all been with individual users and groups with no affiliation to the government. The 1991 coup demonstrated that the coup leaders had outdated ideas about the nature of communication. As a result they were wrong-footed from the very beginning. One thing is certain, those who might be tempted to follow the same road will have learned the lessons afforded by August 1991. Control of television and radio will not be enough. So is there, then, an automatic presumption in favour of IT as the defender – and in the FSU's case – the trail-blazer of the open society? By and large the answer is yes, but with some qualification. The more the FSU can be integrated into the world information exchange, the more difficult it will be for any government to restrict the flow of information, since wealth creation and the free flow of information are inextricably linked. The main dangers are likely to be social-political, arising from the fact that huge numbers of Russians are not going to have their expectations of a higher standard of living realized for many years to come. As a result, the risk of Weimar instability that nourishes political extremism will persist. The creation of a two-tier society in Russia – those who use IT and benefit from it, and those who do not – is something that has to be taken seriously. It is probably unavoidable. Education will exercise only a limited influence in ameliorating this problem, since access is in large part a question of interest, and this tends to be self-selecting. Outside the commercial and academic networks, the penetration of the PC in Russian society is low. An information society requires widespread ownership, or access to the rudiments of IT, access to the necessary data and information from private and public sources. A question to consider is whether the infrastructure and practice of distance learning will strengthen regional identities and undermine the political viability of the Russian Federation. Furthermore, it is likely that the university's traditional allegiance to a geographical area will be weakened in a global market of educational services, given that universities aspire to become global players.

Notwithstanding all these difficulties, new services and products and ever more configurations of IT are being created. Vast amounts of raw intellectual and entrepreneurial energy have been unleashed, and the changes that have already occurred are breathtaking. The very unpredictability of Russia's IT future is exciting. If levels of bureaucratic interference and control can be reduced, or contained, Russia could so easily become an information superpower in the twenty-first century.

6 Concluding Remarks

> Enthusiasm over the way the media were used to overthrow totalitarian regimes in Eastern Europe should not blind citizens to the more sophisticated mind manipulations that governments and politicians will attempt in the future
>
> Alvin Toffler

In one of the many dialogues that made Vasily Grossman's *Life and Fate* an outright and damning rejection of everything Soviet, a group of Russian scientists discuss the state of the world. As they talk, the great life-and-death struggle between Soviet and Nazi troops at Stalingrad is reaching its climax. One of their number makes an eloquent and moving plea for a free press:

> Ah, dear comrades, said Mad'yarov suddenly, can you imagine what it would be like to have a free press? Well, one fine morning after the war you open a newspaper and instead of some frenzied leading article, instead of a worker's letter to the great Stalin, [...] and instead of reports about workers in the United States who in the New Year find themselves in a state of despair, rising unemployment and poverty, you find in the newspaper, do you know what? Information! Can you imagine such a newspaper? A newspaper which provides information!
>
> And you read: there's been a poor harvest in the Kursk district, there's an inspector's report about conditions in the Butyrskiy prison, an argument about whether the White Sea–Baltic canal is really necessary, you read that a certain worker, Golopuzov, has spoken out against the issue of a new loan.
>
> In general you read everything that is happening in the country: good and bad harvests, enthusiasm, thefts and burglaries, the opening of a mine and a disaster in another, a disagreement between Molotov and Malenkov, you read accounts of the course of a strike caused by a factory head who insulted a seventy-year old chemist, you read the speeches of Churchill and Blum, and not what they 'allegedly said', you read through an account of debates in the House of Commons, you find out how many people committed suicide in Moscow yesterday, [...] You know why there is no

buckwheat, and not only that the first batch of strawberries has been flown in from Tashkent to Moscow. [...] Yes, yes and through all this you remain a Soviet citizen.

You go into a book shop and buy a book while remaining a Soviet citizen, you read American, English, French philosophers, historians, economists, political observers. You yourself work out where they are not right, You yourself walk the streets without any nanny.[1]

Such thoughts were the stuff of utter, unforgivable heresy. Worse still, Grossman had no doubts about the fundamentally identical nature of Soviet and Nazi totalitarianism; and said so. In 1961, after he had submitted the manuscript of *Life and Fate* to a leading Soviet journal for publication, it was arrested by the KGB. In a subsequent meeting with the party's chief ideologist, Mikhail Suslov, in a forlorn attempt to regain the manuscript, Grossman was told that publication might be possible in another 250–300 years. As it turned out, *Life and Fate* was published in 1988, the high point of *glasnost'*. In 1991, thirty years after *Life and Fate* was 'arrested', the Soviet Union itself collapsed, undermined, among other things, by its own irreconcilable social, economic and intellectual contradictions. History provides plenty of examples of empires that have collapsed as a result of conquest. One of the two superpowers, the Soviet Union imploded. No other empire has ended this way.

We must turn to Lenin for the blueprint of what followed after 1917, and which survived until the Great August Liberation of 1991. Lenin's deep-rooted hostility to the free flow of information, the approval and use of terror, the frenzied propaganda and agitation, and the new language of class war and hatred, were his unique contributions to the socio-political genre of utopia.

The Marxist-Leninist experiment totally redefined the meaning and scope of 'ideology'. After Lenin ideology – in its Marxist-Leninist variant – was the Final Solution to All Questions for All Time: it is the standard according to which all claims or accusations of ideological thinking and behaviour must be measured. Armed with such an all-powerful answering machine, the party ideologue never had to pause to question his or the party's actions.

Censorship follows ineluctably and paradoxically from such certainty: ineluctably, because once the certainties of ideological exegesis are accepted and are then transmitted as givens of the universal, class condition, all competing ideas can be excluded since they are deemed to be ideologically superfluous; paradoxically, because, despite the scientific pretensions of ideology and the asserted demonstration of irrefutable truths, it is unable to rely on the force of argument alone. Force of a different kind is necessary to uphold it. Ideology and censorship reinforce one another. Without them there can be no totalitarian state.

With regard to the study of the Soviet Union the record of Western social-science disciplines has not been good, to put it mildly. One of the more egregious and damaging errors has been the weakening of the rigour with which ideology is defined, and in so doing, to make it possible to use the concept of ideology as a synonym of doctrine or dogma, or any set of political and economic principles. As a result, all politics is ideology and Marxism-Leninism, it is argued, is just another ideology, no better or no worse than capitalism. Naturally, such inclusiveness does not apply to National Socialism (almost always incorrectly referred to as Fascism) for which special damnation is reserved.

When the media of all states and political systems are lumped together as if they are the same, as if it is a question of degree rather than of unbridgeable differences, then the evidence of our experience is violated, and in the case of the Soviet Union a mass of evidence to the contrary is ignored. The presumption that all systems are more or less the same is the worst kind of question-begging. It leads not to clarity but to an intellectual dead end since differences that should be exposed for all to see are either hidden or blurred. As if to complete the academic rout of Western social scientists (or many of them), concepts and words such as a 'free press', 'objectivity', 'rule of law', 'democracy', 'totalitarian', 'impartiality', 'public opinion' and the 'free flow of information', that throughout a large part of the Cold War period were routinely reviled and sniped at by Western Sovietologists, (and even now are mocked by a politically-correct logocracy), have been wholeheartedly embraced by those who know what 'real-existing socialism' was all about, and enshrined in countless legislative acts.

The contradictions that eventually destroyed the Soviet empire, ensued from a profound failure on the part of Soviet ideologues and leaders: the belief that the human condition was a planned condition, one to be brought to certain ends by whatever means. Planning and the ceaseless issuing of directives excluded the articulation of all differences of opinion. A system of censorship, at first justified as a temporary measure, became a permanent feature of Soviet life, evolving into a bureaucratic monster. Dissent was equated with treachery and ruthlessly persecuted. To repeat Turchin's point: 'The struggle among ideas gives way to the struggle against ideas by means of physical force. From the viewpoint of evolutionary theory, totalitarianism is a malformation, a degeneration, since a lower level of organisation is distorting and suppressing a higher one. A totalitarian society loses the capacity to develop normally, and becomes ossified.'[2]

Soviet censorship failed: it failed on its own terms, that is if the information and ideas reaching people are controlled, specific results will ensue; and it failed in absolute terms since it effectively stifled the intellectual and economic climate necessary for the growth in prosperity, without which the common ownership of the means of production and the incubus of Marxism-Leninism served no purpose other than to maintain a party élite's grip on power. The catastrophic failure of Soviet information policy – prior censorship, mass terror, exile and cultural purges – reveals the dysfunctional nature of Soviet-style omnicensorship. Equally, it reveals some fundamental and universal relationships between prosperity, freedom and the human need to know, and to dispose of information.

First, an open society, that is one that permits the dissemination of ideas and information inside and across its borders, will attract the attention of people in less open or closed societies. People who live in conditions of information-deprivation, such as those that obtained in the former Soviet Union, will make extraordinary efforts to reduce this deprivation. As a plant will grow towards a distant source of light, however faint, if artificially kept in near darkness, so thinking, willing human beings will strive towards information. One might say that they demonstrate positive infotropism. Second, where the state fails to meet the information needs of people (or some of them) because the state believes that access to information has to be controlled, then individuals will make efforts to fill this vacuum. It was this private-information initiative that gave rise to *samizdat*. Third, there is a demonstrable relationship between intellectual freedom and economic prosperity. Fourth, which follows on from this, Soviet-style censorship exerts its most destructive effects on scientific and intellectual endeavour. Fifth, a society that proscribes the dissemination of *Playboy* does not preclude the possibility of its being economically prosperous. In other words, it is the nature of the censorship that is significant. A clear difference between an authoritarian and a totalitarian state emerges. Sixth, the extent, depth, severity and duration of censorship are the predictors of systemic corruption, and ultimate collapse.

The positive correlation between the dissemination of information technologies and economic prosperity should not obscure the fact that it is the *quality* of use rather than the sheer size of a population using, say electronic mail, that is decisive. The dangers from proscribing IT will only arise when academic, business, scientific circles are denied access to them, since these are the driving forces of wealth creation. This is the lesson to be drawn from the massive, Soviet-censorship apparatus. Communication does not have to be equally available to be effective. Beyond a certain level, the convenience of electronic inter-connectivity, that is, the speed, ease and comfort with which people can communicate may actually reduce the quality of communication itself. Access to instant, or near-instant communication does not necessarily lead to better government. In serious and complicated questions, where delay and time for reflection confer definite advan-tages, policy-makers and government officials will be under pressure to react too quickly. This is the debasement of democratic discourse, not its enrichment. As the Internet grows so the problem of informa-tion overload will increase. Hierarchies of usefulness and value will have to be established.

The history of communications and the media is overwhelmingly the history of commercial progress made possible by the private ownership of the means of production (capitalism). The opening act in the fierce competition of approaches towards the flow of information and news, whose dénouement was marked by *perestroyka* and *glasnost'*, began in nineteenth-century London.

London's financial and commercial pre-eminence in the latter half of the nineteenth century grew from Britain's espousal of a free-trade doctrine. Economic liberalism stimulated and encouraged inquisi-tiveness, rewarded the risk takers and created a stable environment for investment. Investment decisions depend on accurate news and information. War, political uncertainty and weather affect markets and government policies. With the advent of telegraph, Morse code and telephony, the speed with which this information was provided also became an important factor. Free trade was impossible without the free, accurate and timely flow of information. Reuters was an agency waiting to be founded. Julius Reuter seized the opportunity.

Another German came to Britain in the nineteenth century but with very different ideas about industrial and economic activity. Karl Marx's self-appointed task was to study the world's leading capitalist economy. He challenged the notion of 'free' trade, arguing that all wealth was created by labour. Only by placing all the means of production into public ownership, asserted Marx, would it be possible to eradicate the inequalities of wealth and opportunity generated by capitalist societies.

Public ownership of the means of production has severe implications for an independent news agency. First and foremost, it destroys the market necessary for survival. But it goes beyond intolerance of unregulated business activity or private ownership of material resources. The success of a news agency is determined by its ability to sell accurate news and information to buyers. Denied an outlet through the destruction of the domestic market, the agency could theoretically sell news to an international market. Conflict will arise between ideology and private reporting. Since there is no separation of ideology from state, and since the ideology purports to be the only accurate statement of the world, its ills, problems and solutions, then the private dispenser of information cannot expect the same tolerance as would be accorded the purveyor of ideologically-correct news.

Business also requires good communication facilities. The innovations and inventions of Reuter, Morse, Bell, Marconi, Bain, Shannon, Wiener, and more recently Murdoch, Turner, Berlusconi, Gates, Jobs, Shockley, Clarke, and many more besides, have created the infrastructure that has made capitalism so conspicuously successful when compared with all other economic systems. Communication products and services are themselves the basis of lucrative industries stimulating ever more research and development. In a society where communication only flows vertically downwards there is no need for such goods and services. As has been suggested, this was one reason that precluded the Soviet Union's matching Western computer and software industries.

As the West's infosphere became ever more open and more liberal, so the Soviet Union's became more closed. Consider the following comparisons. 1934, the year in which socialist realism was declared to be the only permissible doctrine of artistic method in the Soviet Union, was also the year in which the United States government introduced the Communications Act with the aim of placing cheap and reliable communications at the disposal of American citizens. Or consider the fate of the Soviet writers Pasternak, Sinyavsky and Daniel whose crime in the eyes of the party was that they had sent manuscripts abroad to be published. And what of 1974, the year of Watergate in which an American president was forced from office and humiliated as a result of serious improprieties uncovered by two journalists on the *Washington Post*? The Watergate experience, for all the damage it undoubtedly did to the office of president, demonstrated the basic strength of American democracy. It demonstrated that the President of the United States was not above the law. No Soviet leader ever needed to worry about such niceties. Nor need he lose sleep about any unsavoury truths that the comrades on *Pravda* might discover, let alone publish. These points were lost in the welter of gloating and 'liberal' triumphalism over Nixon's fall. Indeed, in the same year as America's media turned on the president, Brezhnev *et al.* ordered the expulsion of Solzhenitsyn. Such bizarre and frequently grotesque contrasts between the West and the Soviet Union destroy any suggestion of convergence. Any comparative study of the two systems that failed to highlight these contrasts would be failing on an intellectual and on a moral level.

Russian citizens now have the information of which Grossman's characters dreamed: they are allowed out onto the street without their ideological keepers. So whither do they go? What do they do? They like Mexican soap operas, Western science fiction, a fair bit of pornography, astrology, game shows, sensational reporting (especially with hefty doses of sex and violence), and the dating columns are packed with lonely hearts. In short, Russian citizens who, we were reliably informed for so long, were loftily indifferent to the offerings of Western-style tabloid journalism, have shown a remarkable capacity for trivia and other media-comestibles. This is not such a bad thing. It confirms that the basic humanity with all its vices and rough decency somehow survived the communist ideological battering ram. Perhaps in the years to come research will reveal the psychological mechanisms that made it possible to survive this onslaught.

Russian journalists are slowly and surely habituating themselves to working in an arena of rights and responsibilities in which juridical persons can be held accountable for breaches of the law. If, to the Western eye Russian media legislation and the judicial process smacks of the American Wild West, then this is not entirely unexpected. The rule of law, the importance of contract and civic self-discipline do not come ready-made. Such a moral and legal infrastructure and its capitalist concomitant take time to develop. Real-existing socialism totally destroyed civil society. One of its most damaging and deadly legacies is the level of crime. In the aftermath of the Great August Liberation Russians are having to learn and to apply what is taken for granted in the West.

This process owes much to Western organizations and individuals, for example, the Eurasian Foundation, the BBC, the Reuter Foundation, The Open Society Institute, The United States Information Agency, The European Union, to name but a few. Alongside these Western influences Russian organizations have sprung up. Some, such as the Glasnost Defence Foundation, have already made their mark, having served notice on the Russian government that media legislation and its enactment will be closely watched and commented on. The Glasnost Defence Foundation's monitoring of the Chechen war and the widespread coverage given to abuses and non-compliance on the part of the Russian federal government were of the greatest importance. It embarrassed the government and kept the abuses in the public eye both inside and outside Russia.

Soviet-style censorship was crude, easy to expose and destructive of the system that employed it. The opportunities and advantages of the digital age are, however, not the exclusive property of private individuals and non-government organizations. The very volatility of the electronic medium makes the Orwellian manipulation of information much easier to carry out, though if a fictional paradigm for the future be required, then it is most likely to be found in the work of Philip K. Dick rather than that of George Orwell. Censorship and the means to combat it are now moving into a new age. For example, the seemingly bland term 'informatization' can cover a multitude of sins. As a result, the role of private organizations is as important as ever. The government harvest of information needs to be watched, justified and controlled, and in this respect it should be noted that freedom-of-information legislation and press services are not necessarily designed with the information requirements of the citizenry in mind.

The technology, ideas and opportunities of what is known as the information society have brought about enormous changes to political structures, the process of wealth creation and the dissemination of knowledge. Long-standing and cherished notions of social and economic equity are now the subject of vigorous reappraisal. In short, the very foundations, on which a civil society is based, are being subjected to simultaneous transformation, or subversion, depending on whether one regards information technology (IT) as something pernicious. Changes of this magnitude benefit individuals and groups of people in different ways: there will be both winners and losers. IT-driven change poses a double challenge to Russia, for it comes at a time when the physical and intellectual detritus of Marxism-Leninism is still being cleared.

Problems of a technical nature dominate much of the discussion about the information society: the provision of sufficient bandwidth, financial backing, telecommunications infrastructure, establishing standards and so on. These are exceptionally important, but we should not lose sight of the fact that among the many legal and competitive battles currently being fought over standards, software, hardware and regulation/deregulation, there are also contesting visions and interpretations of the information society itself. Arguments in the US, for example, over the merits of the *Communications Decency Act* (1996) and proposals put forward by President Clinton in *A Framework for Global Electronic Commerce* (1997) are part and parcel of this attempt to shape the contours of the global information society.

For Russia, even more so than for the West, one of the most pressing problems is whether the information society will be an exclusive or inclusive phenomenon. Both possibilities are of absolute relevance for Russia's nascent information society, since the consequences have a direct bearing on those laying the foundations of the information society in Russia.

Russia has a much more serious problem with official attitudes towards IT and their obstructionism, than in other countries. IT is not an official-friendly technology. IT bypasses the traditional role of the bureaucrat and government official as the mediator of access to data and information. Officials fear the loss of control, and while they can retard the pace of change, they cannot stop it. Global pressures will be too powerful and the exigencies of economic survival and reform will for the foreseeable future outweigh the imperatives of bureaucratic privilege and vested interest – perhaps.

Appendix

The Law of the Russian Federation Concerning the Mass Media

CHAPTER I. GENERAL CONDITIONS

Article 1. The Freedom of Mass Information

The search, receipt, production and dissemination of mass information, the founding of mass media, the ownership, use and disposal thereof, the manufacture, acquisition, preservation and exploitation of technical facilities and equipment, the raw material and material designated for the production and dissemination of the produce of the mass media are, in the Russian Federation, not subject to restrictions, other than to those for which provision is made by the legislation of the Russian Federation concerning the mass media.

Article 2. The Mass Media. Basic Concepts

For the purposes of the present Law:
  mass information is understood to be printed, audio, audio-visual and other reports and materials intended for an unlimited number of persons;
  a mass medium is understood to be a periodical, printed publication, radio, television and video programmes, cinematic and other forms of periodical dissemination of mass information;
  a periodical, printed publication is understood to be a paper, journal, almanac, bulletin or other publication having a fixed title, a current issue and appearing not less than once a year;
  a radio-, tele-, video-, and cinematic programme is understood to be the entire sum of periodical, audio, audio-visual reports and materials (transmissions), having a permanent title and being published (broadcast) not less than once a year;
  a product of the mass media is understood to be the circulation, or part thereof, of a single issue of a periodical, printed publication, a single broadcast of a radio-, tele-, cinematic programme, the circula-

tion, or part thereof, of an audio-programme, or a programme recorded on a videotape;

dissemination of a product of the mass media is understood to be the sale (subscription, delivery, distribution) of periodical printed publications, audio- or video-recorded programmes, the transmission of radio and television programmes (broadcast), or the public showing of cinematic programmes;

a specialized medium of mass information is understood to be such a medium of mass information for which special rules have been established by the present Law for the registration or dissemination of a product;

the editorial staff of a medium of mass information is understood to be the organization, the founders, enterprise or citizen, group of citizens, carrying out the production and broadcast of the medium of mass information;

a journalist is understood to be a person occupied with the editing, creation, collection or preparation of reports and materials for the editorial staff of a registered medium of mass information, and the work and contractual relations linked to the editorial staff, or a person occupied with such activities under the editorial staff's authority;

a publisher is understood to be the publishing house, other institution, enterprise (entrepreneur), carrying out the material-technical provision of the manufacture of a product of a medium of mass information and, additionally, any juridical person or citizen on the same footing in relation to the publisher for whom this activity is not their main one, nor serves as the main source of income;

a distributor is understood to be a person who distributes a product of a medium of mass information in accordance with an agreement with the editorial staff or publisher, or on other legal bases.

Article 3. The Inadmissibility of Censorship

The censorship of mass information, that is, the demand made on the editorial staff of a medium of mass information on the part of official persons, state organs, organizations, institutions or societal bodies to submit reports and materials for advance approval (apart from cases when the official person is the author or interviewee), as well as the imposition of a ban on the dissemination of reports and materials, or separate parts thereof, is not permitted.

The creation and financing of organizations, institutions, of organs or persons whose tasks include the carrying out of censorship of mass information is not permitted.

Article 4. The Inadmissibility of the Abuse of the Freedom of Mass Information

The use of the mass media for the purposes of commissioning criminally punishable acts, for the publicizing of information that comprises state secrets, or other secrets specially protected by law, for an incitement to seize power, for the violent change of the constitutional structure and the integrity of the state, the inflaming of national, class, social, religious intolerance or dissension, for the propaganda of war, and additionally, for the dissemination of broadcasts propagandizing pornography, a cult of violence and cruelty, is not permitted.

The use in tele-, video-, cinematic programmes, documentary and artistic films, and additionally, in information computer files and software for the processing of information files, relating to specialist mass media, of subliminal messages acting exclusively on people's subconscious and (or) having a harmful effect on their health, is forbidden.

Article 5. Legislation Concerning the Mass Media

The Legislation of the Russian Federation concerning the mass media consists of the present Law and other legislative acts and legislation concerning the mass media of the republics of the Russian Federation that are published in connection with it.

If as a result of an intergovernment treaty concluded by the Russian Federation rules are envisaged for the organization and activity of the mass media other than those established by the present Law, then the rules of the intergovernment treaty are to apply.

Article 6. The Application of the Law

The present Law is applicable in relation to the mass media founded in the Russian Federation and for those mass media created beyond its borders, only in that part, which touches the dissemination of their product in the Russian Federation.

Judicial persons and citizens of other states, persons without citizenship, enjoy the rights and bear the obligations envisaged by the present Law on an equal footing with organizations and citizens of the Russian Federation, if provision is not otherwise formulated by the law.

CHAPTER II. THE ORGANIZATION OF THE ACTIVITY OF THE MASS MEDIA

Article 7. The Founder

A citizen, a group of citizens, an enterprise, an institution or organization or state organ can be the founder (co-founder) of a medium of mass information.

A citizen who has not attained the eighteenth year or who is serving a punishment in places involving the deprivation of freedom on the decision of a court or an individual who is mentally ill and has been recognized by a court as being incapable;

a group of citizens, an enterprise, institution or organization whose activity has been banned by law;

a citizen of another state, or one without citizenship who does not reside permanently in the Russian Federation, cannot be a founder.

Co-founders act jointly in their capacity as founder.

Article 8. Registration of a Medium of Mass Information

The editorial staff of a medium of mass information carries out its activity after its registration.

Application for registration of a medium of mass information the product of which is designed chiefly for dissemination:

in all the territory of the Russian Federation, beyond its borders, in the territory of several of the republics of the Russian Federation, in several of its regions and districts – is to be submitted by its founder to the Ministry of Press and Information of the Russian Federation;

in the territory of a republic of the Russian Federation, of a region, district, zone, city, other populated area or micro-region – is to be submitted by the founder to the corresponding territorial organs of the State Inspection for the Protection of the Freedom of Press and Mass Information attached to the Ministry of Press and Information of the Russian Federation.

The founder or person acting on his authority is to be sent (or to be given) notification of the receipt of his application with an indication of the date of arrival. The application for registration is subject to an examination by the registering organ in one month from the indicated date.

The medium of mass information is considered to be registered from the day of issue of the certificate of registration.

The founder maintains the right to start production of the product of the medium of mass information during the first year from the day of dispatch of the certification of registration. In the event that the period of a year passes, the certification of a medium of mass information is declared invalid.

Article 9. The Inadmissibility of Double Registration

A registered medium of mass information may not be registered a second time in the same or other registering organ.

In the event that it is established by the court that a repeat registration has taken place then the first registration, according to the date, will be recognized as legal.

Article 10. Application for Registration

In the application for the registration of a medium of mass information the following must be indicated:

1) information about the founder (co-founders) as determined by the demands of the present Law;
2) the title of the medium of mass information;
3) language (languages);
4) the address of the editorial staff;
5) the form of periodical dissemination of mass information;
6) the proposed territorial dissemination of the product;
7) the approximate thematic area and (or) specialization;
8) the proposed frequency of publication and the maximum volume of the medium of mass information;
9) the sources of finance;
10) Information about the relationship of other mass media of which the applicant is founder, owner, editor-in-chief (editorial staff), publisher or disseminator.

A document certifying payment of the registration fee is to be attached to the application.

The presentation of other demands at registration of a medium of mass information is forbidden.

Article 11. Re-registration and Notification

The replacement of the founder, a change in the composition of the co-founders, and equally any change in the title, of the language or the periodical dissemination of mass information, of the territory in which its product is disseminated are permissible only on the condition of re-registration of the medium of mass information.

Re-registration of a medium of mass information the activity of which has been terminated by a court is not permitted.

When changing the location of the editorial staff, the frequency of publication and the maximum volume of the medium of mass information, the founder is obliged to notify the registering organ of this in writing within one month.

Article 12. Exemption from Registration

Registration is not required for:

any mass media founded by a legislative, executive or judicial authority used exclusively for the publication of their official reports and materials, normative and other acts;

periodical, printed publications with a circulation of less than one thousand copies;

radio- and television programmes disseminated by cable networks and limited to the premises and territory of one state institution, educational establishment or industrial enterprise or having not more than ten subscribers;

audio- and video-programmes disseminated with a video circulation of not more than ten copies.

Article 13. Denial of Registration

The denial of registration of a medium of mass information is possible only on the following conditions:

1) if an application has been submitted on behalf of a citizen, group of citizens, an enterprise, or organization that does not possess the right to found media of mass information in accordance with the present Law;

2) if the information indicated in the application does not correspond to reality;

3) if the title, approximate thematic area and (or) specialization of the medium of mass information represents an abuse of the freedom of mass information in the sense of part 1 of Article 4 of the present Law;

4) if a medium of mass information has already been registered with

the same title and the same form of dissemination of mass information by the registering organ in question or the Ministry of Press and Information of the Russian Federation.

Notice of the denial of registration is to be sent to the applicant in writing indicating the reasons for refusal as laid out in the present Law.

The application for registration for a medium of mass information is to be returned to the applicant without being considered with an explanation for the reasons of the return:

1) if the application was submitted that involved a violation of part 2 of Article 8, or part 1 of Article 10 of the present Law;
2) if the application on behalf of the founder was submitted by a person lacking the authority to do so;
3) if the registration fee has not been paid;

After the grounds for violations have been removed the application will be considered.

Article 14. Registration Fee

A registration fee based on a procedure and within limits determined by the Government of the Russian Federation will be levied for the issue of a certificate of registration. For mass media specializing in reports and materials of an advertising or erotic character an increased rate will be set. For those mass media specializing in reports and materials for children, youths, invalids, and, additionally, those of an educational cultural-enlightening character, a lower registration fee will be set.

In the event that registration is denied and equally in the event that registration is relinquished, the applicant is entitled to the return of the registration fee during the three months from the date indicated on the notification of receipt of the application for registration. The document of payment, on which, at the request of the applicant, the comment 'registration not put into effect' can be entered, is the basis for the return of the money according to the place of payment of the registration fee.

Article 15. Declaration that the Certificate of Registration is Not Valid

The certificate of registration of a medium of mass information can be declared invalid, exceptionally, by a court as a result of civil legal proceedings on the application of the registering organ or the Ministry of Press and Information of the Russian Federation only in the circumstances:

1) if the certificate of registration was received on the basis of deception;
2) if the medium of mass information is not published (broadcast) more than once a year;
3) if the regulations of the editorial staff or the agreement that replaces it are not accepted and (or) not affirmed during the three months from the day of the first publication (broadcast) of the given medium of mass information;
4) if a repeat registration of the given medium of mass information has taken place.

When declaring the certificate of registration to be invalid the registration fee is not subject to return.

Article 16. Cessation and Suspension of Activity

The activity of a medium of mass information can be stopped or suspended only by a decision of the founder or by a court acting on the basis of civil legal proceedings in accordance with a suit of the registering organ or the Ministry of Press and Information of the Russian Federation.

The founder has the right to stop or to suspend the activity of the medium of mass information, exceptionally, in the circumstances, and on the procedure stipulated by the rules of the editorial staff, or by an agreement between the founder and the editorial staff (editor-in-chief).

The basis for the cessation of the activity of a medium of mass information by a court are repeated violations by the editorial staff during a twelve-month period of the requirements of Article 4 of the present Law, on the grounds of which written warnings to the founder and (or) the editorial staff (editor-in-chief) have been made by the registering organ or the Ministry of Press and Information of the Russian Federation, and, equally, the failure to implement the decision of the court concerning the suspension of activity of the medium of mass information.

Only the provision of a suit, as envisaged by part 1 of the present article, can serve as the basis for the suspension by a court (or judge) of the activity of a medium of mass information.

The cessation of the activity of a medium of mass information invalidates the certification of its registration and the rules of the editorial staff.

Article 17. The Source of Rights and Obligations

The rights and obligations of the founder and the editorial staff, provided for in the present Law, arise from the moment of registration of the medium of mass information, and those provided for in the rules of the editorial staff, from the moment of its confirmation. The founder, editorial staff, publisher and distributor can establish additional rights and mutual obligations on a contractual basis. The conditions of the rules and agreements must not contradict the present Law and other legislative acts of the Russian Federation.

Article 18. The Status of the Founder

The founder confirms the rules of the editorial staff and (or) concludes an agreement with the editorial staff of the medium of mass information (editor-in-chief).

The founder has the right to oblige the editorial staff to accommodate, without charge and within a specified period, a report or material in his name (founder's statement). The maximum size of the founder's declaration is to be determined in the rules of the editorial staff, in its contract or in any other agreement with the founder. Responsibility for any claims or suits arising from the founder's declaration will rest with the founder. If the founder's authorship of the indicated report or material has not been disputed by the editorial staff then the editorial staff acquires the status of co-respondent.

With the exception of those cases provided for by the present Law, the rules of the editorial staff, or contract between the founder and the editorial staff (editor-in-chief), the founder does not have the right to interfere in the activity of the medium of mass information.

The founder can transfer his rights and duties to a third person with the agreement of the editorial staff and the co-founder. In the event of liquidation or reorganization of the founder, group of citizens, enterprise, institution, organization, or state organ, its rights and obligations pass in their entirety to the editorial staff provided no alternative provision is included in the rules of the editorial staff.

The founder can also act in the capacity of editorial staff, publisher, distributor and owner of the property of the editorial staff.

Article 19. The Status of the Editorial Staff

The editorial staff carries out its activity on the basis of its professional independence.

The editorial staff can be a juridical person, an independent economic subject, organized in any form that is permitted by law. If the editorial staff of a registered medium of mass information is organized in the capacity of an enterprise, then it is, additionally, subject to registration in accordance with the legislation of the Russian Federation concerning enterprises and entrepreneurial activity, as well as the production and output of a medium of mass information, and has the right to carry out on the basis of the established procedure, other activity, which is not prohibited by law.

During the first two years from the day of the first publication (broadcast) of a product of a medium of mass information the editorial board is exempt from income tax. Re-registration of a medium of mass information has no effect on the calculation of the specified period. In the event that the founder ceases the activity of the medium of the mass information before the expiry of the indicated period, full payment for the entire period will be recovered.

The editorial board may act in the capacity of founder of a medium of mass information, the publisher, distributor and the owner of editorial assets.

The editorial board is to be led by the editor-in-chief who exercises his authority on the basis of the present Law, the rules of the editorial board, an agreement between the founder and the editorial board (editor-in-chief). The editor-in-chief represents the editorial board in its relations with the founder, publisher, distributor, citizens, groups of citizens, enterprises, institutions, organizations and state organs and, additionally, in court. He carries responsibility for the implementation of the requirements arising from the activity of the medium of mass information by the present Law and other legislative acts of the Russian Federation.

Article 20. The Rules of the Editorial Board

The rules of the editorial board of a medium of mass information are adopted at a general meeting of the journalists' collective, the permanent employees, by a majority of votes in the presence of not less than two-thirds of its staff, and confirmed by the founder.

The following must be determined in the rules of the editorial board:

1) the reciprocal rights and obligations of the founder, editorial board and the editor-in-chief;
2) the authority of the journalists' collective and the permanent employees;
3) the procedure for appointing (election) the editor-in-chief, the editorial board and (or) other organs for the administration of the editorial staff;
4) the basis and the procedure of the cessation and suspension of activity of the medium of mass information;
5) the transfer and (or) preservation of the right to the title, other judicial consequences of a change of founder, change to the staff, of the co-founders, the cessation of activity of a medium of mass information, the liquidation or reorganization of the editorial board, or change in its organizational-legal form;
6) the procedure for confirming and changing the rules of the editorial board and, additionally, any conditions provided for by the present Law and other legislative acts.

Before the confirmation of the rules of the editorial board, and, additionally, if the editorial board consists of less than ten persons, its relations with the founder, including questions, enumerated in points 1–5 of part 2 of the present article, can be determined by the rules replacing the existing set by agreement between the founder and the editorial staff (editor-in-chief).

The rules of the editorial staff that is organized in the capacity of an enterprise must simultaneously be the rules of the given enterprise. In this event, the rules of the editorial board must, additionally, be consistent with the legislation concerning enterprises and entrepreneurial activity.

A copy of the rules of the editorial board or the agreement that replaces it is to be sent to the registering organ no later than three months from the day of the first publication (broadcast) of the given medium of mass information. In so doing, the editorial staff has the right to stipulate what information contained in the rules, or the agreement that replaces it, constitutes a commercial secret.

Article 21. The Status of the Publisher

The publisher exercises his rights and assumes his responsibilities on the basis of the given Law, the Federal Law 'Concerning the Procedure for Reporting the Activity of State Organs of Power in the State Mass Media, and of the legislation dealing with publication, enterprises and entrepreneurial activity.

The publisher may act in the capacity of a founder of a medium of mass information, editorial board, distributor or owner of editorial assets.

Article 22. Agreements

The agreement between the co-founders of a medium of mass information is to determine their mutual rights, obligations, responsibility, procedure, conditions, the consequences of changes affecting the composition of the co-founders, and the procedure for resolving disputes between them.

The production, property and financial relations between the founder and the editorial board (editor-in-chief) are determined by the agreement between them: and the procedure for the division and use of the means for the upkeep of the editorial staff, the division of profit, the formation of funds and the refund of losses, the duties of the founder for the provision of the appropriate production and social-personal conditions as well as the work of the employees of the editorial staff.

Each separate co-founder or all co-founders together can be a party to the agreement with the editorial staff.

The production, property and financial relations between the editorial staff and the publisher, the reciprocal allocation of publisher's rights, the obligations of the publisher for the material-technical provision of the manufacture of the product of the medium of mass information and the responsibility of the contracting parties, are to be determined by an agreement.

The founder, editorial staff (editor-in-chief) and publisher may additionally conclude other agreements among themselves, and, additionally, with the distributor.

Article 23. Information Agencies

When applying the present Law in relation to information agencies the status of editorial staff, publisher, distributor and the legal regime of a medium of mass information is simultaneously extended to them.

A bulletin, other publication or programme with a permanent title, founded by an information agency, are registered in accordance with the procedures established by the present Law.

When disseminating reports and materials of an information agency through another medium of mass information reference to the information agency is obligatory.

Article 24. Other Mass Media

The rules, established by the present Law for periodical printed publications, are applicable to periodical dissemination with a circulation of a thousand and more copies or texts, created with the help of computers and (or) stored in their data banks or data bases, and equally in relation to other mass media, the product of which is disseminated in the form of printed reports, materials and images.

The rules, established by the present Law for radio- and television programmes, are to apply in relation to the periodical dissemination of mass information via teletext systems, videotext and other telecommunications networks, if otherwise not established by the legislation of the Russian Federation.

CHAPTER III. DISSEMINATION OF MASS INFORMATION

Article 25. The Procedure of Dissemination

Impeding the legally-based dissemination of a product of the mass media, on the part of citizens, groups of citizens, official persons, enterprises, institutions, organizations and state organs, is not permitted.

The dissemination of a product of mass information is considered to be commercial if payment for it is levied. A product intended for non-commercial dissemination must bear the mark 'Gratis' and may not be the subject of commercial dissemination.

The showing of videotaped programmes in residential accommodation, and equally the making of separate copies therefrom, if no charge is levied, either directly or indirectly, is not considered to be dissemination of a product of mass information in the meaning of the present Law.

Retail sale, including second-hand circulation of periodical printed publications, is not subject to restrictions other than those provided for by the present Law.

The retail sale of the circulation of periodical printed publications in locations that are not generally accessible, in accommodation and in other installations in relation to which a special regime of use has been established by the owner or other person authorized to administer his property, is permitted only with the agreement of those persons indicated.

In the event of a violation by the editorial staff, publisher or distributor of the property or personal non-property rights of authors and in other circumstances provided for by law, the dissemination of the product of a medium of mass information may be terminated on the decision of a court.

Article 26. Publication (Broadcast)

The dissemination of a product of a medium of mass information is permitted only after permission for publication (broadcast) has been given by the editor-in-chief.

Article 27. Publication Data

Each edition of a periodical printed publication must contain the following information:

1) the title of the publication;
2) the founder (co-founder);
3) the surname and initials of the editor-in-chief;
4) the ordinal number of the edition and the date of its publication, and, additionally, for a newspaper the time when it was passed for printing (that established by the schedule and the actual time);
5) an index – for publications disseminated via the enterprises communications;
6) circulation;
7) the price or the note 'Discretionary Price' or the note 'Gratis';
8) the addresses of the editorial staff, publisher and printing house;

With every broadcast of a radio- or television programme, and with continual transmission the editorial staff are obliged to state the name of the programme not less than four times during a 24-hour period.

Every copy of an audio-, video- or newsreel programme must contain the following information:

1) the title of the programme;
2) the date of publication (broadcast) and the number of the edition;
3) the surname and initials of the editor-in-chief;
4) the circulation;
5) the editorial staff and its address;
6) the price or the note 'Discretionary Price' or the note 'Gratis'.

Reports and materials of an information agency must be accompanied by its title.

If a medium of mass information has not been exempted from registration, then, additionally, the organ that registered it and the registration number are to be indicated in the publication data.

Article 28. Circulation

The circulation of a periodical printed publication, of an audio-, video-, newsreel programme is determined by the editor-in-chief in agreement with the publisher.

The withdrawal, and equally the destruction of the circulation, or parts thereof, are only permitted by a court decision's taking effect.

For mass media specializing in the manufacture of a product of an advertising or erotic nature a sliding scale of fees is to be established, and to be levied on the procedure determined by the Government of the Russian Federation.

Article 29. Obligatory Copies

Immediately, on the manufacture of the first edition of the circulation the editorial staff is to send obligatory, free copies of periodical printed publications, including those exempt from registration under article 12 of the present Law, to the founder (co-founders), the organ, registering the given medium of mass information, to the Ministry of Press and Information of the Russian Federation, to the scientific-production association 'All-Union Book Chamber', to the State Library of the USSR named after V.I. Lenin, to the State Public Library named after M.E. Saltykov-Shchedrin, to the Library of the Supreme Council of the Russian Federation and to the Library of the President of the Russian Federation.

The Ministry of Press and Information of the Russian Federation has the right to compel the editorial staffs to send chargeable copies to other institutions and organizations as well.

Article 30. The Federal Commission for Television and Radio Broadcasting

The Federal Commission for Television and Radio Broadcasting works out the state policy in the area of licensing radio- and television broadcasting and implements it directly as well as through the territorial commissions for radio and television broadcasting.

The procedure for creating both the activity of the Federal Commission for Television and Radio Broadcasting and the territorial commissions is determined by the law of the Russian Federation.

Article 31. Licence for Broadcasting

Licences for broadcasting are issued by the Federal Commission for television and radio broadcasting and by the territorial commissions.

The licence for broadcasting confers on the holder the right to carry out, with regard for the licensing terms, the dissemination of a product of the mass media that is registered in accordance with the present Law, using the technical means of the ether, wire or cable television and radio broadcasting including those that he owns.

The issue of a licence must be refused if the technical capability to implement broadcasting with the stated characteristics, or those close to it, is absent.

The issue of a licence can be refused on the grounds provided for by the terms of competition, if the claims are examined on a competitive basis.

Conceding the broadcasting licence to another person is only permitted with the agreement of the body that issued it, with the corresponding redrawing up of the licence.

The scope and procedure for the levying of payment for a broadcasting licence and, additionally, the redrawing up of the licence are established by the Government of the Russian Federation.

Article 32. Annulment of the Licence

The licence is annulled on the following terms:

1) if it was obtained by deception;
2) if the licensing conditions or the rules governing the dissemination of radio- and television programmes provided for by the present Law have been repeatedly violated and on the basis of which written warnings have been made;

3) if the commission for television and radio broadcasting establishes that the licence was granted on the basis of a hidden concession;

Additional grounds for the annulment of the licence may be established by the laws of the Russian Federation.

Annulment of the licence is to be carried out by a decision of the body that issued it or by the Federal Commission of Television and Radio Broadcasting.

When annulling the licence the licence fee is not subject to repayment.

Article 33. Artificial Interference

The creation of artificial interference impeding the regular reception of radio- and television programmes, that is, it impedes the dissemination of radio-, tele-, and other technical signals on the band of frequencies on which the broadcasting is carried out on the basis of a licence, incurs liability in accordance with the legislation of the Russian Federation.

Industrial interference, that is artificial interference arising from the use of technical facilities in the process of economic activity, is subject to elimination at the expense of the persons on whose property (jurisdiction) the sources of this interference are located.

Article 34. The Preservation of Radio- and Television Transmissions

For the purposes of providing evidence possessing a significance for the correct resolution of arguments, the editorial staff of radio and television programmes are obliged:

to preserve the material of their own broadcasts on video;

to record in writing those broadcasts that were transmitted in the registration journal.

The registration journal is to indicate the date and time of the transmission, the subject of the broadcast, its author, presenter and participants.

The periods of preservation:

of broadcast materials for not less than one month from the day of transmission;

of a registration journal – not less than one year from the date of the last entry.

Article 35. Obligatory Messages

The editorial staff are obliged to publish *gratis*, and within the prescribed period:

a decision of the court that has legal force, containing a demand for publication of such a decision via the given medium of mass information;

a message that emanates from the organ registering the given medium of mass information, that concerns the activity of the editorial staff.

The editorial staff of mass media whose founders and (co-founders) are state organs are obliged to publish on the demand of these organs their official messages on the basis of the procedure that is governed by the statutes, or any agreement that replaces it, and equally other materials, the publication of which in the given medium of mass media, is provided for by the legislation of the Russian Federation.

The state mass media are obliged to publish reports and materials of the federal organs of the state and of the subjects of state power of the Russian Federation according to the procedure established by the Federal law 'Concerning the Procedure for Reporting the Activity of State Organs of Power in the State Mass Media'.

The editorial boards of state mass media are obliged, without delay and without any charge, to publish or to broadcast operational information on questions of fire safety on the demand of the State Fire-Prevention Service of the Ministry of Internal Affairs.

Article 36. The Dissemination of Advertising

The dissemination of advertising in the mass media is to be implemented in accordance with the procedure established by the legislation of the Russian Federation concerning advertising.

Article 37. Erotic Publications

A medium of mass information specializing in materials and reports of an erotic character is, for the purposes of the present Law, understood to be a periodical publication, or a programme, which wholly and systematically exploits an interest in sex.

The dissemination of editions of specialized radio and television programmes of an erotic character without a coded signal is only permitted from 2300 hours until 0400 hours local time if not established otherwise by the local administration.

The retail sale of a product of the media of mass information specializing in reports and materials of an erotic character is only permitted for those printed in transparent packaging, and in premises specially designated for that purpose the location of which is determined by the local administration.

CHAPTER IV. THE RELATIONS OF THE MASS MEDIA WITH CITIZENS AND ORGANIZATIONS

Article 38. The Right to Receive Information

Citizens have the right to receive timely and authentic information from a medium of mass information about the activity of state organs and organizations, societal bodies and their official persons.

State organs and organizations, societal bodies and their official persons present information about their activity to the mass media and, additionally, by holding press-conferences the delivery of information and statistical materials and in other forms.

Article 39. Requesting Information

The editorial staff has the right to inquire about information concerning the activity of state organs and organizations, societal bodies and their official persons. A request for information may be made orally or in writing. The leaders of the specified organs, organizations and associations, their deputies, the workers of the press service or other authorized persons are obliged to present the requested information within the limits of their competence.

Article 40. Refusal and Delay in the Presentation of Information

A refusal to present requested information is possible only if it contains information comprising state, commercial or other secrets specially protected by the law. Notification of a refusal is to be submitted to a representative of the editorial staff within a three-day period from the day of the receipt of the written request for information. The following must be indicated in the notification:

1) the reasons why the requested information cannot be separated

from the other information constituting a secret specially protected by law;
2) the official person refusing to provide the information;
3) the date when the refusal to meet the request was taken.

A delay for the request for information is permissible if the information demanded cannot be presented within a seven-day period. Notification about a delay is to be submitted to the editorial staff within a three-day period from the day of the receipt of the written request for information. In the notification the following must be indicated:

1) the reasons why the requested information cannot be made available within a seven-day period;
2) the date by which the requested information will be made available;
3) the official person who initiated the delay;
4) the date on which the decision concerning the delay was taken.

Article 41. Confidential Information

The editorial staff does not have the right to publicize in reports and materials information presented by a citizen on condition that it be kept a secret.

The editorial staff is obliged to keep the source of information secret and has no right to name the person who presented the information subject to the condition that his name not be publicized, with the exception of the circumstance when a corresponding demand comes from a court in connection with court proceedings.

Article 42. Authors' Works and Letters

The editorial staff is obliged to observe the rights to the material being used including the author's rights, publisher's rights and other rights to intellectual property. The author, or another person, owning rights to works can stipulate the conditions and manner of use of the work presented to the editorial staff.

A letter addressed to the editorial staff can be used in reports and materials of the given medium of mass information, if, in so doing, the meaning of the letter is not corrupted and the terms of the present Law are not violated. The editorial staff is not obliged to reply to citizens' letters and to send these letters on to those organs, organizations and official persons, the examination of which falls within their competence.

Nobody has the right to compel the editorial staff to publish a work, letter, or other report which it has rejected, if it is not provided for by law.

Article 43. The Right to Refutation

A citizen or organization has the right to demand that the editorial staff refute information that does not correspond to reality and that defames their honour and dignity, and that was disseminated in the given medium of mass information. The legal representatives of a citizen also have such a right if the citizen himself does not have the opportunity to demand the refutation. If the editorial staff of a medium of mass information is unable to prove that the information that it disseminated corresponds to reality, then it is obliged to refute that information in the same medium of mass information.

If a citizen or organization has presented the text of a refutation then the given text is subject to dissemination on the condition that it meets the demands of the present Law. The editorial staff of a radio or television programme who are obliged to disseminate a refutation can offer the citizen or representative of the organization demanding this the possibility of reading out their own text and broadcast it from a tape-recording.

Article 44. The Procedure for a Refutation

In the refutation it must be shown what information does not correspond to reality, when and how it was disseminated by the given medium of mass information.

The refutation in a periodical printed publication must be set in the same type and accommodated under the heading 'Refutation', as a rule in the same column of the material or report to be rejected. A refutation broadcast by radio or television must be transmitted, as a rule at the same time in the 24-hour period as that of the programme with the material or report to be refuted.

The size of the refutation must not be double the size of the fragment of the disseminated material or report to be refuted. It may not be stipulated that the text of the refutation be shorter by one standard page of typewritten text. A refutation by radio or television must not occupy less broadcast time than that required by the announcer to read one standard page of typewritten text.

A refutation must follow:

1) in the mass media published (broadcast) not less than once a week – during the ten days from the day of receipt of a demand for a refutation or of its text
2) in other mass media – in the edition under preparation or the next planned edition.

In one month from the day of the receipt of a demand for refutation, or of its text, the editorial staff are obliged to notify interested citizens or organizations in writing of the proposed time of the refutation, or of its refusal to disseminate one, with an indication of the grounds for refusal.

Article 45. Grounds for Refusing a Refutation

A refutation must be refused if the given demand or the presented text of a refutation:

1) is an abuse of freedom of the mass information in the meaning of part 1 of article 4 of the present Law;
2) if it contradicts the ruling of a court decision that has become law;
3) if it is anonymous.

A refutation may be denied:

1) if the information to be refuted has already been refuted in the given medium of mass information;
2) if the demand for a refutation, or a submitted text, reaches the editorial staff after the expiry of one year from the day of the dissemination of the information to be refuted in the given medium of mass information.

A refusal to grant a refutation or a violation of the procedure established by the present Law for dealing with refutations may, in the course of one year from the day of the dissemination of the information to be refuted, be the subject of an appeal in connection with the civil or civil-professional legislation of the Russian Federation.

Article 46. The Right to Reply

A citizen or organization in relation to which information not corresponding to reality or which damages the rights and legal interests of a citizen has been disseminated in a medium of mass information has the right to reply (commentary, rejoinder) in the same medium of mass information.

In relation to such a reply or refusal the rules of articles 43–45 of the present Law apply.

A reply to a reply is to be placed no sooner than in the next edition of the medium of mass information. The given rule does not apply to editorial commentaries.

CHAPTER V. A JOURNALIST'S RIGHTS AND OBLIGATIONS

Article 47. A Journalist's Rights

The journalist has the right:

1) to search for, to request, to receive and to disseminate information;
2) to visit state bodies and organizations, enterprises and institutions, societal bodies, or their press-services;
3) to be received by official persons in connection with the request for information;
4) to receive access to documents and materials with the exception of those fragments containing information that constitutes a state, commercial or other secret specially protected by law;
5) to copy, to publish, to publicize or in any other way to reproduce documents and materials provided that the requirements of part 1 of article 42 of the present Law are observed;
6) to make records including those using audio, video, cinematic and photographic equipment with the exception of those cases provided for by the law;
7) to visit specially protected areas, the sites of natural disasters and accidents and catastrophes, mass disorders and mass gatherings of citizens and, additionally, to visit those areas in which a state of emergency has been declared, and to be present at meetings and demonstrations;
8) to check the reliability of the information being given to him;
9) to expound his personal judgements and assessments in reports

and materials designated for dissemination under his by-line;
10) to refuse to sign any materials or reports that contradict his convictions;
11) to remove his signature from reports or materials the content of which, in his opinion, was distorted in the process of editorial preparation, or to forbid, or in any other way to dispute, the conditions and character of the use of the given information and material in connection with part 1 of article 42 of the present Law;
12) to disseminate reports and materials prepared by him under his own by-line, under a pseudonym or without a signature.

The journalist enjoys, in addition, other rights available to him by the legislation of the Russian Federation concerning the mass media.

Article 48. Accreditation

The editorial staff has the right to submit an application to a state organ, organization, institution and societal body for the accreditation with them of its journalists.

State organs, organizations, institutions, organs of societal bodies accredit the journalists who have applied on the condition of the observance by the editorial staff of the rules of accreditation established by those organs, organizations and institutions.

Organs, organizations and institutions that have accredited journalists are obliged to inform them in advance concerning sittings, conferences and other measures, to make stenographic records, minutes, and other documents available, to create favourable conditions for making records.

An accredited journalist has the right to attend sittings, conferences and other measures carried out by the organs, organizations or institutions that have accredited him with the exception of those circumstances when decisions taken at closed meetings are under consideration.

A journalist may be deprived of his accreditation if either he or the editorial staff have violated the rules of accreditation or have disseminated information that does not correspond to reality or that damages the honour and dignity of the organization that has accredited the journalist, and that has been upheld by a decision taken by a court of law.

The accreditation of its own journalists by the editorial staff of mass media is carried out in accordance with the requirements of the present article.

Article 49. The Journalist's Obligations

The journalist is obliged:

1) to observe the regulations of the editorial staff by whom he is employed;
2) to verify the authenticity of the information reported to him;
3) to meet the requests of persons who have given him information concerning the indication of its source, and in addition, concerning the authorization of the utterance being cited, if it is being publicized for the first time;
4) to preserve the confidentiality of information and (or) its source;
5) to acquire the agreement (with the exception of those circumstances when this is necessary for the protection of societal interests) for the dissemination in a medium of mass information of information about the personal life of a citizen from the citizen himself or his legal representatives;
6) when receiving information from citizens and official persons to inform them of the use of any audio, video-recording, cine- or photographic equipment;
7) to inform the editor-in-chief of any possible suits and the presentation of other requirements as provided for by law in connection with the dissemination of reports and materials prepared by him;
8) to refuse a task given to him by the editor-in-chief, or the editorial staff, if either it, or its fulfilment, involves a violation of the law;
9) to present at the first request his editorial identity or other document that confirms his identity and authority as a journalist when carrying out his professional activity.

In addition, the journalist has other obligations established by the legislation of the Russian Federation concerning the mass media.

When carrying out his professional activity the journalist is obliged to respect the rights, lawful interests, honour and dignity of citizens and organizations.

In connection with the journalist's implementing his professional activity, the state guarantees the protection of the journalist's honour, dignity, health, life and property as an individual fulfilling a societal duty.

Article 50. Hidden Recording

The dissemination of reports and materials prepared with the use of hidden audio- and video recording and cine- and photographic equipment is permitted:

1) if this does not violate the constitutional rights and freedoms of a person or citizen;
2) if this is necessary for the protection of societal interests, and if measures have been taken against the possible identification of third parties;
3) if the presentation of a recording is made on the decision of a court.

Article 51. The Inadmissibility of the Abuse of a Journalist's Rights

The use of a journalist's rights established by the present Law for the purposes of concealing or falsifying societally significant information, for the disseminating of rumours under the impression that they are authentic reports, the gathering of information for the advantage of a third party, or organization that does not constitute a medium of mass information, is not permitted.

It is forbidden to use the right of a journalist to disseminate information with the aim of slandering a citizen or separate categories of citizens exclusively on the basis of their sex, age, racial, national allegiance, language, their attitudes towards religion, profession, place of domicile and work and, additionally, in connection with their political convictions.

Article 52. Special Status

The professional status of a journalist established by the present Law extends to:

permanent employees of the editorial staff occupied with the editing, creation, collection or preparation of reports and materials for mass-circulation newspapers and other mass media the products of which are disseminated exclusively in the limits of a single enterprise (association), organization, institution;

authors not linked with the editorial staff of mass media by labour or other contractual relations, but recognized by it to be its freelance authors or correspondents when carrying out an assignment of the editorial staff.

CHAPTER VI. INTERGOVERNMENT COOPERATION IN THE FIELD OF MASS INFORMATION

Article 53. Intergovernmental Treaties and Agreements

Intergovernmental cooperation in the field of mass information is carried on on the basis of treaties concluded by the Russian Federation.

The editorial staffs, professional associations of journalists participate in international cooperation in the field of mass information on the basis of agreements with the citizens and juridical persons of other states and, in addition, with international organizations.

Article 54. The Dissemination of Foreign Information

Citizens of the Russian Federation are guaranteed unimpeded access to the reports and materials of the foreign mass media.

Limiting the reception of direct television broadcast is only permitted in circumstances provided for by intergovernmental treaties concluded by the Russian Federation.

For the dissemination of a product of a foreign periodical, printed publication, that is a medium of mass information not registered in the Russian Federation and having its founder or editorial staff permanently located beyond its borders, and, equally, being financed by foreign states, juridical persons or citizens, it is necessary to receive the authority of the Ministry of Press and Information of the Russian Federation, if the procedure for dissemination has not been established by a treaty concluded by the Russian Federation.

Article 55. Foreign Correspondents

The obligations of representatives of the foreign mass media in the Russian Federation are to be formulated with the permission of the Ministry of Foreign Affairs of the Russian Federation, if no other provision has been made in an international treaty concluded by the Russian Federation.

Foreign representation of media of mass information, registered in the Russian Federation, is to be formulated on the basis of the procedure of the legislative acts of the Russian Federation, and of the country of residence unless otherwise provided for by an international treaty concluded by the Russian Federation.

Accreditation of foreign journalists in the Russian Federation is conducted by the Ministry of Foreign Affairs of the Russian Federation in connection with article 48 of the present Law.

Foreign correspondents, not accredited in the Russian Federation on the basis of the established procedure, enjoy the rights, and assume the obligations, as representatives of a foreign juridical person.

The following are exempt from obligatory accreditation for the carrying out of their professional activity in the Russian Federation:

foreign correspondents who were earlier accredited in the Soviet Union, or in the sovereign states comprising the union;

correspondents of the mass media earlier registered by the state organs of the Soviet Union or sovereign states forming part thereof.

Irrespective of their citizenship the professional status of a journalist established by the present Law extends to correspondents accredited in the Russian Federation. Corresponding restrictions in relation to correspondents of the mass media of those states, in which special restrictions for the implementation of the professional activity of journalists of the mass media registered in the Russian Federation, can be established by the Government of the Russian Federation.

Foreign correspondents of mass media registered in the Russian Federation, irrespective of their citizenship, possess the rights and obligations of a journalist established by the present Law if this does not contradict the legislation of the country of residence.

CHAPTER VII. RESPONSIBILITY FOR THE VIOLATION OF THE LEGISLATION OF THE MASS MEDIA

Article 56. The Imposing of Responsibility

The founders, the editorial staffs, publishers, distributors, state organs, organizations, institutions, enterprises, and societal bodies, official persons, journalists, the authors of disseminated reports and materials, bear responsibility for violations of the legislation of the Russian Federation concerning the mass media.

Article 57. Exemption from Responsibility

The editorial staff, the editor-in-chief and the journalist do not bear responsibility for the dissemination of information that does not correspond to reality and that defames the honour and dignity of citizens and organizations or that limits the rights and lawful interests of citizens which are either an abuse of the freedom of mass information and (or) of the journalist's rights:

1) if this information is present in obligatory reports;
2) if it was received from information agencies;
3) if it is contained in an answer to a request for information or either in the materials of the press-services of state organs, organizations, institutions, enterprises, organs of societal bodies;
4) if it is the *verbatim* reproduction of fragments of announcements of people's deputies at congresses and sessions of the councils of the people's deputies, delegates of congresses, conferences, plenary sessions of societal bodies and, additionally, the official announcements of official persons of state organs, organizations and societal bodies;
5) if it is contained in authors' works that are broadcast without prior recording, or in texts that have not been subjected to any editing in relation to the present Law;
6) if they are the *verbatim* reproduction of reports and materials or fragments thereof disseminated by another medium of mass information that can be established and held to account for the given violation of the legislation of the Russian Federation concerning the mass media.

Article 58. Responsibility for the Limiting of the Freedom of Mass Information

The limitation of the freedom of mass information, that is, the impeding, in whatever form, on the part of citizens, the official persons of state organs and organizations and societal bodies of the lawful activity of founders, editorial staffs, publishers and distributors of a product of a medium of mass information, and in addition, of journalists, including by means of:

the implementing of censorship;

the interference in the activity or violation of the professional independence of the editorial staff;

the unlawful cessation or suspension of the activity of a medium of mass information;

the violation of the right of the editorial staff to a request for and receipt of information;

the unlawful seizure, and equally the destruction of a circulation or parts thereof;

compelling the journalist to disseminate or to refuse to disseminate information;

the establishing of any restrictions on contacts with the journalist and the transfer to him of information, with the exception of that information that constitutes a state, commercial or other secret specially protected by the law;

the violation of the journalist's rights as established by the present Law – entails criminal, administrative, disciplinary and other liabilities in connection with the legislation of the Russian Federation.

The discovery of organs, organizations, institutions or posts of which the tasks of carrying out censorship as a function – entails immediate cessation of their funding and liquidation on the basis of the procedure provided for by the legislation of the Russian Federation.

Article 59. Responsibility for the Abuse of the Freedom of Mass Information

The abuse of the freedom of information, as articulated in the violation of the requirements of article 4 of the present Law – entails criminal, administrative, disciplinary or other liabilities in connection with the legislation of the Russian Federation.

The abuse of a journalist's rights, as articulated in the violation of the requirements of articles 50 and 51 of the present Law, or of the non-observance of a journalist's obligations – entails criminal or administrative liability in connection with the legislation of the Russian Federation.

Article 60. Responsibility for Other Violations of the Legislation Concerning the Mass Media

Violation of the legislation of the Russian Federation concerning the mass media as articulated;

in the setting up of a medium of mass information using a false persona, in the receipt of a registration certificate or a licence for broadcasting by deception, of a licence granted on the basis of a hidden concession, of the evasion of payment of a fee determined on a sliding scale, of evasion of payment of an increased registration fee, or of the illegal receipt of advantages established for specialized mass media;

in the illegal manufacture of a product of a medium of mass information without its registration or either after a decision to stop or to suspend its activity has been taken, or in the evasion of re-registration, and, additionally, the producing, when registering, of requirements not provided for by the present Law;

in the impeding of the dissemination of a product of a medium of mass information carried out on a lawful basis, the establishing of unlawful restrictions on the retail sale of a circulation of periodical printed publications;

in the unlawful dissemination of a product of a medium of mass information without its registration or after a decision to stop or to suspend its activity has been taken or without permission for its publication (broadcast), in the unlawful commercial dissemination, the carrying out of broadcasting without a licence or with a violation of the licensing conditions;

in the violation of the rules governing the dissemination of obligatory reports, advertisements, erotic publications and programmes;

in the violation of the procedure for declaring the publication data, the presenting of obligatory copies, the preservation of the materials of television and radio transmissions;

in the creation of artificial interference, which impedes the regular reception of radio and television programmes – entails criminal, administrative, disciplinary or other liabilities in connection with the legislation of the Russian Federation.

Article 61. The Procedure of Appeal

In connection with the civil and civil-professional legislation of the Russian Federation the following may be the subject of an appeal to a court:

1) the refusal to register a medium of mass information, a violation by the registering organ of the procedure and of the periods of registration, other illegal actions of the registering organ;
2) a decision of the commission for television and radio broadcasting concerning the annulment of a broadcasting licence;

3) a refusal or delay in the presenting of requested information or the failure on the part of official persons, employees of press-services, state organs, organizations, institutions, enterprises, organs of societal bodies to observe the requirements of Article 40 of the present Law;

4) the refusal of accreditation, the removal of accreditation, and, likewise, the violation of the rights of an accredited journalist.

If the court acknowledges the decision or action (or inaction) under appeal to be unlawful, it passes a decision about the foundation of the complaint, the obligations to remove the violation that has occurred, and the reimbursement of losses, including lost income, suffered by the founder, editorial staff and licensee.

Article 62. Compensation for Moral Damage

Moral (non-property damage) caused to a citizen as a result of the dissemination by a medium of mass information, or information not corresponding to reality that defames the honour and dignity of a citizen or causes him other non-property damage is, on the decision of a court, to be compensated by the medium of mass information, and, additionally, by official persons and citizens, and on a scale to be determined by the court.

President of the Russian Federation
B. YELTSIN
Moscow,
House of Councils of Russia
27 December 1991

Notes

CHAPTER ONE: INFORMATION DEFICIT

1. Friedrich Hayek's contention, expressed in *The Road to Serfdom*, that planning the human condition leads to totalitarianism, is totally vindicated. In the post-Soviet period it is worth noting the observations made by Andrei Amalrik in his article, 'Will the Soviet Union Survive until 1984?', which was first published in the journal, *Survey* in 1969. Noting the extreme isolation of the regime and its surrealistic picture of the outside world, he adds: 'Yet the longer this state of affairs helps to perpetuate the status quo, the more rapid and decisive will be its collapse when confrontation with reality becomes inevitable'. See Andrei Amalrik, *Will the Soviet Union Survive until 1984?*, Harper & Row, New York and Evanston, 1970, p. 41.
2. Mikhail Gorbachev, *Perestroika: New Thinking for Our Country and the World*, Collins, London, 1987, p. 83.
3. The proliferation of IT has blurred distinctions between words such as knowledge, data, ideas and concepts. Most people would be quite content to subsume these four words under the apparently simple rubric of information. For the task in hand, I intend to adopt the same pragmatic approach. That said, there are significant differences between these four categories. It was, in part, the failure to cope with these distinctions, or rather the attempt to define them away, which proved so fatal to communism. Theodore Roszak is one of a number of commentators who have tried to take a detached view of IT in the West. Information, he notes, 'smacks of safe neutrality ... in that innocent guise, it is the perfect starting point for a technocratic political agenda that wants as little exposure for its objectives as possible. After all, what can one say against information?' Cf. Theodore Roszak, *The Cult of Information: The Folklore of Computers and the True Art of Thinking*, Lutterworth Press, Cambridge, UK, 1986, p. 19.
4. Francis Fukuyama, *The End of History and the Last Man*, Hamish Hamilton, London, 1992, p. 93.
5. This was certainly the general reaction in the West. A particularly unpleasant shock for the Soviet Union was the condemnation of the invasion by the Non-Aligned Movement and Third World states. The consequences of the Soviet invasion of Afghanistan invite comparison with the effect of the Munich sell-out to Hitler in 1938. It finally brought home the dangers of appeasement to a much wider audience.
6. Western radio broadcasts to the Soviet empire played a vital role in providing accurate information and countering official propaganda. In the introduction to his thorough and comprehensive study of Western radio broadcasts to the Soviet empire Michael Nelson notes that the effects were twofold. First, they broke the monopoly of the mass media

which was essential to the communist Party dictatorship. Second, the cost of jamming was prohibitive. In 1990 Eduard Shevardnadze cited the staggering figure of 700 billion rubles over two decades as the cost of ideological confrontation with the West. Michael Nelson, *War of the Black Heavens: The Battles of Western Broadcasting in the Cold War*, unpublished manuscript, 1995, p. 2. See, too, Julian Hale's explanation of jamming: 'Jamming is expensive for a technical but simple reason. The incoming signal starts at one point, but it ends up over a huge area. If it is transmitted on a number of frequencies, it has to be combated by both sky-wave jamming, in other words by using the same medium as that used by the broadcaster and by ground-wave jamming, which interferes with signals in the immediate vicinity of the jamming transmitter. This requires in a country the size of Russia, innumerable transmitters directed against a single signal. It also requires large teams of monitors to follow the signals around the frequency spectrum and, as jamming is selective, to listen out for the hostile parts. An indirect cost is incurred in the transfer of manpower (estimated to be up to 10,000 technicians in Russia) as well as equipment, which would otherwise have been used to boost domestic broadcasting services.' See Julian Hale, *Radio Power: Propaganda and International Broadcasting*, Paul Elek, London, 1975, p. 133.

7. In the former East Germany, notes Hans Joachim-Maaz, 'teachers would ask children whether their television sets showed dots or lines in order to find out who was watching Western television, who let 'the enemy of the people' into their living rooms. The offenders would have to undergo special 'consciousness-raising' indoctrination.' See *Behind the Wall: The Inner Life of Communist Germany*, trans. Margot Bettauer Dembo, W. W. Norton & Company, New York and London, 1995, p. 24.

8. That collectivist economics had failed in the West did not automatically guarantee the adoption of free-market economics. Despite the cogency of economic liberalism its conclusions were resisted. Those who supported collectivist solutions could quite easily have argued that still more private wealth and personal freedom needed to be arrogated to the state if the state were to succeed. As Robert Skidelsky has noted: 'One response to government failure is to try harder next time. If some regulation is failing to achieve results, strengthen it. If economic planning isn't working out, extend the plan. [...] It was the rejection of such collectivist remedies for failing states which marked out the new terrain of political economy.' See *The World after Communism: A Polemic for Our Times*, Macmillan, London, 1995, p. 118.

9. The problem of the 'objectivity of information' was a source of abiding concern to Marxist-Leninist philosophy. For, if objective information does not depend on the subject then the neutrality of information becomes a serious possibility. Cf. Peter Paul Kirschenmann, *Information and Reflection. On Some Problems of Cybernetics and how Contemporary Dialectical Materialism Copes with Them*, trans. T. J. Blakeley, D. Reidel Publishing Company, Dordrecht, Holland, 1970, p. 120.

10. In the *Bol'shaya Sovetskaya Entsiklopediya*, 3rd edn, vol. 28, Sovetskaya entsiklopediya, Moscow, 1978, censorship is defined as: 'control,

exercised by officials (secular or spiritual), over the content, publication and dissemination of printed material, and over the content (performance or showing) of plays and other dramatic forms, of works, cinema productions, of productions of visual art, radio and television broadcasts, and sometimes even of private correspondence, with the aim of not permitting, or limiting the dissemination of ideas and information, recognized by those authorities as being undesirable or harmful.' 3rd edition, vol. 28, p. 489. In certain circumstances, such as war, this definition, with the elimination of religious censorship, might well apply to the liberal democracies. What the originators of this definition conspicuously fail to mention is that whereas, in the West, such proscription is confined to exceptional circumstances, and in most cases, outside of war, is subject to a public, legal challenge, the nature of censorship in the Soviet Union was altogether more pervasive and destructive. Nor indeed is the existence of the censorship apparatus formally acknowledged. A great deal of what was known in the West about the Soviet censor came to us from defectors, exiles and some diligent and persistent scholarship. However, even before the collapse of the Soviet Union the trickle of information had long been a flood enabling scholars to build up an accurate picture of the extent and nature of the mechanism. New information, made available in the *glasnost'* period, has confirmed the basic picture, and the view repeated many times in various forms, that Soviet censorship was 'a new phenomenon in the history of thought control'. Arkady Belinkov in *The Soviet Censorship*, Martin Dewhirst and Robert Farrell, (eds), Scarecrow Press, Metuchen, NJ, 1973, p. 1. *The Soviet Censorship* is now, understandably, somewhat dated. Nevertheless it contains a great deal of valuable information and personal testimony on the nature and ramifications of Soviet censorship. It is an essential starting point in any study of the problem. Censorship involved a tortuous process of writing, consultations and rewriting and several layers of checking and rechecking before something was deemed fit for publication. For a detailed and personal account of dealings with the censorship see Leonid Finkelstein's experiences in Dewhirst and Farrell, pp. 50–63. A recent publication that builds on the earlier study of Dewhirst and Farrell is Marianna Tax Choldin and Maurice Friedberg (eds), *The Red Pencil: Artists, Scholars, and Censors in the USSR*, Unwin Hyman, Boston and London, 1989. In her survey of censorship in Soviet translations of Western authors, Tax Choldin concludes that whereas the tsarist censors were reactive, that is they tried to limit the perceived damage done by foreign authors, Soviet censors were largely active, that is deletions and amendments had a definite ideological purpose. As she quite rightly suggests the Soviet response has more in common with rewriting or control. Tax Choldin's conclusions are based on a comparative study of English texts and Soviet translations of Senator Fulbright's, *The Arrogance of Power* (1966), Sir Harold Nicolson's, *The Evolution of Diplomatic Method* (1954), Kwame Nkrumah's, *I Speak of Freedom* (1961) and Jawaharlal Nehru's, *India's Foreign Policy: Selected Speeches, September 1946–April 1961* (1961). See Tax Choldin, pp. 29–51.

11. Michael Charlton cites five landmarks in communism's collapse: (i) the breaking of silence by Khrushchev over Stalin; (ii) nationalism within the USSR; (iii) the Pope's influence on Poland; (iv) the collapse of East Germany; and (v) the corruption of language. See *Footsteps from the Finland Station: Five Landmarks in the Collapse of Communism*, The Claridge Press, St Albans, 1992. Censorship is common to all five areas.
12. V. I. Lenin, *Sochineniya*, vol. 5, Gosudarstvennoe izdatel'stvo politicheskoy literatury, Moscow, 1946.
13. Lenin, ibid., p. 341.
14. Any doubts about Soviet attitudes towards neutrality in the dissemination of information can be dispelled by remarks made by V. V. Kuibyshev in early 1931, when forced collectivization was at its height:

> The information part of our press is a sector of this agitation by means of facts. And in these two words is essentially contained the whole Bolshevik definition of the tasks of information. Above all this is agitation – i.e., not the toothless, dispassionate transmittal of facts, but the selection of facts in such a way, in such an order, that they themselves shout out for us, for our cause.

Quoted in *A Country Study: Politics in the USSR*, 3rd ed., F. C. Barghoorn and T. F. Remmington, Little, Brown and Company, Boston and Toronto, 1986, p. 178. A Soviet study defines information as being 'an organic part of propaganda'. Spartak I. Beglov, *Vneshnepoliticheskaya propaganda: Ocherk terminov i praktiki*, Vneshnyaya shkola, Moscow, 1984, p. 359. In the Soviet mind at least, the relationship of information to partisanship is not only inseparable, but also desirable.
15. This is the sin of objectivism. Cf. A. M. Prokhorov (ed.), *Bol'shaya Sovetskaya Entsiklopediya*, 3rd ed., vol. 18, Moscow, 1974, p. 262.
16. See Angus Roxburgh, *Pravda: Inside the Soviet News Machine*, Victor Gollancz Ltd., London, 1987, p. 51.
17. See for example Lenin, *Sochineniya*, vol 5, p. 392 and his thoughts on agitation and propaganda, p. 380.
18. In his detailed description of the workings of the Soviet censorship Leonid Finkelstein comments on the censor's manual, *Index of Information Not to be Published in the Open Press*, known as 'The Talmud'. Among the many forbidden topics were: man-made and natural disasters, information about seasonal price increases, any discussion of better living standards outside the socialist camp, statistics which are not taken from the reports of the Central Statistics Bureau, the existence of GLAVLIT and the jamming of foreign radio stations. The defection of a Polish censor, Tomasz Strzewski, to Sweden in 1977, confirmed the existence of an equally comprehensive censorship mechanism operating in Poland. See *The Black Book of Polish Censorship*, trans. and ed. Jane Leftwich Curry, Random House, New York, 1984. For a wider discussion of censorship in Central and Eastern Europe see Paul Lendvai, *The Bureaucracy of Truth: How Communist Governments Manage the News*, Burnett Books, London, 1981 and George Schöpflin

(ed.), *Censorship and Political Communication in Eastern Europe*, Frances Pinter, London, 1983.

19. Robert Tucker, quoted by Robert Conquest in *Harvest of Sorrow*, 1986, p. 290.
20. Neil Postman, *Technopoly: The Surrender of Culture to Technology*, Alfred A. Knopf, New York, 1993, p. 123.
21. Monroe E. Price, *Television, the Public Sphere, and National Identity*, Clarendon Press, Oxford, 1995, p. 16.
22. Brian McNair. *Glasnost', Perestroyka and the Soviet Media*, Routledge, London, 1991, p. x.
23. Hannah Arendt, *The Origins of Totalitarianism*, Harcourt Brace Jovanovich, New York and London, 1973, p. 469.
24. Arendt, ibid., p. 469. Mikhail Heller has defined ideology 'as a system providing the only possible answers to all questions'. See *Cogs in the Soviet Wheel: The Formation of Soviet Man*, trans. David Floyd, Collins, London, 1988, p. 226.
25. Arendt, ibid., p. 471.
26. Arendt, ibid., p. 471.
27. Edward Shils, quoted in David Apter (ed.), *Ideology and Discontent*, The Free Press, New York and London, 1964, p. 50.
28. Brian McNair, *Glasnost', Perestroyka and the Soviet Media*, Routledge, London, 1991, p. 17.
29. *Politics in the USSR*, Barghoorn and Remington, 1986, p. 186.
30. See for example Brian McNair, *Glasnost', Perestroyka and the Soviet Media*, p. 170.
31. McNair, ibid., p. 170.
32. McNair, ibid., p. 170.
33. Andrei Sakharov, *Memoirs*, trans., Richard Lourie, Hutchinson, London, 1990, p. 165.
34. Brian McNair, *Glasnost', Perestroyka and the Soviet Media*, p. 19.
35. Neil Postman, *Technopoly: The Surrender of Culture to Technology*, p. 124. Recognizing the limitations of language, scientists have more or less solved this problem. The solution is mathematics and the other forms of consistently used symbols which allow scientists to share results, irrespective of language barriers. Later, however, Postman notes: 'Science involves a method of employing language that is accessible to everyone. The ascent of humanity has rested largely on that.' Ibid., p. 194. On the other hand, we might also note that the intellectual ascent of humanity has rested on the efforts of a very limited group of individuals.
36. The problems of the Soviet approach are identified by Angus Roxburgh, who argues that the Soviet media fails because: ... 'as with domestic propaganda, it shows not reality as it is, but an "ideologically correct" version of it – reality honed to fit Marxist precepts – which only the naive can believe in. A country obsessed with Western electronic gadgetry and fashions cannot be expected to accept the image of a West consisting *solely* of unemployment and misery, any more than people who put up with chronic shortages of basic goods can be expected to believe that the Soviet Union "leads the world" in every conceivable field.' *Pravda: Inside the Soviet News Machine*, p. 104.

37. For a discussion of information in the Soviet economy see George R. Feiwel, *The Soviet Quest for Economic Efficiency: Issues, Controversies and Reforms*, Frederick A. Praeger, New York, Washington and London, 1967, pp. 94–6.

38. Quoted in Pryce-Jones, *The War That Never Was: The Fall of the Soviet Empire 1985–1991*, p. 39.

39. Kenneth Kraemer *et al.*, *DATAWARS: The Politics of Modelling in Federal Policymaking*, Columbia University Press, New York, 1987, p. 65.

40. Kraemer *et al*, ibid., pp. 9–10.

41. Tycho Brahe (1546–1601) compiled accurate records without which the discoveries of Kepler and Newton would have been impossible.

42. James Davidson and Lord Rees-Mogg, *The Great Reckoning. How the World Will Change in the Depression of the 1990s*, Sidgwick and Jackson, London, 1992, p. 166.

43. Ludwig von Mises, *Socialism. An Economic and Sociological Analysis*, trans. J. Kahane, Liberty Classics, Indianapolis, 1981, p. 113. The original German-language edition was published in 1922. *Die Gemeinwirtschaft: Untersuchungen über den Sozialismus*, Gustav Fischer, Jena.

44. Von Mises, *Socialism*, p. 105.

45. Von Mises, *Socialism*, p. 118. Note, too, the following: 'It is the speculative capitalists who create the data to which he [the socialist] has to adjust his business and which therefore gives directions to his trading operations.' Ibid., p. 121.

46. Carl Sagan and Iosef Shklovskii, *Intelligent Life in the Universe*, Holden Day, Inc., Amsterdam and London, 1966.

47. *Intelligent Life in the Universe*, p. viii.

48. *Intelligent Life in the Universe*, p. 135.

49. *Intelligent Life in the Universe*, p. 135.

50. *Intelligent Life in the Universe*, p. 136.

51. See, for example, the 18th edition of the *Ozhegov* Russian dictionary, Russkiy yazyk, Moscow, 1987, p. 377.

52. 1966 was also the year in which Daniel and Sinyavsky were put on trial for publishing abroad. From the Soviet point of view, therefore, the timing of publication of the Sagan–Shklovskii book was not unwelcome, since it served to deflect attention from the restrictions imposed on Soviet scientists generally.

53. Andrei Sakharov, *Progress, Coexistence, and Intellectual Freedom*, trans., *The New York Times*, with introduction, afterword and notes by Harrison Salisbury, W. W. Norton & Company Inc, New York, 1970. See ch. 7, 'The Threat to Intellectual Freedom'. In his third proposal Sakharov notes: 'A law on press and information must be drafted, widely discussed, and adopted, with the aim not only of ending irresponsible and irrational censorship, but of encouraging self-study in our society, fearless discussion, and the search for truth. The law must provide for the material resources of freedom of thought.' p. 87.

54. Sakharov, *Progress*, p. 67.

55. Sakharov, *Progress*, p. 67.

56. Andrei Sakharov, *Memoirs*, trans. Richard Lourie, Hutchinson, London, 1990, p. xiv.
57. Sakharov, ibid., p. 200. Of interest here is the observation from Sakharov that when he visited Igor Kurchatov, director of the Atomic Energy Institute to discuss his fears about nuclear testing, Kurchatov took notes in a notebook, 'camouflaged with the dust-cover of Nehru's *Memoirs*'. p. 208.
58. Quoted in Sakharov, *Memoirs*, p. 234.
59. Sakharov, *Memoirs*, p. 680.
60. Valentin Turchin, *The Inertia of Fear and the Scientific Worldview*, trans. Guy Daniels, Martin Robertson, Oxford, 1981, p. 45.
61. Turchin, ibid., p. 3.
62. Turchin, ibid., p. 4.
63. Turchin, ibid., p. 229.
64. Turchin, ibid., p. 78.
65. Turchin, ibid., pp. 78–9. Zhores Medvedev notes that the attacks on cybernetics – dismissed as 'bourgeois pseudo-science' – held back the development of the computing industry in the Soviet Union. See *Soviet Science*, W. W. Norton, New York, 1978, pp. 53–4. Some applications of computing were clearly more important to the party than others. For example, the KGB maintained a computer database known by the acronym SOOD to which all the communist satellites, with the exception of Romania, contributed information. The East German STASI are known to have contributed at least 75 000 personal dossiers for computer storage, which is in addition to the material contributed by the Hauptverwaltung Aufklärung (HVA), the agency responsible for espionage abroad. See David Pryce-Jones, *The War That Never Was: The Fall of the Soviet Empire 1985–1991*, Weidenfeld & Nicolson, London, 1995, p. 253. Richard Cummings, formerly of RFE in Munich, suggests that the acronym is SOUD *System for Institutional and Operational Data* (*Sistema dlya uchreditel'nykh/ustanovlennykh i operativnykh dannykh?*), not SOOD as given in Pryce-Jones.
66. For a full account of the attacks on scientists, especially during the immediate post-war period, see George Counts and Nucia Lodge, *The Country of the Blind: The Soviet System of Mind Control*, Houghton Mifflin, Boston, MA, 1949.
67. Andrei Amalrik, *Will the Soviet Union Survive until 1984?*, no translator, Harper & Row, New York and Evanston, 1970, p. 8.
68. Norbert Wiener, *The Human Use of Human Beings, Cybernetics and Society*, Houghton Mifflin, Boston, 1954, p. 93.
69. For Lenin's ideas on literature, see 'Partiynaya organizatsiya i partiynaya literatura', *Polnoe sobranie sochinenii*, vol. 10, OGIZ, Moscow, 1947, pp. 26–31.
70. Norbert Wiener, *The Human Use of Human Beings*, 1954, p. 17.
71. Some of the first people to notice and to react to the emergence of a specifically Soviet language were writers such as Evgeniy Zamyatin, Mikhail Zoshchenko, Andrey Platonov and Mikhail Bulgakov. It is perhaps not surprising that all of these writers suffered under the Soviet system. Zamyatin's anti-utopian novel *We* was first published in

the Soviet Union in 1987, some 60 years after it was written.
72. Quoted in Remington, *The Truth of Authority*, p. 86.
73. Mikhail Heller, *Cogs in the Soviet Wheel*, p. 270.
74. Quoted in Heller, *Cogs in the Soviet Wheel*, p. 272.
75. Quoted in Heller, *Cogs in the Soviet Wheel*, p. 272.
76. *Ozhegov*, 18th edn, 1987, p. 302.
77. *Ozhegov*, 1987, p. 229.
78. *Ozhegov*, 1987, p. 20.
79. For a discussion of Amsterdamski's ideas see Heller, *Cogs in the Soviet Wheel*.
80. Another aspect of SDI, that tormented Soviet strategists, and one which assumed great importance in expediting the final collapse of the Soviet empire, was the ability of the SDI system to be able to manipulate vast amounts of data in real time. This requirement, as Richard Pearle noted, plays to an American strength. See David Pryce-Jones *The War That Never Was: The Fall of the Soviet Empire 1985–1991*, Weidenfeld & Nicolson, London, 1995, p. 122. Pryce-Jones's title is something of a misnomer. Both superpowers fought proxy wars and the Soviet empire's appetite for suppression and military intervention continued throughout the Soviet period. Yeltsin has continued this tradition beyond 1991. There was also the war on the front of ideas and the practical application of these ideas; that is the battle between a free-market economy and the central-command economy. We should also bear in mind the election of Thatcher and Reagan, crucial events in the ending of the Cold War.
81. The Soviet propaganda machine made some determined efforts to persuade American academic and public opinion that SDI, or Star Wars as the propagandists dubbed it, was a waste of money, and that it represented the militarization of space.
82. The fact that in the West defence requirements – such as ARPANET, for example – have given a massive impetus to the development of IT technology in no way undermines those achievements. What can we conclude from the fact that in the Soviet Union the percentage of GNP on defence was much higher than that of the USA, but without the corresponding pre-eminence in IT?
83. General Leonid Shebarshin, head of the KGB's First Main Directorate between 1989–91, argues that: 'Since war was never a realistic prospect in the nuclear age, the West skilfully picked trade as an arena of competition in which its superiority was assured.' *The War That Never Was*, p. 363. There is something to this argument. But it should be noted that the possession of a nuclear arsenal counts for nothing if the willingness to use it has been undermined. Soviet sponsorship of various peace fronts and related organizations was designed to achieve this end. It failed. Had the West's resolve to use nuclear weapons been undermined, and been perceived to have been undermined, then a conventional war against NATO, or some limited military action on NATO's periphery, would have been a serious option for the Soviet military leadership. Whether such an option could have avoided an escalation to the use of nuclear weapons is a moot point.

84. I base this interpretation in part on conversations I had with a number of Soviet army officers in Berlin in 1982. They were clearly impressed with Britain's performance, despite the fact that the Argentine military enjoyed numerical superiority and the advantage of operating very close to home bases.

85. These speculative implications of the British victory for the outcome of the Cold War were prompted by Brian Crozier's assessment of the campaign in his autobiography, 'In terms of grand strategy and of the wider war that concerns us here, the Falklands War was an expensive sideshow.' See *Free Agent: The Unseen War 1941–1991*, Harper Collins, London, 1994, p. 265. The British victory came at a time when domestic and international pressures were forcing the Soviet Union to make some very painful decisions. Crozier also notes the Soviet interest in the Anglo-Argentine conflict and the decision to launch a propaganda campaign in support of Argentina (a typical Soviet *volte-face*): 'Henceforth, Argentina was to be described as an "ally", and pejorative terms such as "junta" or "dictatorship" were to be avoided. There was an ironical side to these guidelines, as the Soviet Union had vilified the military regime during the terror campaign, in which it [the Soviet Union] had played a significant, though indirect, role.' Crozier, ibid., p. 266.

86. Ithiel de Sola Pool, *Technologies of Freedom*, The Belknap Press of Harvard University Press, Cambridge, MA and London, 1983.

87. Mikhail Gorbachev, *Perestroika: New Thinking for Our Country and the World*, Collins, London, 1987, p. 19.

88. Gorbachev, *Perestroika*, p. 21.

89. Gorbachev, *Perestroika*, p. 25. A further reference to Lenin, can be found in Gorbachev's paraphrasing of a well-known Leninist principle, first articulated in *What is to be Done?* (See V. I. Lenin, *Sochineniya*, vol. 5, 4th edn, OGIZ, Moscow, 1946, p. 341.): 'No revolutionary movement is possible without a revolutionary theory – this Marxist precept is today more relevant than ever.' Ibid., p. 49.

90. Gorbachev, *Perestroika*, p. 25.

91. Gorbachev, *Perestroika*, p. 40.

92. See Robert Conquest, *The Harvest of Sorrow: Soviet Collectivization and the Terror-Famine*, Hutchinson, London, 1986. Conquest notes that 14.5 million are likely to have died as the result of the war waged against the peasants. Conquest regards this as a conservative estimate, p. 306. Note that Gorbachev was a specialist in agronomy, which makes his comments about collectivization in *Perestroika* all the more difficult to fathom. Also, collectivization was intended to destroy self-reliance and initiative, the very qualities that Gorbachev wished to see unleashed in *perestroyka*.

93. Gorbachev, *Perestroika*, p. 79.

94. Gorbachev, *Perestroika*, p. 79.

95. Gorbachev, *Perestroika*, p. 105.

96. Viktor Chebrikov, 'Results of the Work of the KGB in Investigating Authors of Anonymous Materials of a Hostile Nature', Top Secret, Special Folder, To the Central Committee of the CPSU, 21 March

1988, No. 458–Ch, Moscow. Hereafter Chebrikov. File available at the Library of Congress in /pub/soviet.archive/text.english. See *KGB Report of Publications Hostile to Soviet Government*, af2bdlit.doc, documents loaded 17 June 1992.

97. Chebrikov.
98. One example which typifies the sort of intellectual exercise in damage-control which I have in mind is the collection of articles in Robin Blackburn (ed.), *After the Fall: The Failure of Communism and the Future of Socialism*, Verso, New York and London, 1991.
99. Charles S. Maier, 'The Collapse of Communism: Approaches for a Future History', *History Workshop*, issue 31, Spring 1991, p. 39.
100. It is inaccurate to say that 'the West eventually opted for the discipline of the world market'. (Maier, p. 39). Rather it was the decisions of political leaders such as Thatcher and Reagan who decided that market discipline had to be applied. In so doing they set a trend that at the time it was advocated encountered vociferous opposition but that subsequently has been emulated world-wide.
101. Maier, p. 50.
102. Maier, p. 52.
103. I am grateful to Walter Laqueur for pointing this out. He notes: 'Franco's Spain was not totalitarian. There was no central ideology and no political mass party, only an old-fashioned if altogether unattractive military dictatorship. For this reason, after Franco's death the transition to a democratic regime proceeded without great difficulty.' See *The Dream that Failed: Reflections on the Soviet Union*, Oxford University Press, New York and Oxford, 1995, p. 84.
104. Eric Hobsbawm, 'Goodbye to All That', in Robin Blackburn (ed.), *After the Fall: The Failure of Communism and the Future of Socialism*, Verso, New York and London, 1991, p. 121.
105. *After the Fall*, p. 121.
106. *After the Fall*, p. 121.
107. *After the Fall*, p. 121.
108. Two articles published in the latter half of 1990 in *Kommunist* are worth quoting. The first shows a lamentable understanding of just how bad things were, even at this late stage. See for example, Dzherman Gvishiani *et al*, 'Sotsial'nye apsekty informatizatsii', *Kommunist*, 10, July 1990, pp. 48–56. The authors propose sensible measures. The trouble is that what they are proposing is far too little, and above all too late in order to save the Soviet Union. In July 1990 the system was beyond reform. They note:

> The increasing volumes and the ever increasing speed required for the processing and transmission of economic information (in the widest sense including production-technological, administrative, statistical and financial planning) are creating a fundamentally new economic situation. The processing of information constitutes the basis for the structural *perestroyka* of industrial production, of integrated processes in our country's economy, and in the world economy (p. 50).

The belief that merely building an information structure could solve the Soviet Union's problems fails to realize that such an information structure, that is one with computers and IT would presuppose a totally different Soviet Union. Just grafting a modern information infrastructure onto the ailing Soviet body politic would do no good at all. The authors note the hostility on the part of the bureaucracies to anything that might break their information monopoly. Problems of information reconstruction are, 'in the first place', they argue, 'problems of science, not ideology' (p. 54). This surely misses the point: they are problems of ideology since considerations of ideology are put before the considerations of science and solving real situation problems. A second article shows understanding, but any solutions are of course far too late. See V. Makarov, 'Informatizatsiya v novom ekonomicheskom mekhanizme', *Kommunist*, 12, August 1990, pp. 51–5:

> We are sometimes surprised as to why, in a country of centralised planning, statistical data concerning economic and social processes are much more sparse than in countries with a market economy. But you see control from the centre, according to an idea, must be based on the knowledge of what is happening in the regions. The paradox is explained by the fact that every institution only needs information and indicators for which it is responsible. The institution tries to keep this information secret by truths and lies so as, on the one hand, to avoid control, and on the other hand, to raise its status and to be able to dispose of a resource, which can be realised in a market of exchange in kind. [...] (p. 52).

> [...] The striving of the administrative-command system to block the horizontal flows of information is corroborated by the total concealment of banking information which reflects the economic interaction between organisations. This is a priceless source of the most reliable and timely data of economic processes. It is precisely banking information that in the West is the foundation of all economic statistics. Up till now we have sealed the secret with seven seals. Yet, the computerization of banking is one of the high priority spheres of informatization where the greatest effect is possible (p. 52).

and note too:

> Throughout the country in the course of one year banking operations to the sum of three trillion rubles are carried out. The majority of these follow on after the corresponding material relocations – deliveries products and so on. In general the delay constitutes anything from ten or more days. It is as if we live in another financial world which moves at a slower speed. If we are to march in step with the West, then there is no other way than to create the very same (technically) banking system, where every operation is measured in seconds, where cashless transactions with the help of cards and other means increasingly drive out cash, where fundamental economic decisions are taken in banks, and not mechanically processed (p. 52).

109. It is not widely known that the Kalashnikov assault rifle is based on the design of a German airborne, assault-rifle, the Fallschirmjäger Gewehr 43, used in the Second World War.

110. 'Out of the Ashes', in *After the Fall*, p. 318.

111. Robert X. Cringely, *Accidental Empires*, Penguin, Harmondsworth, Middlesex, 1996, p. 15.

112. As exemplified by Moore's Law. Gordon Moore, one of the founders of Intel, stated that the number of transistors that can be built on a given piece of silicon will double every 18 months.

113. Bill Gates, *The Road Ahead*, Viking, London, 1995, p. 15.

114. Cringely, *Accidental Empires*, pp. 124–5.

115. Ronald Reagan, Speech at London's Guildhall, *Los Angeles Times*, 14 June 1989, p. 10.

116. Frank Ellis 'The Media as Social Engineer: The Failed Experiment, 1953–1991, *Russian Cultural Studies*, Oxford University Press, Oxford, 1998, p. 221.

117. The use of camcorders to record the activities of the security forces in Czechoslovakia during demonstrations in 1988 is one example. This had the same sort of explosive effect as the Rodney King video in Los Angeles.

118. See Bob Travica and Matthew Hogan, Syracuse University, USA, 'Computer Networking in the XUSSR: Technology, Uses and Social Effects', The Department of the History of Science, Johns Hopkins University, 1992.

119. Ibid. A similar example of the use of computer networks in an emergency, but in a political context which bears no relation to the Soviet circumstances, is cited by Randy Reddick. Immediately after the large earthquake struck California's San Fernando valley on 17 January 1994, state employees used the Emergency Digital Information Service (EDIS) to keep people informed of rescue operations. See Randy Reddick, *The Online Journalist: Using the Internet and Other Electronic Resources*, Harcourt Brace College Publishers, New York, 1995, p. 102.

120. Paul Kennedy, *The Rise and Fall of the Great Powers: Economic Change and Military Conflict from 1500 to 2000*, Unwin and Hyman, London, 1988, p. 439.

CHAPTER TWO: MASS MEDIA LEGISLATION OF THE RUSSIAN FEDERATION

1. They are: *Article 6*: 'Everyone has the right to recognition everywhere as a person before the law.' [which was clearly at odds with Marxist-Leninist ideology and its glorification of class war. There were no individuals only classes]. *Article 12*: 'No one shall be subjected to arbitrary interference with his privacy, family, home or correspondence, nor to attacks upon his honour and reputation. Everyone has the right to the protection of the law against such interference or attacks.' *Article 13*: '1. Everyone has the right to freedom of movement and residence

within the borders of each state. 2. Everyone has the right to leave any country, including his own, and to return to his country.' *Article 18*: 'Everyone has the right to freedom of thought, conscience and religion; this right includes freedom to change his religion or belief, and freedom, either alone or in community with others and in public or private, to manifest his religion or belief in teaching, practice, worship and observance.' *Article 20*: '1. Everyone has the right to freedom of peaceful assembly and association. 2. No one may be compelled to belong to any association.' *Article 27*: '1. Everyone has the right freely to participate in the cultural life of the community, to enjoy the arts and to share in scientific advancement and its benefits. 2. Everyone has the right to the protection of the moral and material interest resulting from any scientific, literary or artistic production of which he is author.'

2. Article 50 of the Soviet Constitution (adopted 7 October 1977) guaranteed citizens of the USSR, freedom of speech, the freedom of the press, assembly, processions and demonstrations. Article 50 also states that: 'The exercise of these political freedoms is guaranteed by making available public buildings, streets and squares to the workers and their organisations and by the widest dissemination of information, and by the opportunity to use the press, television and radio.' See *Konstitutsiya (osnovnoy zakon) Soyuza Sovetskikh Sotsialisticheskikh respublik*, Yuridicheskaya literatura, Moscow, 1980, p. 18. Soviet constitutions were promulgated in 1918, 1922, 1936 and 1977.

3. Article 19 states: 'Everyone has the right to freedom of opinion and expression; this right includes freedom to hold opinions without interference and to seek, receive and impart information and ideas through any media regardless of frontiers.' quoted in Andrei Sakharov, *Memoirs*, trans., Richard Lourie, Hutchinson, London, 1990, p. 362.

4. The demands for legislation protecting the rights of free speech are of course inextricably linked with the horrendous memories of the Lenin and Stalin periods. As Solzhenitsyn documents in great detail in vol. 1 of the *GULAG Archipelago*, NKVD terror relied heavily on the provisions of the 14 sections of Article 58 of the Criminal Code of 1926. Section 10 of Article 58 was used extensively against any manifestation of free speech since any criticism could easily be construed under the section as an appeal to overthrow or subvert Soviet power. The sections of Article 58 were worded in such a way that anything can be made to fit the definition of a crime. As Solzhenitsyn noted: 'Wherever the law is, crime can be found.' p. 67. See *The Gulag Archipelago 1918–1956, An Experiment in Literary Investigation*, vol. 1, trans. Thomas Whitney, Harper Collins, New York, 1991, p. 67. For Solzhenitsyn's discussion of Article 58 see pp. 60–92.

5. Yuriy M. Baturin, Vladimir Entin and Mikhail Fedotov state that the idea was raised in *Vedomosti Verkhovnogo Soveta SSSR* (*Newspaper of the Supreme Soviet*). See 'The Road to Freedom for the Soviet Press', *Journal of Media Law and Practice*, vol. 13, No. 1, 1991, p. 43.

6. Baturin *et al.*, ibid., p. 43.

7. Baturin *et al.*, ibid., p. 43.

8. Baturin *et al.*, p. 44.

9. A full English translation of the 1990 Press Law can be found in *The Current Digest of the Soviet Press*, Vol. XLII, No. 25, 1990, pp. 16–20. Unless otherwise stated all quotations are taken from this translation.
10. Article 55 of the draft put forward by Baturin *et al.* proposed the following definition of censorship which was omitted from the 1990 Media Law: [...] 'demands on mass media by officials, state bodies and public organisations to coordinate well in advance materials and reports (except in cases when an official is an author or an interviewed person), the banning of the dissemination of materials and reports or parts thereof'. See Baturin *et al.*, ibid., p. 44. GLAVLIT was transformed into the General Authority on the Protection of Secrets attached to the Council of Ministers of the USSR. The new body offered to vet, for a small fee, all material prior to publication. As the authors note, there is no legislative basis for this vetting since the 1990 Press Law prohibits the publication of state secrets (Article 5 'The Impermissibility of Abuse of the Freedom of Speech').
11. The 1990 Media Law made no provision for the specific electronic transmission of data and news via computer networks.
12. Article 10 ('Cases of the Dissemination of News without Registration') of the 1990 Media Law stated that: 'Registration is not required for media outlets issuing printed output with a press run of fewer than 1,000 copies.' This effectively legalized *samizdat*.
13. From a purely chronological point of view the 1990 Press Law is of course a Soviet law.
14. Monroe Price argues that the Leninist criterion of *partiynost'* bedevils the question of a 'founder' in Russian press law and thus the nature of independence. He notes: 'Without a sense of the Leninist past, without the concept of *partiinost*, the important status and function of a publication's 'founder' in the time of transition were difficult to translate into Western terms.' See *Television, the Public Sphere, and National Identity*, Clarendon Press, Oxford, 1995, p. 90. In response, one can say that by the time the Soviet Union ceased to exist the criterion of *partiynost'* meant very little, in fact *glasnost'* brutally exposed the deadening hand of *partiynost'* on the Soviet media. The questions that bedevil the notion of 'founder' owe more to the commercial control of the paper rather than to any ideological legacy, which by the time these questions were on the agenda, had been totally and publicly discredited.
15. For the full text of the law see 'Zakon Rossiyskoy federatsii o sredstvakh massovoy informatsii', *Rossiyskaya gazeta*, 8 February 1992, pp. 3–4. A full English translation of this law is included in Appendix A.
16. Article 57 ('Exemption from Responsibility') raises similar problems to those discussed in Article 38 of the 1990 Press Law. Categories of exemption are: (i) if the information was present in 'obligatory messages' (*obyazatel'nye soobshcheniya*). What constitutes an 'obligatory message' is not made clear. (ii) if the information is received from information agencies. (iii) if the information comes from official sources. (iv) if it is the *verbatim* reproduction of officials at conference and state sessions. (v) if the information is contained in texts which

were not subject to any editing. (vi) if they originate from other mass media that can be held responsible under the law.

17. The information could be construed as being commercially sensitive. It is not clear from the law whether the information required for registration will be supplied on request to members of the general public and media rivals.

18. The nine members of the Court were: Professor Anatoliy Borisovich Vengerov (Professor of Law); Aleksey Evgen'evich Voinov (student of the School of Law of Mass Information); Anatoliy Stepanovich Ezhelev (chairman of the St Petersburg Union of Journalists); Igor' Yur'evich Eremin (member of the Committee for Mass Media of the former Supreme Council of the Russian Federation); Aleksandr Konstantinovich Kopeyka (member of the Committee for Mass Media of the Supreme Council of the Russian Federation); Viktor Nikolaevich Monakhov (State Inspection for the Protection of the Freedom of the Press and Mass Information Russian Federation); Mar'yana Viktorovna Panyarskaya (student of the School of Law of Mass Information); Aleksey Kirillovich Simonov (chairman of the governing board of the Glasnost Defence Foundation); Vladimir Valentinovich Sukhomlinov (first deputy chairman of the International Confederation of Journalists' Unions).

19. The provisions and implementation of the Statute are subject to the force of the 1992 Mass Media Law. Of particular relevance are Articles 4 and 58, as noted in Point 19, paragraph a. and Point 21 of the Statute.

20. 'Ob utverzhdenii polozheniya o Sudebnoy palaty po informatsionnym sporam pri Prezidente Rossiyskoy Federatsii', Presidential Decree N 228, 31.1.94.

21. The Judicial Chamber is to deal with disputes arising from the following areas: (i) any damage to the freedom of the mass media outside those provided for by the Mass Media Law, particularly demands for information on the part of journalists as provided for by Article 38; (ii) the requirement to provide timely correction or refutation of mistakes; (iii) disputes concerning the nature of reports that are not objective and are unreliable, including those 'based on rumours, unverified data, false information' (Point 9, para. 3); (iv) violation of the principle of equality of rights, particularly those cases involving violations based on political, social, linguistic, racial or religious allegiance; (v) damage to the moral interests of children and youth; (vi) allocation of broadcast time.

22. Chapter III, Point 23 states that the most important decisions of the Judicial Chamber are to be published in *Rossiyskaya gazeta*, and they are to be widely disseminated throughout the mass media.

23. For details of disputes see Vladimir Klimov, 'Reshenie okonchatel'noe. Obzhalovaniyu ne podlezhit', *Rossiyskaya gazeta*, 13.5.95, p. 1.

24. Frances Foster, 'Freedom with Problems: The Russian Judicial Chamber on Mass Media', a paper presented at the Conference, *Post-Soviet Media in Transition*, University of Stirling, 2–4 February 1996, p. 4. Most of the original members of the Arbitration Information Tribunal transferred to the Judicial Chamber.

25. Chapter I, Point 16 of the Statute defining the Judicial Chamber's role and competence states that the Judicial Chamber must submit an annual report on this matter to the President of the Russian Federation.
26. Vladimir Klimov, 'Reshenie okonchatel'noe. Obzhalovaniyu ne podlezhit', *Rossiyskaya gazeta*, 13.5.1995, pp. 1 and 6.
27. Klimov, ibid., p. 6.
28. Article 46 is published in Chapter 2, 'The Rights and Freedoms of the Person and Citizen'. Paragraph 2 states: 'The decisions and actions (or non-action) of the organs of state power, organs of the local government, of social associations and official persons may be the subject of an appeal to a court.'
29. Foster, 'Freedom with Problems', p. 4. In her study of the Judicial Chamber Frances Foster has identified six trends or 'fact patterns' in its rulings. They are: (i) ethnic, that is those publications that have launched attacks on the basis of ethnicity; (ii) publications that discredit state institutions; (iii) information that discriminates on the basis of a person's sex; (iv) undermining public morality; (v) information that causes physical harm; (vi) information that causes financial harm. See pp. 11–15.
30. Foster, ibid., p. 28.
31. Article 8 ('Degrees of Secrecy of Information and the Seals of Secrecy of the Bearers of this Information'), paragraph 2 specifies three categories of classification: 'of special importance' (*osoboy vazhnosti*); 'top secret' (*sovershenno sekretno*); and 'secret' (*sekretno*).
32. The provisions of Article 7 of the Secrecy Law are reinforced by Article 10 ('Information Resources According to Categories of Access') of the Information Law (1995).
33. The Commission is not the sole government body with an interest in the protection of secrets. Article 20 ('Organs of Protection of State Secrecy') lists others who have a vital interest: the Ministry of Security of the Russian Federation; the Ministry of Defence of the Russian Federation; the Federal Agency of Government Communication and Information of the Office of the President of the Russian Federation; the Foreign Intelligence Service of the Russian Federation; and the State Technical Commission of the Office of the President of the Russian Federation.
34. The law was adopted on 15.12.1994 and enacted on 13.1.1995.
35. 'Federal'nyy zakon ob informatsii, informatizatsii i zashchite informatsii', N 24–F3, 20.2.1995.
36. Paragraph 1 of Article 3 states: 'State policy in the sphere of the formation of information resources and informatization is aimed at the creation of conditions for the effective and qualitative information provision in the solution of the strategic and operational tasks of the societal and economic development of the Russian Federation.'
37. Yet paragraph 3 of Article 6 states that: 'The state has the right of purchase of documentary information [defined in Article 2, paragraph 3] from physical and juridical persons in the event that this information is placed in the category of a state secret.'
38. The danger of government bias and the threat of censorship were

manifest in the first Statute of *Roskompechat'*, promulgated and confirmed by a Presidential resolution dated 3.3.1994. Paragraph 8, part 13 of the Statute provided for: 'the presentation in accordance with the established procedure of written warnings to the founders or editorial staffs (editors-in-chief) of publishers of the periodical press in the event of a violation of current legislation, of international treaties and of inflicting damage on the Russian Federations's inter-state relations with foreign countries.' While this part has been omitted from the later and current Statute dated 1.11.1994, its very inclusion in the first Statute bears witness to some very powerful groupings within the state and government apparatus who are quite unready to tolerate the sort of activities and freedoms to which Russian journalists aspire.

39. The decree of 3.3.1994 states that the total personnel of *Roskompechat'*, excluding maintenance and security personnel, numbers 439 persons in the central agency alone.

40. Corporate Russia is also aware of the value of a press service, and corporate secrecy and public relations go hand-in-hand. According to Mikhail Gulyaev: 'The top executives as well as middle management are rarely available to the media, and the recently created press-services often pose as guards rather than providers of information.' See 'Media as Contested Power in Post-Glasnost Russia', p. 9.

41. The technical and material resources at the disposal of the Presidential press service are indeed considerable. The director has access to state and government communications networks, access to the data bases of the Presidential administration, and has the right to secure information from other government agencies. Unlike *Roskompechat'*, no numbers are given for the staff. In view of the press service's access to various resources, there may well be other tasks for the service, which are not stated in the Statute.

42. See 'Voprosy Mezhvedomstvennoy komissii po zashchite gosudar-stvennoy tayny', N 71, 20.1.1996.

43. As in the case of the Judicial Chamber and *Roskompechat'*, both the chairman and the deputies of the Inter-Departmental Commission are appointed, and can be relieved of their duties, by the President of the Russian Federation.

CHAPTER THREE: RUSSIAN JOURNALISM'S TIME OF TROUBLES

1. The first use of the term 'fourth estate' has been attributed to Edmund Burke by Thomas Carlyle.

2. Frances Foster, '*Izvestiya* as a Mirror of Russian Legal Reform: Press, Law and Crisis in the Post-Soviet Era', *Vanderbilt Journal of Transnational Law 26*, 1993, p. 675. Quoted by Monroe Price, *Television, the Public Sphere, and National Identity*, Clarendon Press, Oxford, 1995, p. 127.

3. The title of chapter 5 in Price's book, *Television, the Public Sphere and National Identity*.
4. Peter Krug, 'From "Rules of Socialist Community Life" to the 1995 Civil Code: Private and Public Interests in Russian Civil Defamation and Constitutional Law', Part 1, 1996, p. 28.
5. V. I. Bakshtanovskiy *et al.*, *Stanovlenie dukha korporatsii: pravila chestnoy igry v soobshchestve zhurnalistov*, Nachalo-Press, Moscow, 1995. These remarks are taken from the editorial introduction, pp. 9–10.
6. Ibid., p. 10.
7. These conclusions are drawn from a study of the attitudes of journalists and editors (see Bakshtanovskiy *et al.*), backed up by a detailed survey carried out by the Glasnost Defence Foundation (see *Zhurnalist i Zhurnalistika rossiyskoy provintsii, Opyt issledovaniya*, Sept.–Dec. 1994, Fond zashchity glasnosti, Nachalo-Press, Moscow, 1995). The essays merit close attention for they cast considerable light on the problems of contemporary Russian journalism. The GDF survey represents one of the most comprehensive undertaken since the end of the Soviet Union.
8. O. G. Lobyzova, in *Stanovlenie dukha korporatsii*, pp. 136–7.
9. Lobyzova, ibid., p. 139.
10. Lobyzova, ibid., p. 144.
11. *Stanovlenie dukha korporatsii*, p. 5.
12. *Stanovlenie dukha korporatsii*, quoted p. 5.
13. Yakovlev, *Stanovlenie dukha korporatsii*, p. 66.
14. Yakovlev, ibid., p. 68.
15. Yur'ev, *Stanovlenie dukha korporatsii*, p. 200.
16. Yur'ev, ibid., p. 200.
17. Yur'ev, ibid., p. 201.
18. Yur'ev, ibid., p. 205.
19. Iosif Dzyaloshinskiy, *Rossiyskiy zhurnalist v posttotalitarnuyu epokhu: nekotorye osobennosti lichnosti i professional'noy deyatel'nosti*, Vostok, Moscow, 1996.
20. Dzyaloshinskiy, ibid., p. 249.
21. *Stanovlenie dukha korporatsii*, p. 3.
22. Mikhail Gulyaev, 'Media as a Contested Power in Post-Glasnost Russia', a paper presented at *Post-Soviet Media in Transition*, University of Stirling, 2–4 Feb. 1996, p. 1.
23. Mostbank, one of Russia's largest banks, has invested in the daily *Segodnya*, the television company NTV and the radio station *Ekho-Moskvy*.
24. Up to 1995 the following allocations have been made: national regional publications 72; children's papers and journals 52; youth papers and journals 70; cultural-educational 55; sport 18; women's 12; literature-arts 29; social-political 30; popular science 45; teaching 30; economic 7; various administrative regions 225; former party publications 13; central republican publishers 69; industrial, medicine and agricultural 92; others 7. See Iosif Dzyaloshinskiy, *Rossiyskiy zhurnalist v posttotalitarnuyu epokhu*, p. 13.
25. Gulyaev, 'Media as a Contested Power in Post-Glasnost Russia', p. 4.

26. *Stanovlenie dukha korporatsii*, p. 21.
27. Gol'dberg, *Stanovlenie dukha korporatsii*, p. 21.
28. Monroe Price, *Television, the Public Sphere, and National Identity*, p. 86.
29. Price, ibid., p. 89.
30. Price, ibid., p. 90.
31. Price, ibid., p. 91.
32. Price, ibid., pp. 91–2.
33. Price, ibid., p. 92.
34. Price, ibid., p. 93.
35. See Aleksey Simonov (ed.), *Zhurnalisty na chechenskoy voyne: Fakty, Dokumenty, Svidetel'stva, November 1994–December 1995*, Prava cheloveka, Moscow, 1995. In his introductory remarks Simonov observes that 'Tiredness is the mother of despair' (p. 9). He argues that the state of tiredness works in favour of the authorities who through various bureaucratic devices and procedures are trying to wear journalists down. Also, according to Simonov, the Russian state, having declared its belief in the freedom of the word, is nevertheless waging a war against journalists with the intention of limiting the very freedom of the word it claims to uphold. Simonov also contends – and it is difficult to disagree with him – that in the Chechen war Russian journalists have defended and upheld their journalistic freedoms, a fact supported by the numbers of deaths and wounded. The Chechen war has proved to be the first real test of the journalists' freedoms and the willingness (or lack of) of the government to guarantee them in a conflict situation after the fall of the Soviet Union.
36. See Aleksey Simonov (ed.), *Presledovanie zhurnalistov i pressy na territorii byvshego SSSR v 1994 godu*, Moskovskaya Pravda, Moscow, 1995, pp. 5–7.
37. Grigoriy Baklanov, 'Professiya: pogibshiy reporter', *Obshchaya gazeta*, No 42, 21.10.94, p. 1.
38. Kronid Lyubarskiy, 'Terror kak forma tsenzury', *Novoe vremya*, No 43, 1994, p. 6.
39. Andrey Bayduzhiy, 'Po komu zvonit kolokol?', *Nezavisimaya gazeta*, 21.10.94, p. 2.
40. See Larisa Kislinskaya, 'List'ev stal chetvertym ubitym rukovoditelem reklamnogo konsortsiuma', *Golos*, 11, 1995, p. 2.
41. 'Versii ubiystva', *Izvestiya*, 3.3.1995, p. 4. Unattributed.
42. An article in *Krasnaya zvezda* speculated that one of the aims of the murderers was to intimidate the press and destabilize Russia. See 'Eshche odno ubiystvo, potryasshee obshchestvo: gosudarstvo obyazano ostanovit' etot bespredel', *Krasnaya zvezda*, 3.3.1995, p.1.
43. On 17 June 1995 Natalya Alyakina, a freelance correspondent working for the German news service RUFA and the magazine *Focus*, was shot dead by a Russian soldier after she had been allowed through a Russian military checkpoint. By an unusual coincidence Alyakina was shot dead on the day in the (West) German calendar marking the uprising in East Berlin in 1953.

44. See the CPJ web site for this article, 'Murdering Journalists with Impunity', 1996.
45. See Simonov, *Chechenskaya voyna*, p. 210.
46. Quoted in Simonov, *Chechenskaya voyna*, p. 157.
47. Quoted in Simonov, *Chechenskaya voyna*, p. 158. Nikolay Egorov seems to have no doubt about the well-organized nature of the enemy's media campaign. In *Rossiyskaya gazeta* (15 February 1995) he noted: 'We have lost the information war to Dudaev not only because he has been deliberately nurturing people for the last three years and creating a massive counter-propaganda mechanism ...', Ibid., p. 80.
48. Quoted in Simonov, *Chechenskaya voyna*, p. 158. Less sensational and more persuasive are Gryzunov's remarks on the responsibility of the press: 'By means of its abstract-humanist response to the operations of the power ministries Russian journalists have noticeably deepened the conflict itself, making it more pervasive and a solution more difficult. Moreover, by their 'eye-witness accounts' they have subjected the whole experience of democratic transformations in Russia to doubt and inflicted a very heavy blow on the institution of presidential authority and given a mass of arguments to those who for a long time have been searching for signs of a 'national crime' in the acts of the reformers. In so doing the press has, as it were, created a psychological basis for future coup attempts. Its one-sided view of events has definitely furthered a situation in which brutality on both sides has been manifested on levels much greater than that dictated by concrete circumstances (Quoted in Simonov, *Chechenskaya voyna*, p. 182).
49. Quoted in Simonov, *Chechenskaya voyna*, p. 157. Subsequently, an open letter to Yeltsin, signed by leaders of a number of media organizations challenged Yeltsin to substantiate these accusations.
50. Quoted in Simonov, *Chechenskaya voyna*, pp. 344–5.
51. Quoted in Simonov, *Chechenskaya voyna*, pp. 158–9. Amid the wave of official and semi-official criticism, the Judicial Chamber judged that: 'nobody and nothing alters the direct effect of the Constitution of the Russian Federation, including in this respect the freedom of the word, the rights of citizens to receive reliable and objective information'. See Zayavlenie No 11, 26 Dec. 1994, 'O zashchite svobody sredstv massovoy informatsii v svyazi s sobytiyami v Chechne'.
52. Consider the case of the British *Guardian's* Richard Gott, who in 1994 was identified as being a KGB agent of influence (*agent vliyaniya*). See Alisdair Palmer, 'How the KGB ran the *Guardian's* Features Editor', *The Spectator*, 10.12.94., pp. 9–12. For a discussion of Soviet front organizations in the West see Clive Rose, *The Soviet Propaganda Network: A Directory of Organisations Serving Soviet Foreign Policy*, Pinter Publishers, London and St Martin's Press, New York, 1988.
53. See Simonov, *Chechenskaya voyna*, pp. 121–2.
54. Quoted in Simonov, *Chechenskaya voyna*, p. 146.
55. Quoted in Simonov, *Chechenskaya voyna*, p. 147. It is also clear that the provision to give priority in accreditation to the major media outlets discriminates against the smaller ones. Again, size of a media enterprise is not a consideration when determining accreditation (Article 48

of the Mass Media Law). Note too that the requirement that the journalist be accompanied by a member of the various security forces when filming and recording is also a contradiction of the 1992 Mass Media Law.

56. Quoted in Simonov, *Chechenskaya voyna*, p. 152.

57. The problem is by no means unique to the Russian Federal Army. The British Army's problems with the press in the Falklands war and in Northern Ireland come to mind. In the Falklands War journalists at one stage were forbidden to broadcast details about the weather since this would have given information to the Argentine military concerning the location of the task force. See D. Mercer et al., *The Fog of War*, Heinemann, London, 1987.

58. Simonov, *Chechenskaya voyna*, p. 154.

59. Quoted in Simonov, *Chechenskaya voyna*, p. 250.

60. What one might term the 'media wars' among the Yugoslav republics began in earnest in the mid-1980s. The republican leaderships were not satisfied with just controlling the media, they were now using them in their internal and external power struggles. The major republican television networks – Belgrade Television, Zagreb Television and Llubljana Television – were instruments in this policy. Opponents were demonized in accordance with national stereotypes: Croats portrayed as genocidal, religious zealots, Serbs as oriental despots; Croatia as Europe's guardian against the Eastern threat and so on. See Stan Markotich, 'Government Control over Serbia's Media', *RFE/RL Research Report*, vol. 3, no. 5, 4 Feb. 1994, pp. 35–9 and Pedrag Simic, 'The Former Yugoslavia: The Media and Violence', *RFE/RL Research Report*, vol. 3, no. 5, 4 Feb. 1994, pp. 40–7.

61. Quoted in Simonov, *Chechenskaya voyna*, p. 203.

62. Erskine, quoted in F. Knight Hunt, *The Fourth Estate: Contributions Towards a History of Newspapers and of the Liberty of the Press*, vol 1., David Bogue, 86 Fleet Street, London, 1850, p. 267.

CHAPTER FOUR: A SURVEY OF RUSSIA'S CULTURE AND MEDIA WARS

1. Hedrick Smith, *The New Russians*, Hutchinson, London, 1990, p. 402.

2. Hedrick Smith, p. 401.

3. Neil Postman, *Amusing Ourselves to Death: Public Discourse in the Age of Show Business*, Heinemann, London, 1986, p. 84.

4. Postman, *Amusing Ourselves to Death*, p. 126.

5. In his essay 'Psychological Culture', Alexander Etkind, notes: 'The only way for a patient to get out of the psychiatric prison was to renounce incorrect views and embrace the official line. Again, the healthy psyche was equated with discursiveness, the ability to spout correct verbiage, the eagerness with which one was willing to present ideologically correct precepts as personal convictions.' See *Russian Culture at the Crossroads: Paradoxes of Postcommunist Consciousness*,

Dmitri N. Shalin (ed.), Westview Press, Colorado and Oxford, 1996, p. 121.

6. *Selected Works of Mao Tsetung*, 1st edn., vol. 5, Foreign Languages Press, Peking, 1977, p. 405.

7. Mikhail Dunaev's blistering attack on Western rock music and its Russian imitators, a mixture of speculative hyperbole and some serious insights, typifies the state of mind that equates rock music with a satanic plot to destroy Russia, while ignoring the spiritual devastation of communism. If we filter out any conspiracy theories, then there is much in the article worth reading. Dunaev notes, for example, the way rock music in all its varieties undermines hierarchies of artistic achievement, and that this, in turn, has profound consequences on moral behaviour and choices. He notes: 'The absence of any precise criteria of truth, which is known as relativism, arises from a consumer mentality whose survival requires extremely flexible day-to-day principles [...] In evaluating life's phenomena relativism recognises a host of individual assessments which for all their diversity are just as equal and therefore entitled to equal treatment. As a consequence of this, the most wretched and most repulsive phenomena can be considered to be good and beautiful. A similar manner of thinking must, inevitably, lead to the idea that: all is permitted.' See *Nash sovremennik*, vol. 2, 1988, p. 167.

8. George Orwell, 'The Prevention of Literature', *Inside the Whale and Other Essays*, Penguin, Harmondsworth, Middlesex, 1983, p. 173.

9. A word coined by Marianna Tax Choldin in 'The Censorship of Foreign Books in Russia and the USSR', trans. Yurii Fridshtein, May 1992. See http://carousel.lis.uiuc.edu/~iris/choldin.html.

10. Neil Postman, *Amusing Ourselves to Death: Public Discourse in the Age of Show Business*, Heinemann, London, 1986, p. 141.

11. Czesław Miłosz, *The Captive Mind*, trans. Jane Zielonko, Penguin, Harmondsworth, 1985, p. xiv.

12. Cited by Price in *Television, the Public Sphere, and National Identity*, p. 149.

13. Price does not go far enough in rejecting Schudson's absurd comparison: 'Of course, while there is a superficial resemblance between the strategies of the socialist realism of the past and "capitalist realism", the differences are vital, and they should be mentioned even before the similarities.' See Monroe Price, *Television, the Public Sphere, and National Identity*, p. 149. A similar misunderstanding can be found in Aldous Huxley's *Brave New World Revisited*. See chs. 4–6. As Ludwig von Mises has noted in *Human Action*, high pressure advertising alone cannot compel consumers to buy what they do not want to buy: 'If this were true, success or failure in business would depend on the mode of advertising only. However, nobody believes that any kind of advertising, would have succeeded in making the candlemakers hold the field against the electric bulb, the horsedrivers against the motorcars, the goose quill against the steel pen ...'. See *Human Action: A Treatise on Economics*, 3rd revised edn, Fox and Wilkes, San Francisco, 1966, p. 321. Consumer items can be tested by consumers to see whether the

item meets the consumer's expectations. Political and religious ideas, as von Mises notes, cannot be tested in such a manner. However, it is not entirely accurate that: 'The statements of religious, metaphysical, and political propaganda can be neither verified nor falsified by experience' (p. 321). A dissatisfied consumer hurts the businessman and damages his profits. The whole nation is not turned upside down, as is the case with the grand utopian schemes of social engineering. Political ideas have consequences that reveal themselves well after they have first been disseminated, the claims of National socialism and Soviet socialism, being two obvious examples, by which time of course it is too late to prevent the misery and carnage. Nevertheless, von Mises is right to argue that: 'political and business propaganda are essentially different things, although they often resort to the same technical methods' (p. 322). In this respect we should also note the remarks of Friedrich Hayek: 'The only point that needs to be stressed is that neither propaganda in itself, nor the techniques employed, are peculiar to totalitarianism, and that what so completely changes its nature and effect in a totalitarian state is that all propaganda serves the same goal, that all the instruments of propaganda are co-ordinated to influence the individuals in the same direction and to produce the characteristic *Gleichschaltung* of all minds. As a result, the effect of propaganda in totalitarian countries is different not only in magnitude but in kind from that of the propaganda made for different ends by independent and competing agencies. See *The Road to Serfdom*, Routledge & Kegan Paul, London, 1993, p. 114.

14. The study of Russian literature in the West throughout the Cold War more or less avoided the damaging fashions that did so much to undermine history, sociology and economics. Could it be that the continuity factor, that is the nineteenth-century legacy, provided some kind of standard for Western scholars as much as it did for Russian readers; that socialist-realist texts inspired not so much admiration but a mixture of horror and entertainment?

15. A recent example is Valentin Rasputin's 'Senya edet'. See *Movska*, 7, 1994, pp. 3–7.

16. Quoted in Tax Choldin, *The Red Pencil*, 1989, p. 93.

17. Dmitri N. Shalin (ed.), *Russian Culture at the Crossroads: Paradoxes of Postcommunist Consciousness*, Westview Press, Colorado and Oxford, 1996, p. 33.

18. For example, Evgeniy Zamyatin's *We* and Andrey Platonov's, *The Foundation Pit*. The growth of critical methodologies specifically geared to the rise of independent television and the media in general is almost certain in the next few years. These critics will study the works of McLuhan and other media theorists, formulating their own critical approach. Their contribution to our understanding is likely to be significant. For their part Western researchers will need to study the growth of this new discipline.

CHAPTER FIVE: THE INTERNET IN RUSSIA

1. Bill Gates, *The Road Ahead*, Viking, London, 1995, p. 5.
2. *Bangemann Report*, p. 4.
3. *Bangemann Report*, p. 4.
4. *Bangemann Report*, p. 4.
5. *Bangemann Report*, p. 4.
6. *Bangemann Report*, p. 16.
7. *Bangemann Report*, p. 6.
8. *Bangemann Report*, p. 5.
9. *Bangemann Report*, p. 5.
10. *Bangemann Report*, p. 6.
11. *Bangemann Report*, p. 6.
12. *Bangemann Report*, p. 6.
13. *Bangemann Report*, p. 6.
14. Bureaucracies are of course not the sole group with a vested interest in mitigating the effects of IT. The authors state: 'The arrival of the information society comes in tandem with changes in labour legislation and the rise of new professions and skills.' (*Bangemann Report*, p. 6). The trouble is that many of those who will create these new jobs are not likely to feel any allegiance towards the trade union movement, among other things because they will need to be able to pursue flexible employment practices.
15. *Bangemann Report*, p. 6.
16. *Bangemann Report*, p. 8.
17. *Bangemann Report*, p. 12.
18. At the 1994 RELARN conference in Moscow the incompatibility of many servers was, it was argued, responsible for a poor service. The situation was described as 'elemental' and 'unsystematic'. See D. V. Kurakin, '*O razrabotke gosudarstvennogo profilya standartov, obespechivayushchego sovmestimost' federal'nykh telekommunikatsionnykh setey s regional'nymi, vedomstvennymi, kommercheskimi i mezhdunarodnymi setyami i o vedenii domena EDU.RU*', RELARN conference 5–6 Dec. 1994, Moscow.
19. *The Road Ahead*, the title of chapter 8.
20. *The Road Ahead*, p. 256.
21. *The Road Ahead*, p. 254.
22. *The Road Ahead*, p. 5.
23. See Robert H. Anderson *et al.*, *Universal Access to E-Mail: Feasibility and Societal Implications*, Rand Organization, Santa Monica, CA, 1995.
24. Anderson *et al.*, p. 115.
25. Anderson *et al.*, p. 39.
26. Anderson *et al.*, p. 44.
27. Anderson *et al.*, p. 46.
28. Anderson *et al.*, p. 48.
29. Anderson *et al.*, p. 49.
30. A useful starting point was a review of the study carried out by Travica and Hogan. Three years on, a lot has been achieved. In their survey Travica and Hogan noted four major networks: (i) IASNET (Institute

for Automated Systems Network), that was established by the Academy of Sciences. (ii) RELCOM (Russian Electronic Communications), established in 1990 by DEMOS. Bulk of users are private. (iii) GlasNet (Glasnost' Network). This is a joint venture of the Institute of Global Communications (IGC), San Francisco and the International Foundation. It began operating on 30 May 1991. Aimed at the private market. (iv) SUEARN (SU = Soviet Union + EARN = European Academic and Research Network). Operates under the Academy of Sciences.

31. *Roskominform* also has responsibility for the international protection of the Russian Federation's interests in the sphere of informatization (point 18, paragraph 4). The interests are not defined. There is, here, I suggest, a real risk of banning cultural products and certain services on the basis that they damage Russian interests. At the time of writing I am not aware that this part of the statute has been invoked by the Russian government. See below discussion of the implications of the CDA's becoming law in the US. On the question of governments setting standards the Rand study notes: 'In principle, entry into the e.mail service provision business could be regulated and a service obligation imposed on each licensed entrant. However, regulating entry would go strongly against the dynamic of the innovative computer networking industry. Indeed, erecting successful barriers to entry appears improbable. The history of innovation in digital technology is one of an increasing number of alternative ways of representing and transmitting information. Bootleg messaging systems would likely circumvent any regulatory effort.' See Anderson *et al.*, p. 113.

32. A letter clarifying certain provisions of the Information Law was published by the Supreme Arbitration Court of the Russian Federation on 7 June 1995 (Pis'mo ot 7 iyunya 1995 g. N C1–7/03–316). The chairman of the Court, V. F. Yakovlev, pointed out that a document that had been corroborated with an electronic signature would be admissible as evidence in any case consideration by the Arbitration Court.

33. Article 19 ('The Certification of Information Systems, Technologies and the Means of Provision Thereof and the Licensing of the Activity in the Formation and Use of Information Resources') suggests a different approach for private and state bodies. Point 1 requires compulsory certification of 'information systems, databases and data banks, intended to meet the information needs of citizens and organisations' in accordance with the procedure laid down in the 'Federal Law Concerning the Certification of Products and Services'. With regard to information systems operated by the state, then the 'Procedure of Certification is to be determined by the legislation of the Russian Federation' (point 2). Unlike the requirement for privately-owned information systems no specific piece of legislation is indicated.

34. When describing the global information exchange the law uses the adjective *edinyy*. Translation of this adjective is not entirely straight-

forward in the context of its use. It can mean 'one', 'common', 'united'. Since it is possible to have more than one global network with competing architecture and carrier standards, the distinction between one among many or only one is not academic. Given the thrust of this law and the provisions of other Russian Federation legislation dealing with standards (*Roskominform* for example), then the aspiration of the legislators will be taken to mean a single global network.

35. Russian owners are qualified by the adjective *otechestvennyy*, a word with very powerful emotional connotations, the presence of which in a formal legal document is unusual. *Otechestvennyy* suggests 'patriotic', 'of the Fatherland', as in for example, the Great Fatherland War. Its use hints perhaps at a state of mind that sees Russia as being under siege from foreign information and ideas, as an inferior player and thus deserving special consideration and protection.

36. Article 13 ('The Inadmissibility of Monopolization in the International Exchange of Information') notes the need to combat monopolies. Nothing is said about the state's monopoly which is the biggest obstacle to progress, especially deregulation of the telecommunications industry.

37. Two provisions of section 502 of the CDA were challenged: 223(a) and 223(d). Plaintiffs argued that the provisions of the CDA aimed at communications that might be considered 'indecent' or 'patently offensive' for minors' infringed rights protected by the First Amendment and the Due Process Clause of the Fifth Amendment. See *American Civil Liberties Union et al. v. Reno*, Communications Decency Act Challenge, In the United States District Court For the Eastern District of Pennsylvania, Civil Action 96–963, Before: Sloviter, Chief Judge, United States Court of Appeals for the Third Circuit; Buckwalter and Dalzell, Judges, United States District Court for the Eastern District of Pennsylvania, 11 Jun 1996, Introduction (hereinafter *ACLU et al. v. Reno*).

38. The full text of the ruling can be found on the Electronic Frontier Foundation web site http://www.eff.org/pub/EFF.

39. In the Preliminary Injunction Standard, the judges concluded that the Government's failure to define 'indecent' was a negative pregnant. They stated:

> Subjecting speakers to criminal penalties for speech that is constitutionally protected in itself raises the spectre of irreparable harm. Even if a court were unwilling to draw that conclusion from the language of the statute itself, plaintiffs have introduced ample evidence that the challenged provisions, if not enjoined, will have a chilling effect on their free expression. Thus, this is not a case in which we are dealing with a mere incidental inhibition on speech [...], but with a regulation that *directly penalizes speech* [emphasis added].

40. Communist China has supported calls to ban the dissemination of pornography, but one suspects that the real worry for the Communist

party is the Internet itself and the opportunities it offers for political dissenters.

41. Beglov, *Vneshnepoliticheskaya propaganda*, 1984, p. 364.
42. Note the Soviet definition of the New International Information Order: 'a programme of the decolonisation of the mass media put forward by the developing countries which envisages the liquidation of the gap between the industrialised countries of the West and their former colonies in the material provision of information resources, as well as the removal of the ideological and political dominance of the capitalist monopolies of press in the structure and content in the flow of information broadcast by them'. See Beglov, *Vneshnepoliticheskaya propaganda*, 1984, pp. 360–61.
43. Monroe Price, *Television, the Public Sphere, and National Identity*, 1995, p. 79.
44. Michael Specter, 'World, Wide, Web: 3 English Words', *New York Times*, 14 April 1996, p. A1.
45. Vladimir Ermakov, one of the network's developers asserts that there is: 'hidden resistance of our administration to development of networking in IEM. These are common problems in scientific institutions in Russia, I believe, because of intrinsic independence of networking from administration.' See http://www.iem.ac.ru/~ermak.
46. RELARN charter adopted 20 March 1993, paragraph 2.1
47. In the period 5–6 December 1994 the first RELARN conference took place in Moscow. The RELARN Web site has a full bibliography and full texts of all papers given. See too details of the 1995 conference (19–20 Dec.) with bibliography and papers.
48. As can be seen a number of the scientific networks were operational before the August coup attempt of 1991. Systems administrators were contacted by e-mail and asked to clarify the extent to which these dedicated lines were used during the coup to circumvent the restrictions imposed on television, radio and the selective press blackout. None of those who agreed to reply did reply.
49. See http://www.glasnet.ru/~vega/nato/index.html.
50. See Peter Knight's paper, 'Networking in Support of Training for Market-Oriented Development in Russia and other States of the FSU'.
51. Knight, 'Networking'.
52. Knight, 'Networking'.
53. For an overview of the problems of SIW see Roger C. Molander *et al.*, *Strategic Information Warfare: A New Face of War*, Rand Corporation, 1996 at http://www.rand.org/
54. Knight, 'Networking'.
55. Gordon Cook, 'Oral Presentation of Gordon Cook', *Cook Report on Internet*, 29.9.94.
56. Norbert Wiener, *The Human Use of Human Beings: Cybernetics and Society*, Houghton Mifflin Company, Boston, 1954, pp. 121–2.

CHAPTER SIX: CONCLUDING REMARKS

1. Vasiliy Grossman, *Zhizn' i sud'ba*, Knizhnaya palata, Moscow, 1988, pp. 258–9.
2. Valentin Turchin, *The Inertia of Fear and the Scientific Worldview*, 1981, p. 4.

Bibliography

Amalrik, Andrei. *Will the Soviet Union Survive until 1984?*, no translator, Harper & Row, New York and Evanston, 1970.

——. *Notes of a Revolutionary*, trans., Guy Daniels, with an introduction by Susan Jacoby, Weidenfeld and Nicolson, London, 1982.

American Civil Liberties Union et al. v. Reno. Communications Decency Act Challenge, In the United States District Court For the Eastern District of Pennsylvania, Civil Action 96-963, Before: Sloviter, Chief Judge, United States Court of Appeals for the Third Circuit; Buckwalter and Dalzell, Judges, United States District Court for the Eastern District of Pennsylvania, 11 June 1996.

Anderson Robert H. *et al. Universal Access to E-Mail: Feasibility and Societal Implications*, Rand Publications, Santa Monica, CA. 1995.

Apter, David, ed. *Ideology and Discontent*, The Free Press, New York and London, 1964.

Arendt, Hannah. *The Origins of Totalitarianism*, Harcourt Brace Jovanovich, New York and London, 1973.

Baiter, Stephen. 'Albania's First Press Law', *Journal of Media Law and Practice*, vol. 15, No. 3, 1994, pp. 70–72.

Baklanov, Grigoriy. 'Professiya: pogibshiy reporter', *Obshchaya gazeta*, No 42, 21.10.94, p. 1.

Bakshtanovskiy, V.I. *et al.*, eds. *Stanovlenie dukha korporatsii: pravila chestnoy igry v soobshchestve zhurnalistov*, Izdatel'stvo, Nachala-Press, Moscow, 1995.

Barghoorn, F.C. and Remmington, T.F. *A Country Study: Politics in the USSR*, 3rd edn, Little, Brown and Company, Boston and Toronto, 1986.

Batygin, Aleksandr. 'Pressu prosyat ne bespokoit'sya', *Rossiyskaya gazeta*, 29.4.94, p. 4.

Baturin, Yuriy M., Entin, Vladimir L. and Fedotov, Mikhail A. 'The Road to Freedom for the Soviet Press', *Journal of Media Law and Practice*, vol. 12, No. 1, 1991, pp. 43–7.

——. *Zakon o sredstvakh massovoy informatsii: Respublikanskiy variant*, Initsiativnyy avtorskiy proekt, Yuridicheskaya literatura, Moscow, 1991.

Bayduzhiy, Andrey. 'Po komu zvonit kolokol?', *Nezavisimaya gazeta*, 21.10.94, p. 2.

Beglov, Spartak I. *Vneshnepoliticheskaya propaganda: Ocherk teorii i praktiki*, Vneshnyaya shkola, Moscow, 1984.

Benn, David Wedgwood. *From Glasnost to Freedom of Speech: Russian Openness and International Relations*, The Royal Institute of International Affairs, Pinter Publishers, London, 1992.

Blackburn, Robin, ed. *After the Fall: The Failure of Communism and the Future of Socialism*, Verso, London and New York, 1991.

Bol'shaya Sovetskaya Entsiklopediya, vol. 28, 3rd edn, Sovetskaya entsiklopediya, Moscow, 1978.

Bukovsky, Vladimir. *To Build a Castle: My Life as a Dissenter*, trans. Michael Scammell, Andre Deutsch, London, 1978.

Charlton, Michael. *Footsteps from the Finland Station: Five Landmarks in the Collapse of Communism*, The Claridge Press, St Albans, 1992.

Choldin Tax, Marianna and Friedberg, Maurice, eds. *The Red Pencil: Artists, Scholars, and Censors in the USSR*, Unwin Hyman, Boston and London, 1989.

Choldin Tax, Marianna. 'The Censorship of Foreign Books in Russia and the USSR', trans. Yurii Fridshtein, May 1992. See http://carousel.lis.uiuc.edu/~iris/choldin.html.

Commission of the European Communities. *The Martin Bangemann Report, Europe and the Global Information Society: Recommendations to the European Council*, 1994.

——. *Learning in the Information Society: Action Plan for a European Education Initiative (1996–1998)*, Brussels, 1996.

Conquest, Robert. *The Harvest of Sorrow: Soviet Collectivization and the Terror-Famine*, Hutchinson, London, 1986.

Counts, George and Lodge, Nucia, *The Country of the Blind: The Soviet System of Mind Control*, Houghton Mifflin, Boston, MA, 1949.

——, ed. *The Politics of Ideas in the USSR*. The Bodley Head, London, 1967.

Cringely, Robert X. *Accidental Empires*, Penguin, Harmondsworth, Middlesex, 1996.

Crozier, Brian. *Free Agent: The Unseen War 1941–1991*, Harper Collins, London, 1994.

Curry, Jane Leftwich, trans. and ed. *The Black Book of Polish Censorship*, Random House, New York, 1984.

Davidson, James and Rees-Mogg, Lord. *The Great Reckoning. How the World Will Change in the Depression of the 1990s*, Sidgwick and Jackson, London, 1992.

Dewhirst, Martin and Farrell, Robert, eds. *The Soviet Censorship*, Scarecrow Press, Metuchen, NJ, 1973.

Dunaev, Mikhail. 'Rokovaya muzyka', *Nash sovremennik*, vol. 1, 1988, pp. 157–68 and *Nash sovremennik*, vol. 2, 1988, pp. 163–72.

Dzyaloshinskiy, Iosif. *Rossiyskiy Zhurnalist v posttotalitarnuyu epokhu: neko-torye osobennosti lichnosti i professional'noy deyatel'nosti*, Vostok, Moscow, 1996.

Eide, Asbjørn, ed. *et al. The Universal Declaration of Human Rights: A Commentary*, Scandinavian University Press, Oslo, Norway, 1992.

Ellis, Frank. 'The Media as Social Engineer: The Failed Experiment, 1953–1991', *Russian Cultural Studies*, Oxford University Press, Oxford, 1998, pp. 208–22.

Ellman, Michael and Kontorovich, Vladimir, eds. *The Disintegration of the Soviet Economic System*, Routledge, London and New York, 1992.

'Eshche odno ubiystvo, potryasshee obshchestvo: gosudarstvo obyazano ostanovit' etot bespredel', *Krasnaya zvezda*, 3.3.1995, p. 1.

Feiwel, George R. *The Soviet Quest for Economic Efficiency: Issues, Controversies, and Reforms*, Frederick A. Praeger, New York and London, 1967.

Foster, Frances H. 'Freedom with Problems: The Russian Judicial Chamber on Mass Media', 1996, pp. 1–29, a paper presented at the Stirling Media Research Institute, 2–4 February 1996.

Fukuyama, Francis. *The End of History and the Last Man*, Hamish Hamilton, London, 1992.

Gates, Bill. *The Road Ahead*, Viking, London, 1995.

Glasnost Defence Foundation (Fond zashchity glasnosti):

——. *Zhurnalist i Zhurnalistika rossiyskoy provintsii, Opyt issledovaniya*, September–December 1994, Fond zashchity glasnosti, Nachalo-Press, Moscow, 1995.

——. Simonov, Aleksey, ed. *Zhurnalisty na chechenskoy voyne: Fakty, Dokumenty, Svidetel'stva*, November 1994–December 1995, Prava cheloveka, Moscow, 1995.

——. Simonov, Aleksey. *Presledovanie zhurnalistov i pressy na territorii byvshego SSSR v 1994 godu*, Moskovskaya Pravda, Moscow, 1995.

Golikov, A.G. *Rossiyskie monopolii v zerkale pressy (gazety kak istochnik po istorii monopolizatsii promyshlennosti)*, Izdatel'stvo Moskovskogo universiteta, Moscow, 1991.

Gorbachev, Mikhail. *Perestroika: New Thinking for our Country and the World*, Collins, London, 1987.

Grossman, Vasily. *Zhizn' i sud'ba*, Knizhnaya palata, Moscow, 1988.

Gulyaev, Mikhail. 'Media as a Contested Power in Post-Glasnost Russia', a paper presented at the Stirling Media Research Institute, 2–4 February 1996, pp. 1–13.

Gvishiani, Dzherman, *et al.* 'Sotsial'nye aspekty informatizatsii', *Kommunist*, 10, July 1990, pp. 48–56.

Hale, Julian. *Radio Power: Propaganda and International Broadcasting*, Paul Elek, London, 1975.

Hayek, Friedrich. *The Road to Serfdom*, Routledge & Kegan Paul, London, 1993.

Head, Brian William. *Ideology and Social Science: Destutt de Tracy and French Liberalism*, Martinus Nijhoff Publishers, Dordrecht, Boston and Lancaster, 1985.

Heller, Mikhail. *Cogs in the Soviet Wheel: The Formation of Soviet Man*, trans. David Floyd, Collins, London, 1988.

Hogan, Matthew and Travica, Bob. 'Computer Networking in the XUSSR: Technology, Uses and Social Effects', The Department of the History of Science, John Hopkins University, USA, 1992.

Hunt, F. Knight. *The Fourth Estate: Contributions towards a History of Newspapers and of the Liberty of the Press*, 2 vols., David Bogue, 86 Fleet Street, London, 1850.

Hutchings, Raymond. *Soviet Secrecy and Non-Secrecy*, Macmillan, Basingstoke and London, 1987.

Huxley, Aldous. *Brave New World Revisited*, Harper and Row, New York, 1958.

International Covenant on Economic, Social and Cultural Rights and *International Covenant on Civil and Political Rights*, Government Printer, Hong Kong, 1993.

Ioffe, Olimpiad S. *Soviet Law and Soviet Reality* in the series *Law in Eastern Europe*, Martinus Nijhoff Publishers, Dordrecht, Boston and Lancaster, 1985.

'Versii ubiystva', *Izvestiya*, 3.3.95, p. 4. Unattributed.

Kapuściński, Ryszard. *Imperium*, trans. Klara Glowczewska, Granta Books, London, 1994.

Kennedy, Paul. *The Rise and Fall of the Great Powers: Economic Change and Military Conflict from 1500 to 2000*, Unwin Hyman, London, 1988.

Kirchin, Yu. G. *et al.* 'Informatsionnye uslugi seti RUNNET: model' samorazvitiya', RUNNet Web site, 1996.

Kirschenmann, Peter Paul. *Information and Reflection: On Some Problems of Cybernetics and How Contemporary Dialectical Materialism Copes with Them*, trans. T. J. Blakeley, D. Reidel Publishing Company, Dordrecht, Holland, 1970.

Kislinskaya, Larisa. 'List'ev stal chetvertym ubitym rukovoditelem reklamnogo konsortsiuma', *Golos*, 11, 1995, p. 2.

Klimov, Vladimir. 'Reshenie okonchatel'noe. Obzhalovaniyu ne podlezhit', *Rossiyskaya gazeta*, 13.5.1995, p. 1.

Konstitutsiya (osnovnoy zakon) Soyuza Sovetskikh Sotsialisticheskikh respublik. Yuridicheskaya literatura, Moscow, 1980.

Kraemer, Kenneth *et al. DATAWARS: The Politics of Modelling in Federal Policymaking*, Columbia University Press, New York, 1987.

'The Law on the Press and Other Media', *The Current Digest of the Soviet Press*, vol. XLII, No. 25, 1990, pp. 16–20.

Krug, Peter. 'From "Rules of Socialist Community Life" to the 1995 Civil Code: Private and Public Interests in Russian Civil Defamation and Constitutional Law', part 1, *Cardozo Arts & Entertainment Law Journal*.

——. 'Civil Defamation Law and the Press in Russia: Private and Public Interests, the 1995 Civil Code, and the Constitution', Part II.

Kurakin, D.V. 'O razrabotke gosudarstvennogo profilya standartov, obespechivayushchego sovmestimost' federal'nykh telekommunikatsionnykh setey s regional'nymi, vedomstvennymi, kommercheskimi i mezhdunarodnymi setyami i o vedenii domena EDU.RU', RELARN Conference 5–6 December 1994, Moscow.

Lanham, Richard. *The Electronic Word: Democracy, Technology and the Arts*, The University of Chicago Press, Chicago and London, 1993.

Laqueur, Walter. *The Dream That Failed: Reflections on the Soviet Union*, OUP, New York and Oxford, 1995.

'The Law on the Press and Other Media', *The Current Digest of the Soviet Press*, Vol. XLII, No. 25, 1990, pp. 16–20.

Lendvai, Paul. *The Bureaucracy of Truth: How Communist Governments Manage the News*, Burnett Books, London, 1981.

Lenin, V.I. *Sochineniya*, Gosudarstvennoe izdatel'stvo politicheskoy literatury, Moscow, 1946.

Littleton, Suellen M. *The Wapping Dispute: An Examination of the Conflict and its Impact on the National Newspaper Industry*, Avebury Publishing Limited, Aldershot, 1992.

Lyubarskiy, Kronid. 'Terror kak forma tsenzury', *Novoe vremya*, No. 43, 1994, p. 6.

Maaz, Hans-Joachim. *Behind the Wall: The Inner Life of Communist Germany*, trans. Margot Bettauer Dembo, W. W. Norton, New York and London, 1995.

Maier, Charles S. 'The Collapse of Communism: Approaches for a Future History', *History Workshop*, issue 31, Spring 1991, pp. 34–59.

Makarov, V. 'Informatizatsiya v novom ekonomicheskom mekhanizme', *Kommunist*, 12, August 1990, pp. 51–5.

Malia, Martin. 'From Under the Rubble, What?', *Problems of Communism*, January–April 1992, Vol. XLI, pp. 89–106.

Markotich, Stan. 'Government Control over Serbia's Media', *RFE/RL Research Report*, vol 3, No. 5, 4 February 1994, pp. 35–9.

Materski, Wojciech, ed. *KATYN, Documents of Genocide*, Documents and Materials from the Soviet Archives Turned Over to Poland on 14 October 1992, with an introduction by Janusz K. Zawodny, trans. Jan Kolbowski and Mark Canning, Institute of Political Studies, Polish Academy of Sciences, Warsaw, 1993.

McElvoy, Anne. *The Saddled Cow: East Germany's Life and Legacy*, Faber and Faber, Boston and London, 1992.

McNair, Brian. *Glasnost', Perestroyka and the Soviet Media*, Routledge, London, 1991.

McQuail, Denis. *Mass Communication Theory, an Introduction*, 2nd edn, Sage Publications, London, 1990.

Medvedev, Zhores. *Soviet Science*, W.W. Norton & Company, Inc., New York, 1978.

Miłosz, Czeław. *The Captive Mind*, trans. Jane Zielonko, Harmondsworth, 1985.

Milton, John. *Areopagitica and Of Education*, ed. K. M. Lea, Clarendon Press, Oxford, 1973.

Mises, Ludwig, von. *Human Action: A Treatise on Economics*, Fox and Wilkes, San Francisco, 1966.

——. *Socialism: An Economic and Sociological Analysis*, trans. J. Kahane, Liberty Classics, Indianapolis, 1981.

Murray, John. *The Russian Press from Brezhnev to Yeltsin: Behind the Paper Curtain*, Studies of Communism in Transition, Edward Elgar, Aldershot, England, 1994.

Nelson, Michael. *War of the Black Heavens: The Battles of Western Broadcasting in the Cold War*, Brassey's, London, 1997.

Orwell, George. 'The Prevention of Literature', *Inside the Whale and Other Essays*, Penguin, Harmondsworth, Middlesex, 1983.

Ozhegov, S.I., ed. *Slovar' russkogo yazyka*, 18th edn, Russkiy yazyk, Moscow, 1987.

Palmer, Alisdair., 'How the KGB Ran the *Guardian*'s Features Editor, *The Spectator*, 10.12.94, pp. 9–12.

Plamenatz, John. *Ideology*, Pall Mall Press, London, 1970.

Pool, de Sola Ithiel. *Technologies of Freedom*, The Belknap Press of Harvard University Press Cambridge, MA and London, 1983.

Popper, Sir Karl. *The Poverty of Historicism* (1957), Routledge, New York and London, 1991.

Postman, Neil. *Amusing Ourselves to Death: Public Discourse in the Age of Show Business*, Heinemann, London, 1986.

——. *Technopoly: The Surrender of Culture to Technology*, Alfred A. Knopf, New York, 1993.

Press Complaints Commission, 'Code of Practice', February 1996.
Price, E. Monroe. *Television, The Public Sphere, and National Identity*, Clarendon Press, Oxford, 1995.
Pryce-Jones, David. *The War That Never Was: The Fall of the Soviet Empire 1985–1991*, Weidenfeld and Nicolson, London, 1995.
Rasputin, Valentin. 'Senya edet', *Moskva*, 7, 1994, pp. 3–7.
Read, Donald. *The Power of News: The History of Reuters*, Oxford University Press, 1992.
Reading, Anna. 'The People v. the King – Polish Broadcasting Legislation, *Journal of Media Law and Practice*, vol. 15, No. 1, 1994, pp. 7–12.
Reagan, Ronald. Speech at London's Guildhall, *Los Angeles Times*, 14 June 1989, p. 10.
Reddick, Randy. *The Online Journalist: Using the Internet and Other Electronic Resources*, Harcourt Brace College Publishers, New York, 1995.
'Rekomendatsii Sudebnoy palaty po informatsionnym sporam pri Prezidente Rossiyskoy Federatsii i Soyuza zhurnalistov 'O Svobode massovoy informatsii i Otvetstvennosti zhurnalistov', *Rossiyskaya gazeta*, 11 July 1995, p. 6.
Remington, Thomas. *The Truth of Authority: Ideology and Communication in the Soviet Union*, University of Pittsburgh Press, Pittsburgh, PA, 1988.
'Results of the Work of the KGB in Investigating Authors of Anonymous Materials of a Hostile Nature', Committee of State Security of the USSR (KGB), 21 March 1988, No. 458-Ch, Moscow to The Central Committee of the Communist Party of the Soviet Union (CPSU), Top Secret, Special Folder. File available at the Library of Congress in /pub/soviet.archive/text.english. See *KGB Report of Publications Hostile to Soviet Government*, af2bdlit.doc, documents loaded 17 June 1992.
Richter, Andrey, ed. *Zakonodatel'stvo i praktika sredstv massovoy informatsii*, Monthly Bulletin, Eurasian Foundation & Glasnost' Defence Foundation, Moscow.
Rose, Clive. *The Soviet Propaganda Network: A Directory of Organisations Serving Soviet Foreign Policy*, Pinter Publishers, London and St. Martin's Press, New York, 1988.
Roszak, Theodore. *The Cult of Information: The Folklore of Computers and the True Art of Thinking*, Lutterworth Press, Cambridge, UK, 1986.
Roxburgh, Angus. *Pravda: Inside the Soviet News Machine*, Victor Gollancz Ltd, London, 1987.
Sagan, Carl and Shklovskii, Iosef. *Intelligent Life in the Universe*, Holden-Day, Inc., Amsterdam and London, 1966.
Sakharov, Andrei. *Progress, Coexistence, and Intellectual Freedom*, trans. *The New York Times*, with introduction, afterword and notes by Harrison Salisbury, W. W. Norton & Co. Inc., New York, 1970.
——. *Memoirs*, trans. Richard Lourie, Hutchinson, London, 1990.
Schöpflin, George, ed. *Censorship and Political Communication in Eastern Europe*, Frances Pinter, London, 1983.
Selected Works of Mao Tsetung, 1st edn, vol. 5, Foreign Languages Press, Peking, 1977.
Shalin, Dmitri N., ed. *Russian Culture at the Crossroads: Paradoxes of Postcommunist Consciousness*, Westview Press, Boulder, CO and Oxford, 1996.

Shanor, Donald R. *Behind the Lines: The Private War against Soviet Censorship*, St. Martin's Press, New York, 1985.

Shentalinsky, Vitaly. *The KGB's Literary Archive*, trans. John Crowfoot, with an introduction by Robert Conquest, The Harvill Press, London, 1995.

Sherman, Barrie. *The New Revolution: The Impact of Computers on Society*, John Wiley and Sons, Chichester, UK, 1985.

Simic, Pedrag. 'The Former Yugoslavia: The Media and Violence', *RFE/RL Research Report*, vol. 3, No. 5, 4 February 1994, pp. 40–47.

Skidelsky, Robert. *The World After Communism: A Polemic for Our Times*, Macmillan, London, 1995.

Skilling, H. Gordon. *Samizdat and an Independent Society in Central and Eastern Europe*, Macmillan Press, Basingstoke and London, 1989.

Smith, Hedrick. *The New Russians*, Hutchinson, London, 1990.

Solzhenitsyn, Aleksandr. *The Gulag Archipelago 1918–1956, An Experiment in Literary Investigation*, vol. 1, trans. Thomas P. Whitney, Harper Collins, New York, 1991.

Specter, Michael. 'World, Wide, Web: 3 English Words', *The New York Times*, 14.4.96, pp. 1 and 5.

——. 'Russians' Newest Space Adventure: Cyberspace', *The New York Times*, 9.3.96, pp. A1 and D2.

Stokes, Gale. *The Walls Came Tumbling Down: The Collapse of Communism in Eastern Europe*, Oxford University Press, New York and Oxford, 1993.

Strassman, Paul. *Information Payoff: The Transformation of Work in the Electronic Age*, The Free Press, New York, 1985.

The Information Infrastructure and Technology Act of 1992 (United States).

Thom, Françoise. *Newspeak: The Language of Soviet Communism*, trans. Ken Connolly, The Claridge Press, London, 1989.

Tikhonov, A.N. *et al.* 'RUNNET – Federal'naya universitetskaya komp'yuternaya set' Rossii', RUNNet Web site, 1996.

Todai Symposium '86: Information and Its Functions, Institute of Journalism and Communication Studies, University of Tokyo, Tokyo, 1988.

Toffler, Alvin. *Powershift: Knowledge, Wealth and Violence at the Edge of the 21st Century*, Bantam Books, New York and London, 1990.

Turchin, Valentin. *The Inertia of Fear and the Scientific Worldview*, trans. Guy Daniels, Martin Robertson & Co. Ltd., Oxford, 1981.

Tusa, John. 'The Diplomat and the Journalist – Sisters Under the Skin', Montague Burton Memorial Lecture, Leeds University, 14 May 1996, pp. 1–15.

Urban, George R., ed. *Can the Soviet System Survive Reform? Seven Colloquies about the State of Soviet Socialism Seventy Years after the Bolshevik Revolution*, Pinter Publishers, London and New York, 1989.

USTAV Assotsiatsii nauchnykh i uchebnykh organizatsiy pol'zovateley elektronnykh setey peredachi dannykh – 'RELARN', adopted 20 March 1993.

Vasil'ev, V.N. *et al.* 'RUNNET: Realizatsiya vtorogo etapa', RUNNET Website, 1996.

Wiener, Norbert. *The Human Use of Human Beings: Cybernetics and Society*, Houghton Mifflin Company, Boston, 1954.

——. *Cybernetics: or Control and Communication in the Animal and the*

Machine, MIT Press and John Wiley & Sons, New York and London, 1961.

Woodward, Kathleen, ed. *The Myths of Information: Technology and the Postindustrial Culture*, Routledge & Kegan Paul, London and Henley, 1980.

'Zakon Rossiyskoy Federatsii o sredstvakh massovoy informatsii', *Rossiyskaya gazeta*, 8 February 1992, pp. 3–4.

Zinoviev, Aleksandr. *Katastroyka: Povest' o perestroyke v Partgrade*, L'Age d'Homme, Lausanne, Switzerland, 1990.

BIBLIOGRAPHY OF MEDIA LEGISLATION OF THE RUSSIAN FEDERATION

Note: Unless otherwise stated the source of documentation was the Inforis Legal Database. Material is in chronological order.

'Zakon Rossiyskoy Federatsii o sredstvakh massovoy informatsii', N 2124–1, 27.12.91.

'O zashchite gosudarstvennykh sekretov Rossiyskoy Federatsii', *Prezident Rossiyskoy Federatsii*, ukaz, N 20, 14.1.92.

'Zakon Rossiyskoy Federatsii o vnesenii izmeneniy i dopolneniy v grazhdanskiy kodeks RSFSR', N 3119/1–1, 24.6.92.

'Zakon Rossiyskoy Federatsii o pravovoy okhrane programm dlya elektronnikh vychislitel'nykh mashin i baz dannykh', *Prezident Rossiyskoy Federatsii*, zakon, No 3523–1, 23.9.92.

'Otraslevye osobennosti sostava zatrat, vklyuchaemykh v sebestoimost' produktsii (rabot, uslug) po izdatel'skoy deyatel'nosti', *Ministerstvo pechati i informatsii Rossiyskoy Federatsii*, pis'mo, N 02–68–a/18, 8.4.93.

'Ob utverzhdenii perechnya vykhodnykh svedeniy, razmeshchaemykh v neperiodicheskikh pechatnykh izdaniyakh', *Ministerstvo pechati i informatsii Rossiyskoy Federatsii*, prikaz, N 127, 28.6.93.

'Zakon Rossiyskoy Federatsii ob avtorskom prave i smezhnykh pravakh', zakon, N 5351–1, 9.7.93.

'Zakon Rossiyskoy Federatsii o gosudarstvennoy tayne', zakon, N 5485–1, 21.7.93.

'Ob informatsionnykh garantiyakh dlya uchastnikov i zbiratel'noy kampanii 1993 goda', *Prezident Rossiyskoy Federatsii*, ukaz, N 1792, 29.10.93.

'O neotlozhnykh merakh podderzhki gosudarstvennogo teleradioveshchaniya', *Prezident Rossiyskoy Federatsii*, ukaz, N 2206, 18.12.1993.

'Ob obespechenii deyatel'nosti Rossiyskogo informatsionnogo agentstva "Novosti"', *Prezident Rossiyskoy Federatsii*, ukaz, N 2278, 23.12.93.

'Voprosy formirovaniya edinogo informatsionno-pravovogo prostranstva Sodruzhestva Nezavisimykh Gosudarstv', *Prezident Rossiyskoy Federatsii*, ukaz, N 2293, 27.12.93.

'O dopolnitel'nykh garantiyakh prav grazhdan na informatsiyu', *Prezident Rossiyskoy Federatsii*, ukaz, N 2334, 31.12.93.

'Ob osnovakh gosudarstvennoy politiki v sfere informatizatsii', *Prezident Rossiyskoy Federatsii*, ukaz, N 170, 20.1.94.

'Ob utverzhdenii Polozheniya o Sudebnoy palate po informatsionnym sporam pri Prezidente Rossiyskoy Federatsii', *Prezident Rossiyskoy Federatsii*, ukaz, N 228, 31.1.94.

'Polozhenie o Komitete pri Prezidente Rossiyskoy Federatsii po politike informatizatsii', N 328, 17.2.94.

Voprosy deyatel'nosti komiteta pri prezidente Rossiyskoy Federatsii po politike informatizatsii', *Prezident Rossiyskoy Federatsii*, ukaz, N 328, 17.2.94.

'O sovershenstvovanii deyatel'nosti v oblasti informatizatsii organov gosudarstvennoy vlasti Rossiyskoy Federatsii', *Prezident Rossiyskoy Federatsii*, ukaz, N 361, 21.2.94.

'Voprosy komiteta Rossiyskoy Federatsii po pechati', *Pravitel'stvo Rossiyskoy Federatsii*, Postanovlenie, N 180, 3.3.94.

'Ob upravlenii informatsionnogo obespecheniya administratsii prezidenta Rossiyskoy Federatsii', *Prezident Rossiyskoy Federatsii*, ukaz, N 449, 4.3.94.

'O likvidatsii gosudarstvennoy inspektsii po zashchite svobody pechati i massovoy informatsii pri byvshem ministerstve pechati i informatsii Rossiyskoy Federatsii', *Pravitel'stvo Rossiyskoy Federatsii, postanovlenie*, N 810, 6 July 1994.

'O programme "Stanovlenie i razvitie chastnogo prava v Rossii", *Prezident Rossiyskoy Federatsii*, ukaz, N 1473, 7.7.94.

'Ob utverzhdenii pravil akkreditatsii i prebyvaniya korrespondentov inostrannykh sredstv massovoy informatsii na territorii Rossiyskoy Federatsii', *Pravitel'stvo Rossiyskoy Federatsii*, Postanovlenie, N 1055, 13.9.94.

'O poryadke primeneniya soglasheniya o sozdanii mezhgosudarstvennoy teleradiokompanii "Mir"', *Gosudarstvennaya Nalogovaya sluzhba Rossiyskoy Federatsii*, Pis'mo, N HP-6–06/390, 12.10.94.

'O vnesenii izmeneniy i dopolneniy v polozhenie o komitete rossiyskoy federatsii po pechati', *Pravitel'stvo Rossiyskoy Federatsii, postanovlenie*, N 1221, 1.11.94.

'O litsenzirovanii televizionnogo veshchaniya, radioveshchaniya i deyatel'nosti po svyazi v oblasti televizionnogo i radioveshchaniya v Rossiyskoy Federatsii', *Pravitel'stvo Rossiyskoy Federatsii*, Postanovlenie, N 1359, 7.12.94.

'Ob obespechenii gosudarstvennoy bezopasnosti i territorial'noy tselostnosti Rossiyskoy Federatsii, zakonnosti, prav i svobod grazhdan, razoruzheniya nezakonnykh vooruzhennykh formirovaniy na territorii Chechenskoy Respubliki i prilegayushchikh k ney regionakh Severnogo Kavkaza', *Pravitel'stvo Rossiyskoy Federatsii*, Postanovlenie, N 1360, 9.12.94.

'Zakon o poryadke osveshcheniya deyatel'nosti organov gosudarstvennoy vlasti v gosudarstvennykh sredstvakh massovoy informatsii', zakon, N 7–F3, 15.12.94.

Sudebnaya palata po informatsionnym sporam, zayavlenie, 27.12.94, No. 11., 'O zashchite svobody sredstv massovoy informatsii v svyazi s sobytiyami v Chechne'.

'O vnesenii izmeneniy i dopolneniy v zakon Rossiyskoy Federatsii 'o sredstvakh massovoy informatsii' ', Federal'nyy zakon, N 6–F3, 13.1.95.

'Ob informatsii, informatizatsii i zashchite informatsii', zakon, *Rossiyskaya Federatsiya*, N 24–F3, 25.1.95.

'Zakon o svyazi', Federal'nyy zakon, N 15 F-3, 16.2.95.

'O poryadke primeneniya ST.19 chasti 2 zakona RF "o sredstvakh massovoy informatsii", raz"yasneniya, S. P. Gryzunov, predsedatel' Komiteta PF po pechati & A. B. Vengerov, predsedatel' Sudebnoy palaty, 24.5.95.

'O vnesenii izmeneniy i dopolneniy v zakon rossiyskoy federatsii 'o sredstvakh massovoy informatsii ', Federal'nyy zakon, N 87–F3, 6.6.95.

Vysshiy arbitrazhnyy sud Rossiyskoy Federatsii, pis'mo, N C1–7/03–316, 7.6.95.

'O vnesenii izmeneniya i dopolneniya v stat'yu 4 zakona rossiyskoy federatsii 'o sredstvakh massovoy informatsii' 'Federal'nyy zakon, N114–F3, 19.7.95.

'O vnesenii izmeneniy i dopolneniy v ukazy prezidenta Rossiyskoy Federatsii ot 20 yanvarya 1994 g. N 170 "ob osnovakh gosudarstvennoy politiki v sfere informatizatsii" i ot 17 fevralya 1994 g. N 328 "voprosy deyatel'nosti komiteta pri prezidente Rossiyskoy Federatsii po politike informatizatsii"', *Prezidente Rossiyskoy Federatsii*, ukaz, N 764, 26.7.95.

'Polozhenie o gruppakh kontrolya i izbiratel'nykh komissiy za soblyudeniem uchastnikami izbiratel'nogo protsessa poryadka i pravil provedeniya predvybornoy agitatsii v sredstvakh massovoy informatsii pri vyborakh deputatov gosudarstvennoy dumy federal'nogo sobraniya Rossiyskoy Federatsii', Prilozhenie N 2 k Postanovleniyu Tsentral'noy izbiratel'noy komissii Rossiyskoy Federatsii, N 47/398–11, 18.11.95.

'O gosudarstvennom fonde televizionnykh i radioprogramm', *Pravitel'stvo Rossiyskoy Federatsii*, Postanovlenie, N 1232, 13.12.95.

'Ob uluchshenii informatsionnogo obespecheniya naseleniya Rossiyskoy Federatsii', *Pravitel'stvo Rossiyskoy Federatsii*, Postanovlenie, N 11, 12.1.96.

'Voprosy mezhvedomstvennoy komissii po zashchite gosudarstvennoy tayny', *Prezident Rossiyskoy Federatsii*, ukaz, N 71, 20.1.96. Note the 'Polozhenie o mezhvedomstvennoy komissii po zashchite gosudarstvennoy tayny', attached to this ukaz.

'O komitete pri prezidente Rossiyskoy Federatsii po politike informatizatsii', *Prezident Rossiskoy Federatsii*, ukaz, N 414, 22.3.96.

'O dopolnenii sostava mezhvedomstvennoy komissii po zashchite gosudarstvennoy tayny po dolzhnostyam', *Prezident Rossiyskoy Federatsii*, ukaz, N 573, 21.4.96.

'O press-sluzhbe prezidenta Rossiyskoy Federatsii', *Prezident Rossiyskoy Federatsii*, ukaz, N 645, 2.5.96.

'Ob uchastii v mezhdunarodnom informatsionnom obmene', federal'nyy zakon, N B5–F3, 5.6.96.

BIBLIOGRAPHY OF INTERNET SOURCES

Committee for the Protection of Journalists (http://www.cpj.org/pubs/russ96/murder.html)

Inforis (http://www.inforis.nnov.ru).

Internews (http://www.internews.ras.ru).

Izvestiya Information Agency (http://www.izvestia.ru).

Open Media Research Institute (OMRI), (http://www.omri.cz).

Rand Foundation (http://www.rand.org/publications/).

Russia-On-Line (http://www.online.ru).

Russian Library and Literature (http://www.laum.uni-hannover.de/iln/
bibliotheken/buecher.html).

Russian Newsletter (http://www.essex.ac.uk/plus/ruselect/maill.txt).

East European Media and Cinema Studies (http://www.utexas.edu/ftp/pub/
eems/main.html), 1996.

The Electronic Frontier Foundation (http://www.eff.org/pub/EFF).

Zakon i praktika SMI (http://www.internews.ras.ru/Zip/).

http://www.glasnet.ru/~vega/nato/index.html.

Index